The Two Hendricks

The Two Hendricks

Unraveling a Mohawk Mystery

Eric Hinderaker

Harvard University Press
Cambridge, Massachusetts
London, England
2010

Library of Congress Cataloging-in-Publication Data
Hinderaker, Eric.
   The two Hendricks : unraveling a Mohawk mystery / Eric Hinderaker.
         p. cm.
   Includes bibliographical references and index.
   ISBN 978-0-674-03579-9 (alk. paper)
   1. Theyanoguin, Hendrick Peters, 1692–1755. 2. Tejonihokarawa, Hendrick,
ca. 1660–ca. 1735. 3. Mohawk Indians—Biography. 4. Mohawk Indians—
History—18th century. 5. Six Nations. 6. Great Britain—Colonies—America.
7. Indians of North American—History—Colonial period, ca. 1600–1775.
8. United States—History—Colonial period, ca. 1600–1775. I. Title.
   E99.M8H56 2010
   974.7004'975542—dc22   2009020267

For Carrie, always

Contents

Illustrations

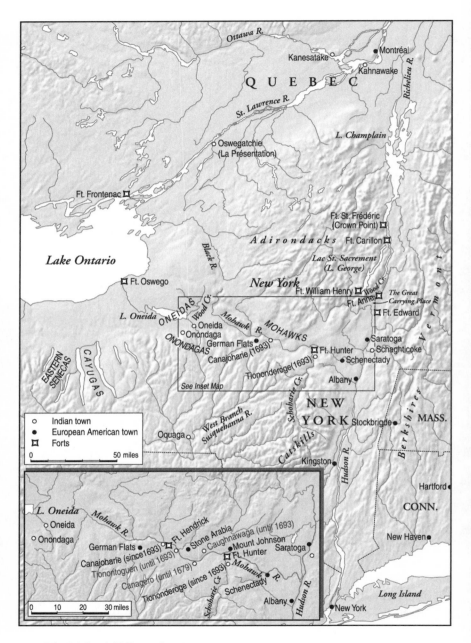

The Mohawk Valley and environs, 1670–1755

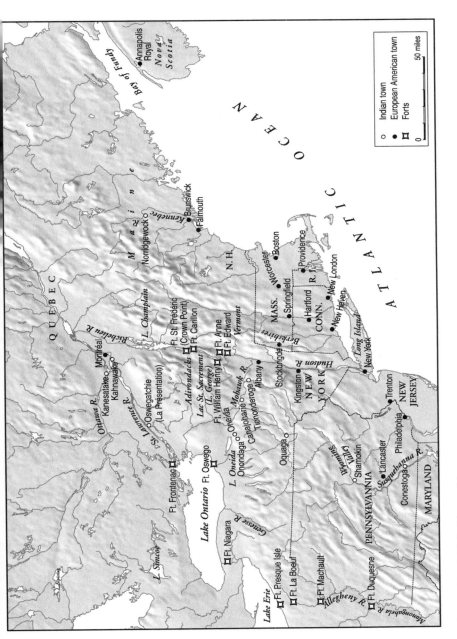

The two Hendricks' wider world

The Two Hendricks

Introduction:
Fame and Obscurity

Early on a September morning in 1755, a thousand Anglo-American provincial troops and two hundred Iroquois warriors marched from their camp alongside Lac St. Sacrement—soon to be called Lake George—to reconnoiter a French force they believed to be moving south toward Fort Edward. They were led by the most famous Indian in the English-speaking world, a Mohawk named Theyanoguin. His baptismal name was Hendrick: Britons knew him as Chief Hendrick, King Hendrick, or "the antient Mohawk." He would not survive the day's events.

The encounter that killed him has come to be known as "the bloody morning scout," the opening act of the Battle of Lake George, which was won by the British but at an appalling cost. About sixty-five years old and far past his fighting prime, Hendrick was the only member of his party on horseback that morning, "being," as a contemporary chronicler explained, "somewhat corpulent as well as old." But as a central figure in the Anglo-Iroquois alliance, he had to be there. Though he lost his life, his prominent position at the front of the combined force of provincial soldiers and Iroquois warriors may have saved many others. They were marching into an ambush. The French soldiers and their Indian allies had strict orders to hold fire and remain silent until the trap could be sprung. Instead, on seeing Hendrick, one of the French-allied Indians—also a Mohawk, from the St. Lawrence River town of Kahnawake—called out to him in his native tongue. The firing started prematurely and the trap was spoiled; the ensuing battle dragged on through a long and bloody day. Hendrick's end, however, came early. A "heavy old Man as grey haired as Silver," he "lit off his horse" and tried to get back to camp. Instead he fell in with the young Indian boys and women who were guarding the French baggage. He was stabbed in the back and clumsily scalped.[1]

The story of Hendrick's death and the battle that followed was recounted in newspapers throughout Britain's American colonies and in the pages of the *Gentleman's Magazine* in London. Already famous before the battle, afterward Hendrick became an icon of the British cause. Taverns and sailing ships were named for him, and a print of the "brave old Hendrick" was advertised for sale in London bookstalls.

His midcentury fame resonated with that of another, earlier Mohawk, also named Hendrick, who gained renown on both sides of the Atlantic—though he was known in Britain as Tee Yee Neen Ho Ga Row (Figure 1), a stylized version of his Mohawk name, which was Tejonihokarawa (Tay yon´ a ho ga rau´ a). The earlier Hendrick developed a close relationship with powerful residents of the frontier town of Albany, in the colony of New York, and became a stalwart supporter of their efforts to manage Indian relations. In 1710 he traveled to London as one of the "four Indian kings." He met Queen Anne and many other dignitaries, had his portrait painted three times, and sampled many of the city's entertainments. The visit was a sensation in London; crowds gathered wherever the four kings went, and a flurry of pamphlets, prints, ballads, and squibs amplified its significance. At the moment of his London visit, this Hendrick, too, could have been accurately described as the most famous Indian in the English-speaking world.

The two Hendricks, Tejonihokarawa and Theyanoguin, were important for what they did, but also for what they symbolized. The Anglo-Iroquois alliance was a cornerstone of Britain's imperial vision for

North America, and the two men at the center of this book, perhaps more than any other figures of the era, gave physical form and meaning to that alliance. The Mohawks were the most pro-British of the Six Nations of the Iroquois Confederacy, and the two Hendricks were among the most pro-British Mohawks of their respective generations. Theyanoguin's death in an early engagement of the Seven Years' War marked the end of an era in Anglo-Iroquois relations. For three quarters of a century, France and Britain competed for control of northeastern North America, and both empires regarded the Iroquois as central players in that competition. During that period the two Hendricks were essential to the Anglo-Iroquois alliance, and their images—conveyed in paintings, prints, and accounts of speeches—shaped its potential in the minds of Britons. At war's end, the Treaty of Paris of 1763 ceded all of France's claims in North America east of the Mississippi River to Britain. Thereafter, both the Iroquois Confederacy and the British Empire faced new challenges as the era of the two Hendricks gave way to the more familiar sequence of events leading toward American independence and revolution.

Surprisingly, given their eighteenth-century renown, the lives of the two Hendricks have been consigned to obscurity. Many historians have written about their two moments of transatlantic celebrity, but little beyond those episodes is known about them. Indeed, for more than two hundred years historians have presented these two men, almost without exception, as a single individual.[2] They are best known from two widely reproduced portraits that are among the most familiar images of American Indians to survive from the colonial era.

The older man, Hendrick Tejonihokarawa, was born around 1660, baptized in Albany by the Dutch Reformed minister Godfridius Dellius in July 1690, and apparently died around 1735. He signed his name to colonial documents by sketching a wolf, his clan totem. In the accompanying illustration (Figure 2), taken from a 1701 land deed, his signature is second from the top. (The clan totems are drawn upside down, since the sachems

Figure 1. *Tee Yee Neen Ho Ga Row*, by John Verelst, 1710. Painted by order of Queen Anne, this portrait of Hendrick Tejonihokarawa was a landmark in the visual representation of American Indians. Painted according to the conventions of European portraiture, it accentuates Hendrick's humanity and civility. Courtesy of the Portrait Gallery, Library and Archives of Canada.

would have been across the table from the scribe, for whom the document was right side up.)

The younger Hendrick, Hendrick Peters Theyanoguin (Figure 3), was born around 1691, was baptized by Reverend Dellius in Albany as an infant two years after the baptism of the first Hendrick, and died in the Battle of Lake George. His signature, probably learned in Henry Barclay's mission school, was a stylized pair of block initials (Figure 4). On legal documents he was designated Hendrick Peters (or, occasionally,

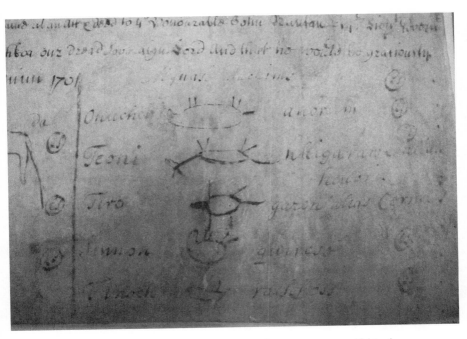

Figure 2. Deed of 1701, detail. Tejonihokarawa's signature—a wolf, his clan totem—is second from the top. It is upside down because he would have been standing across the table from the scribe when he drew it. His name appears alongside in phonetic English. Courtesy of the National Archives, United Kingdom. Photo by the author.

The brave old Hendrick the great SACHEM or Chief of the Mohawk Indians, one of the Six Nations now in Alliance with & Subject to the King of Great Britain. Sold by Eliz: Bakewell opposite Birchin Lane in Cornhill.

Figure 3. *The brave old Hendrick, the great Sachem or Chief of the Mohawk Indians* (London, 1755). This print, widely considered to be the most accurate likeness of Hendrick Peters Theyanoguin, was advertised for sale in London shortly after his death at the Battle of Lake George. Note the distinctive facial markings and the flowing white hair. Courtesy of the John Carter Brown Library at Brown University.

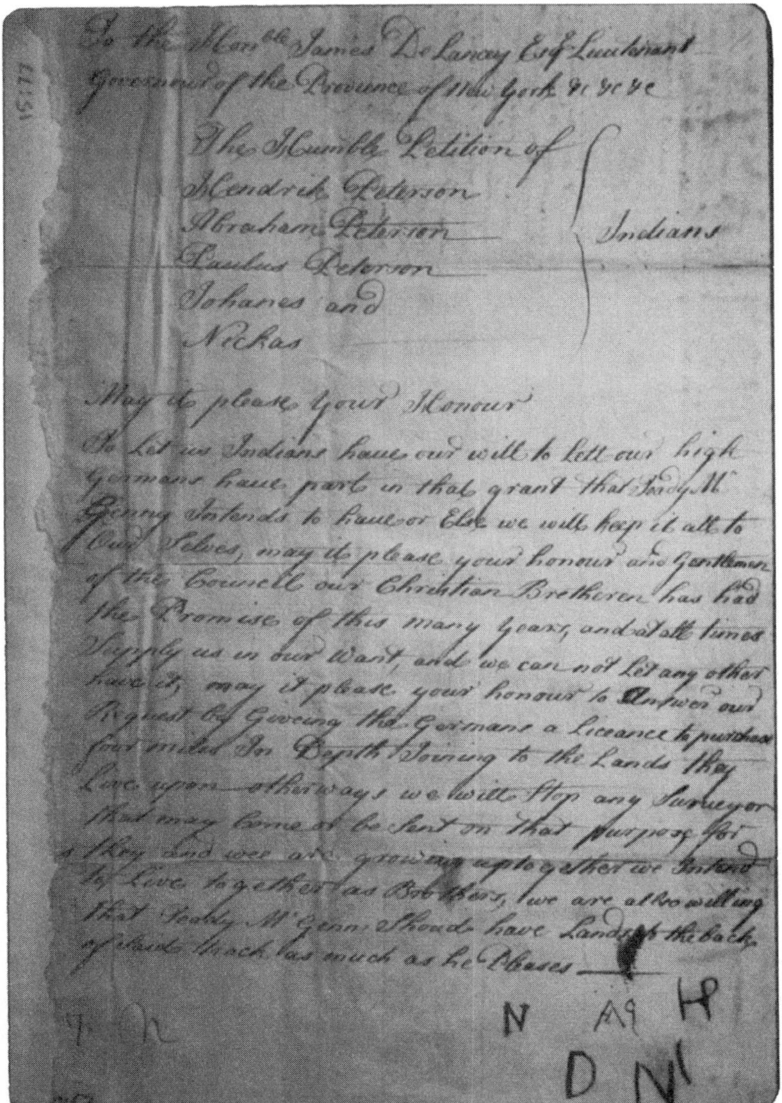
To the Honble James DeLancey Esq Lieutenant
Governour of the Province of New York &c &c &c

The Humble Petition of
Hendrik Peterson
Abraham Peterson
Paulus Peterson
Johanes and
Nickas
Indians

May it please your Honour
To Let us Indians have our will to Lett our high germans have part in that grant that Lady Mc Genny Intends to have or Else we will keep it all to Our Selves, may it please your honour and Gentlemen of the Council our Christian Brethren has had the Promise of this many years, and at all times Supply us in our Want, and we can not Let any other have it, may it please your honour to Answer our Request by Giveing the Germans a Licence to purchase four miles In Depth Joining to the Lands they Live upon otherways we will Stop any Surveyor that may Come or be Sent on that purpose for they and wee are growing up together we Intend to Live together as Brothers, we are also willing that Lady Mc Genn Should have Lands at the back of their Track as much as he Pleases

N AQ HP
D N

Figure 4. The "Humble Petition" of Hendrik Peterson et al. to Gov. James DeLancey, 1753, with alphabetic signatures, including Hendrick's "HP." Courtesy of the New York State Archives. Ann Aronson Photography; reproduced by permission.

Peterson), so the initials are "HP." They are clearly visible on the bottom right of a letter he sent to Governor James DeLancey.

Both Hendricks were well known to the circle of colonists and administrators most closely involved in Indian affairs, and both gained influence among their fellow Mohawks as their reputations grew in the colonies and the empire. Their high profiles, the frequency with which they appear in colonial records, and the large number of extant portraits and prints depicting their likenesses make it all the more surprising that there could have been so much confusion about their identities.

They were easily confused, in part, because the roles they played and the meanings they took on for those around them were so similar. The fact that they shared the same name was mere coincidence: the name Hendrick—a common Dutch name, whose English equivalent is Henry—was probably chosen by Reverend Dellius. There is no evidence that the two baptisms were linked in any way. The two Hendricks belonged to different generations, and their public careers never overlapped. But both men dressed (sometimes) as English gentlemen, cultivated a cosmopolitan bearing, and maintained close relationships with colonial officials. Among their fellow Mohawks, the two Hendricks were strong Anglophiles who argued for the benefits the Anglo-Iroquois alliance could confer upon their communities. For colonial administrators, each Hendrick, in his time, represented the hope that Indian allies would aid Britain in its conflicts with France in North America. More than that, Indians who converted to Christianity and accepted European norms of comportment embodied the possibility that they might cooperate with, and ultimately be absorbed by, the empire. Both Tejonihokawara and Theyanoguin struggled with these expectations as they sought to advance their interests and protect their communities.

The two Hendricks were ennobled in memory, but their real identities were elided and obscured. For contemporary British and Anglo-American observers, Hendrick Peters's battlefield death had less to do with the fate of the Mohawks or the Iroquois than with the protean power of the British Empire. It symbolized the way that imperial identity might transcend racial destiny. His loyalty in death suggested that the differences between Europeans and Indians could be subsumed beneath the banner of empire. Following the American Revolution, as the imperial wars of the eighteenth century faded in memory in the United States, "Hendrick"—now remembered as a single individual—came to represent something almost antithetical to the transatlantic, imperial roles played by Tejonihokarawa and Theyanoguin. The nineteenth-century image of "Hendrick" was shaped by a combination of half-remembered anecdotes, sketchy investigation, and imaginative invention. Local historians, antiquarians, and artists populated the landscape with colorful ghosts and invented a mythic past for their infant republic. "Hendrick" became a particular kind of culture hero, one who evoked a lost era and personified a uniquely American identity. A skeletal figure, bones without flesh, safely wrapped in the shroud of distant recollection, he came to represent the enduring legacy of an Indian past for a generation of Americans who could recover it only in fragments.

What did it mean to be the world's most famous Indian in the eighteenth-century Anglo-American world? The two Hendricks attracted attention by doing the unfamiliar and the unexpected. Their fame was largely a product of the British imagination. It took shape first in the minds of governors in the colonies, ministers in London, army officers posted to the frontier, traders, and land speculators, all of whom relied on the Iroquois as partners: all these people had a stake in the Anglo-Iroquois alliance, and all had a reason to elevate the Hendrick they knew to prominence. But these two Mohawks were not pawns. They had minds and motives of their own, and they tried to use the power generated by their fame to pursue their own ends. Though they allied themselves with Britain, they often challenged officials and demanded aid and cooperation. They earned their fame; they learned to manipulate it, even as they were manipulated in turn by the men to whom they were useful.

They became famous because they were Mohawks, and the Mohawk Nation belonged to the Iroquois Confederacy. During the first half of the eighteenth century, Britons became convinced that the Iroquois were a power to be reckoned with. Many observers believed that the Iroquois Confederacy, positioned as it was between New York and New England, on one side, and French Canada on the other, held the balance of power in the northeast, and that an alliance with it could mean the difference between victory and defeat in the imperial wars between France and Britain that repeatedly spilled over into the American borderlands. From a modern perspective this may appear to overstate the power of the Iroquois, who, after all, rarely brought more than a couple of hundred warriors into the field, and who often tried to remain neutral in imperial wars. But the American empires of Britain and France were precariously balanced systems. Small events could have enormous consequences, capable of rippling from the North American borderlands to colonial capitals and even across the Atlantic to the British Isles and the European continent. The power of the Iroquois, though limited, was real.

Heightened awareness of Iroquois power gave rise to a mythic view of the Confederacy. The myth of the Iroquois, which gained currency in the eighteenth century and has retained considerable power into recent times, held that the Iroquois constituted a uniquely powerful and enlightened Native American polity, one that was described alternately as either republican or imperial in character. The myth originated in efforts by colonial administrators to extend British authority and territorial claims through the Anglo-Iroquois alliance, which became a critical part of Britain's strategy to contest French power in North America. The idea gained popularity on both sides of the Atlantic in part because of the fame of Tejonihokarawa and Theyanoguin. Their performances on behalf of the British alliance dovetailed with the efforts of colonial administrators, provincial writers, and metropolitan pamphleteers to promote the Iroquois as uniquely fitted to sustain an imperial partnership. The speeches, portraits, appearances, and heroics of the two Hendricks were an indispensable element in the creation of the Iroquois myth.

The eighteenth-century idea that the Iroquois were suitable partners in empire has given way, in the last generation or two, to two parallel ideas. The first, widely discredited among scholars but astonishingly durable in the popular imagination and in primary and secondary school curricula, is the notion that the Iroquois Confederacy served as a model for the United States Constitution. There is little in the historical record to support this claim.[3] The other idea, which has gained much more widespread acceptance among scholars, holds that the Iroquois were extraordinarily canny politicians and diplomats who played imperial interests off against each other and, after 1701, maintained a consistent policy of neutrality toward France and Great Britain. There is something to this: the Iroquois played the cards that were dealt them with exceptional skill for a very long time. But Iroquois leaders were often divided and factionalized. To speak of "the Iroquois" in this period as if they acted with one voice obscures much of the confusion, conflict, and drama that accompanied an era of wrenching change. Their actions were often contradictory, their understanding of circumstances partial and imperfect. Desperation, as often as thoughtful calculation, drove the two Hendricks and their contemporaries to make the choices they did. It does not diminish the Iroquois, as individuals, constituent communities, or a collective polity, to acknowledge the profound disorientation unleashed by their long proximity to European colonies and the rivalries they engendered.[4]

This book restores flesh to the bones of two extraordinary individuals who lived in tumultuous and momentous times. Their efforts to ensure the survival of their communities have been largely lost to historical memory and deserve to be remembered on their own terms, at the same time that each Hendrick takes his proper place in the story of the imperial struggle to control North America.

The older Hendrick was deeply influenced by his Protestant Mohawk identity and was extraordinarily loyal to his Protestant Christian brethren, be they Mohawk, Dutch, or English. Though he gained strength and confidence in public as he matured, he initially appears in the records of New York as an ambivalent, enigmatic figure. Caught in a devastating war between empires, he did not have much stomach for the fight. This Hendrick gradually learned to defend the interests of his community, but at times in his early public career he almost seemed to be hastening its demise. When he played the role of an Indian "king" on a trip to London and gained international fame, he won influence among his fellow Mohawks and began to come into his own as a public figure. He gradually discovered how to balance the demands of the British Empire with the needs of his people. Only in the last phase of his long career does he emerge from the records, vividly and powerfully, as his own man.

The later Hendrick jumped much more suddenly onto the imperial stage. Absent from any documented public role until he was more than fifty years old, from that point forward he is ubiquitous in the colonial records. His newfound prominence owed much to the close relationship he developed with William Johnson, whose influence with his Mohawk neighbors won him an appointment first as colonel of the Six Nations, then as commissioner for Indian affairs for the northern colonies—both titles without precedent in Anglo-America—and eventually earned him a baronetcy. As Johnson became the central figure in the Anglo-Iroquois alliance, Hendrick emerged alongside him.

But Hendrick was not a retiring figure who attracted attention only because of his proximity to Johnson. On the contrary: he was an extraordinarily forceful, charismatic man who made a strong impression everywhere he went. A lifelong Christian who was exposed from child-hood to European influences, under Johnson's tutelage he quickly came to understand how to present himself in the Anglo-American world. His public personality owed little to Christian piety, though his mission school education stood him in good stead. He made his reputation as a fearsome warrior, then cemented it with the extraordinary confidence and energy—even fire and bluster—he showed as a speaker. He was a clever strategist and savvy politician. More secure in his hybrid identity, perhaps, than his predecessor, in the end he was better able to fulfill the expectations of his British partners than to recognize and defend the in-terests of his own community. In that sense, his death on the battlefield in a global war for empire was perhaps a fitting conclusion to his event-ful life.

This book explores the construction of imperial power through symbols of authority and reflects on the paradox of historical memory. But it is, at its heart, a biography conceived along traditional lines. To a degree that most students and scholars of early America do not fully ap-preciate, the very survival of Tiononderoge and Canajoharie, the Mo-hawk River communities that were home to the two Hendricks, was in doubt through nearly the entire span of both their lives. These two men played pivotal roles in assessing the fortunes of their people and search-ing out a path to the future.

What value is there in a biography of the Hendricks, sunk in obscu-rity for more than two hundred years? In part, it highlights the distant and alien qualities of a lost world. "The past," novelist L. P. Hartley wrote, "is a foreign country: they do things differently there."[5] We strain to imagine the violence and valor of Mohawk warriors, the efforts of Dutch traders to carve out a recognizable life for themselves in the tiny frontier villages of Albany and Schenectady, the mystery of baptism for a Mohawk convert, the glory and squalor of eighteenth-century London, the complex net of imperial entanglements that imparted meaning to the chaos of borderlands warfare. Among these elements of the unfamiliar, though, the essential, enduring humanity of this book's central characters and situations—above all, the enduring humanity of the two Hendricks, Tejonihokarawa and Theyanoguin—shines through. In recovering their stories we recover an essential dimension of the early American past: the dense web of human entanglements, the imperfect calculations of interest, and the deeply contingent sequence of events that shaped the contest to control North America.

1 New Birth

On a summer day in 1690, Tejonihokarawa opened the door of a squared log chapel in Albany and crossed beneath the lintel. He had come to be reborn. It was not the first time: rebirth, or requickening, was a familiar though momentous event in a Mohawk's life. Tejonihokarawa, which means "open the door," was not the sort of name an infant would be given. He must already have been reborn once before to be called "open the door." The name suggests that Tejonihokarawa played a particular ceremonial role on behalf of the Five Nations of the Iroquois. It was probably his job to "open the door" of the Iroquois longhouse to strangers who traveled through the woods to visit with the council of sachems. Such a position brought honor as well as responsibility. Tejonihokarawa had recently married a woman who belonged to the leading clan of the Mohawk nation; perhaps it was his wife's status that brought him his name and role. Yet he must have been an impressive figure in his own right (Figure 5). He stood nearly six feet tall. Contemporary portraits and descriptions suggest that he was thoughtful, perceptive, and serious—a man of substance, well suited to the role that had been granted him.[1]

Now, in Albany, he was opening a different door that would bring him another name, another identity, new responsibilities. He had come to be baptized.

Land of shadows

In the last half of the seventeenth century, the Mohawks lived in a land of shadows between a dream of peace and a nightmare of warfare, disease, death, and destruction. The Mohawks guarded the eastern "door" of Iroquoia, which extended from the Mohawk River Valley some two hundred miles west to Seneca country on the Genesee River. The Five Nations of the Iroquois Confederacy—from east to west, the Mohawks, Oneidas, Onondagas, Cayugas, and Senecas—controlled this territory and occupied the middle ground between New France, New Netherland, and New England. (The Confederacy's sixth nation, the Tuscarora, was not added until about 1720.) Beginning in the 1630s, with the support of a Dutch trading connection that supplied them with arms and enticed them with desirable trade goods, Iroquois warriors drove one neighboring Indian group after another into oblivion: the Wenros in 1638, Hurons in 1649, Petuns and Algonquins in 1650, Neutrals in 1651, Eries in 1657. This was the era of the Beaver Wars, when the Iroquois made ferocious war on many neighbors, particularly the French-allied Algonquian-speaking peoples to the west. In an escalating cycle of conflict they won many victories and took many captives, but also made powerful enemies and lost many warriors. Successive campaigns carried them farther and farther afield; by the 1650s, Iroquois war parties were ranging as far as the Illinois country, nearly all the way to the Mississippi River.

Iroquois men proved their masculinity in war. While historians have often tried to explain the Beaver Wars by stressing the economic or political imperatives that drove the Five Nations to fight, the ever-expanding cycle of warfare went far beyond economic or political need and can only be understood as a cultural phenomenon. The mourning war, in which a community responded to the loss of members by going to war to replace

I: Faber Fecit & Excud.' 1710.

Tee yee Neen Ho Ga Row. Emperour
of the Six Nations

Sold by J. Faber near y̆ Savoy. & J. King in the Poultry Lond̃.

Figure 5. Tejonihokarawa, engraved by John Faber, Sr. (London, 1710), based on a lost portrait. Though this likeness was created when Tejonihokarawa was about fifty years old, his youthful appearance allows us to imagine him as a younger man. Print collection, Miriam and Ira D. Wallach Division of Art, Prints, and Photographs, The New York Public Library, Astor, Lenox and Tilden Foundations.

them with captives, was central to Iroquois communal identity. As contact with Europeans triggered devastating cycles of epidemic disease, mourning wars took on a new importance. The intensity of Iroquois raids was greatest in the wake of epidemics that killed large numbers of people as warriors sought to replace the residents of their villages. Yet even in victory, warriors were lost. The logic of mourning war was unforgiving; when warriors died in battle they had to be replaced. The Iroquois' response to misfortune in war was usually more war.[2]

Their raids inspired universal terror. Most often, Iroquois attacks relied on the element of surprise. When news of their approach preceded Iroquois war parties, residents of a village under attack might spend hours or days wondering what lay in store for them. When it came, the attack was chilling. In these years the Iroquois were pioneering a Native American version of total war. In its intensity as well its geographical scope, Iroquois warfare was aberrant and perverse. Though the Iroquois carried flintlocks at a time when most of their victims did not, superior firepower was not always the key to their dominance. (The sound of guns often did more to terrify and demoralize the enemies of Indian warriors who carried firearms than lead bullets did to reduce their numbers.) War clubs were the traditional weapons of Iroquois warriors; the Dutch trade also brought them iron hatchets, scalping knives, and brass- and iron-tipped arrowheads. All were used with brutal efficiency. Iroquois forces, sometimes more than a thousand strong, attacked villages and made victims or captives of women, children, and the elderly. Fire followed blade to ensure that nothing—not huts, or cornfields, or stores of food—survived. Their opponents were defenseless in the face of the Iroquois' furious valor.[3]

Many died in these attacks; many more were captured. Few were left behind. The torment continued as Iroquois warriors escorted captives— often hundreds at a time—back to their home villages. The very young and very old were almost certain to die so they would not slow down the group's progress. Occasionally, Iroquois warriors killed and ate some of their captives before marching the rest of them homeward. At the slightest provocation they might inflict torture and pain to see how it would be endured. In 1677 Wentworth Greenhalgh and Arnout Cornelise traveled through Iroquoia; on their way they encountered a war party traveling with fifty prisoners. On meeting with the travelers, the Iroquois warriors stopped their captives and "made [them] sing, and cut off their fingers, and slashed their bodies with a knife, and when they had sung each man confessed how many men in his time he had killed."[4]

Captives marching toward Iroquoia must have experienced a bottomless sense of dread. Those who survived until they reached the gates of a village might have felt that the worst was yet to come. Most Iroquois communities were surrounded by a double row of palisades—tall, sharpened poles standing side by side to form walls that protected the residents from attack. They were formidable enough that Europeans who visited Iroquois towns commonly called them "castles." Returning war parties were usually greeted outside the palisades by their fellow villagers, who formed two lines and forced the captives to run the gantlet. The phrase has become a meaningless cliché, but in Iroquoia this was a harrowing and brutal experience in which prisoners were beaten on the head with clubs, poked, punched, and kicked. A captive who faltered and fell might be beaten to death. Those who survived proceeded through a narrow gate in the palisade and entered the village, where they would have seen an orderly arrangement of perhaps two dozen longhouses: large structures made from saplings, bark, and moss that were big enough to contain four or five fires and house twenty to thirty people.

Villagers drew the captives aside to continue their torments as clan matrons discussed their fates. Some might be subjected to further torture. They might have fingers painfully severed from their hands, one by one. Slow burning was especially common. Though prisoners might eventually burn to death, their captors would seek to prolong their suffering as long as possible. Finally, some captives would be chosen for adoption. Iroquois tradition held that new members replaced those who had died—this was the logic of the mourning war. A captive was requickened in a ceremony that would give him or her a new identity with a clearly defined place in the adoptive community. For the lucky few, it was possible to imagine that they had now, at last, come home.[5]

Clans were the sinews of Iroquois community and stood at the heart of the adoption process. Every Mohawk was a member of one of three clans: Turtle, Bear, or Wolf. Clan identity was matrilineal (so Tejonihokarawa, like his mother, was a Wolf) and marriage patterns were exogamous (so he would be expected to marry outside the Wolf clan). In the seventeenth century, most Mohawk longhouses contained extended family units. In principle the extended families gathered under longhouse rafters were all related through mothers' lines, and each Iroquois village was the special province of a particular clan; in practice, the Iroquois were pragmatic and flexible about such matters, and the extended families of a single longhouse might be configured in a variety of ways.[6]

Clans structured Mohawk life and governance and shaped Mohawk participation in the Iroquois League. By the late seventeenth century the league was perhaps two hundred years old. At its inception, tradition tells us, the Five Nations were fighting constantly. A man named Hiawatha lost his family and was overwhelmed by grief. Wandering into the forest, he encountered a spirit-being named Deganawidah, "the peacemaker." Deganawidah eased Hiawatha's suffering through words of condolence, then taught him a series of rituals—condolence ceremonies—that he could carry back to his people. Hiawatha returned with a new gospel: the Good News of Peace and Power. Once its rituals were accepted, the Five Nations could bring the perpetual bloodshed of their mourning wars with one another to an end. To adopt the new gospel and enact the rituals of condolence, the Five Nations created the Grand Council, which met annually to ease one another's sorrows, air grievances, and sustain good relations through ritualized diplomacy. League ritual was built around the words of condolence, sealed with the exchange of wampum strings and belts. Through wampum—beads painstakingly fashioned from seashells by Indian craftsmen and woven into belts and strings—the Iroquois made their public statements authoritative and ensured that they would be remembered.

Each of the Five Nations had its own clan system, and the Grand Council was comprised of the clans' representatives. The Mohawks, Onondagas, and Senecas were designated the older brothers of the league, the Oneidas and Cayugas the younger brothers. Each nation had its complement of league chiefs, representing various clans, who sat on the Grand Council. When a league chief died, his passing was mourned in a condolence ceremony, and then another member of his clan was requickened to adopt the deceased member's identity and take his place on the council.

The Turtle clan was said to be the oldest of the three Mohawk clans. Its senior sachem on the league council was called Tekarihoken, a name that suggests division and has been translated "of two opinions" or "between two statements," implying judiciousness or an ability to hear both sides of an issue. According to Iroquois tradition, Tekarihoken was the first sachem to accept Hiawatha's message of condolence and peace; he was therefore the first sachem named in the league's "roll call of the founders," the eulogy chant that recited the names of the league sachems. The Wolf clan was held to be the youngest of the three Mohawk clans. The Mohawks contributed nine sachems to the Grand Council, which had about fifty members in all.[7]

Mohawk villages moved periodically, sometimes because of depleted resources, sometimes in response to the devastation of epidemic disease or war. Settlement patterns in the last half of the seventeenth century were especially unstable. Visitors' accounts tell us that in 1634 there were eight Mohawk communities, in the mid-1640s three, in 1653 four, in the 1660s seven, then three, and after 1679 two. These reports capture villages in motion: when travelers visited six, seven, or eight town sites, we can generally infer that some were in the process of being settled while others were being abandoned. In these dramatic fluctuations, we can read the ebb and flow of Mohawk fortunes in an especially turbulent time. Despite the frequent moves, village names often persisted—though no two travelers heard them quite the same, and we have a multitude of spellings for each. In the era of Tejonihokarawa's youth, we can speak generally of three Mohawk villages whose sites shifted repeatedly. At the western end of Mohawk country stood Tionontoguen, in the vicinity of modern Fort Plain, New York. The largest of the three villages according to most reports, it had about thirty longhouses in 1677. With fifteen to twenty residents per longhouse, the village population in 1677 would have been between five and six hundred. After 1693, this village was called Canajoharie. Canagero occupied a series of sites in the middle of Mohawk territory, a short distance downriver from the modern town of Canajoharie. Reported to contain sixteen longhouses in 1677, it disappeared from the records after 1679, at which point the number of Mohawk villages dropped from three to two. The easternmost village, Caughnawaga, appears as a new name for the first time in 1659, around the time of Tejonihokarawa's birth. Located just upriver from modern Fonda, New York, in 1677 it consisted of twenty-four longhouses and a population just over four hundred.[8]

As the Beaver Wars progressed, each Mohawk village evolved into an imperfect amalgamation of natives and captives. In its traditional form, the mourning war would bring a small, steady trickle of captives into a village, who would then be requickened and assigned a stable place in an orderly community. Ideally, a captive's assimilation into Iroquois villages, clans, and families would be complete. But the warfare, epidemic disease, and mass adoptions of the second half of the seventeenth century strained the bonds of community. By the last quarter of the century, visitors reported that two-thirds to three-fourths of the residents of Iroquois villages had been adopted, and large numbers of former captives stood apart from the Iroquois among whom they lived. Hurons, for example, were a distinct and identifiable population within Iroquois towns for decades after their defeat and capture. While new members continued to be requickened and to receive nominal membership in particular clans and lineages, villages in which so many residents had been born elsewhere, in communities destroyed by war, must have taken on something of the quality of refugee camps, bound together by necessity but not by deep ties of family, community, and culture.[9]

In the mid-1660s the consequence of unrestrained aggression and conquest came home to Iroquois country. Frustrated by the terror inflicted on their Indian allies, New France's leaders grew steadily more destructive in their response. In 1665 a new governor, Louis de Buade de Frontenac, arrived in the colony, along with eleven hundred elite royal troops and instructions to "exterminate" the Iroquois. Instead the governor convinced the four westernmost nations to agree to peace, but the Mohawks held out. The effort to bring the Mohawks to heel culminated in the fall of 1666, when a force of more than a thousand French troops marched through Mohawk country. The residents fled, but the soldiers looted their longhouses, burned their villages, and destroyed enough food "to nourish all Canada for two entire years." In the following year the last of the Mohawk holdouts joined the rest of the Iroquois Confederacy in accepting a peace agreement that would bring Jesuit missionaries to the Mohawk towns—towns that were just being rebuilt after the previous year's campaign. This was a blow of inestimable proportions to the Mohawks. Of all the Iroquois nations, they were the most closely identified with the Dutch connection and the era of military domination that was now passing; they were the most confident of their own power. Of the defeat and peace of 1666–1667, the esteemed anthropologist William Fenton has written, "The Mohawks were never the same afterward."[10]

Tejonihokarawa would have been six or seven years old.

The French ascendancy

The arrival of the Jesuits in Mohawk country marked the beginning of a new era. In bringing Christian instruction, the French fathers also brought humiliation, intimidation, and reversal to Mohawk towns. The humiliation began as the priests Jacques Frémin, Jean Pierron, and Jacques Bruyas made their way to the Mohawk towns in the summer of 1667. Traveling south from Montreal in the company of Christian Iroquois guides, they paddled down Lake Champlain and Lac St. Sacrement. As they reached the southern end of Lac St. Sacrement, with a ninety-mile overland march to Caughnawaga still ahead of them, they encountered a Mohawk war party lying in wait for any French army that might make its way to Iroquoia in violation of the previous summer's agreement. Discovering them, Father Frémin's party demanded their help. In this way the Mohawk "Lions . . . became our menials, and served us very opportunely as porters,—being furnished us by Providence to take charge of our baggage."[11]

The humiliation of the warrior party turned to intimidation on a larger scale when Father Frémin introduced himself in the village of Tionontoguen, "the Capital of this whole country," to an audience drawn from all the Mohawk communities. He spoke to the assembled crowd about the blessings of peace, he reproached the Mohawks for their cruelty and untrustworthiness, and he declared that the fathers would teach them "to live like men, and then to be Christians." To emphasize the threat that underlay that promise, Frémin then had his supporters erect a forty- to fifty-foot-high gallows with a wampum belt suspended from its top and warned his listeners that anyone who killed a Frenchman or one of their allies would be hung from the pole and strangled by the belt.[12]

The Mohawks responded to this gesture with intense anxiety and astonishment. Of all the humiliations ever inflicted on them by a victorious enemy, perhaps none had so simply and perfectly inverted the moral order of their communities as this symbolic gesture. In itself sacred and precious, when wampum was woven into a belt or string it became the Iroquois' central symbol of communal identity and collective will. Wampum belts and strings were exchanged in diplomatic councils to seal agreements and preserved as permanent reminders of the commitments a community had entered into. Their public use was carefully prescribed by ritual. To have a wampum belt used in this way, torn from its proper context and raised up as a symbol of strangulation, violated the most sacred artifact of public life and inverted its meaning. Symbolic of collective speech, it was presented to the crowd by Father Frémin as a means to silence and suffocate. The audience "remained for a long time with their heads down, without daring either to look at this spectacle or talk about it." Then an elder, "the most prominent and most eloquent of their Orators," stood to address the crowd. His performance struck the French writer who recorded the scene as ridiculous, but must have conveyed to his audience something of the fear and outrage they shared.

> It is impossible to describe all the gesticulations made by this man, who was more than sixty years old. What looks of surprise at the sight of this spectacle, as if he had not known its meaning! What exclamations, upon finding out its secret and interpretation! How often he seized himself by the throat with both his hands, in a horrible manner,—squeezing it tightly to represent, and at the same time to inspire a horror of, this kind of death, in the

multitude of people who surrounded us! In a word, he employed all the artifices of the most excellent Orators, with surprising eloquence; and, after discoursing on this theme for a very long time, continually manifesting mental traits which were out of the ordinary, he ended by delivering to us the captives for whom we asked, and giving us the choice of a site for the erection of our Chapel, in the construction of which they offered to work with all diligence.

Father Frémin had made himself understood.[13]

Humiliation and intimidation were accompanied by reversal as the Jesuit fathers began their work. Frémin's first act on reaching Caughnawaga was to search its longhouses for Huron and Algonquin captives, "who alone compose two-thirds of the Village." Among them were ten children, whom he baptized immediately as the "blessed first-fruits of the new Mission." In a similar manner, the missionaries raised up the captive population of every Mohawk village: Hurons and Algonquins who had already been baptized and instructed in Christianity prior to their capture—the fathers thought of them as their "old-time Christians"—became the honored first members of the new missions. Frémin, Pierron, and Bruyas seem initially to have regarded Mohawk country primarily as a vehicle for reaching non-Mohawks. "As the Iroquois have made conquests in all parts of Canada," one noted, "they give us the means of opening the Treasures of grace to every kind of Nation, by instructing their Captives." Women captives, in particular, attracted the missionaries' attention. The first Mohawks to receive instruction were also women, and they chose to listen to the Jesuits at considerable cost to their local reputations. One twenty-five-year-old wife and mother won the confidence of Father Frémin and received baptism, only to have her son fall ill and her husband die in battle. Her relatives blamed her new faith for her suffering and urged her to renounce it. She refused; she fell ill herself; Mohawk shamans unsuccessfully attempted a cure; then the Jesuit fathers credited a Christian Huron with healing her. She and her son remained firmly in the missionary fold.[14]

From the margins of the Mohawk villages, Frémin and his colleagues moved slowly toward the center. Their progress was linked to the fortunes of the Mohawk communities. In the late 1660s and early 1670s, the Mohawks were continuously at war with the Mahicans, whose territory lay to the east along the Hudson River, and various other New England Algonquian peoples. (Tejonihokarawa may have been born a Mahican. Though the evidence is slight, if it is correct then he was likely captured at this time.)[15] In the ebb and flow of these conflicts, some Mohawks were impressed by the Jesuits' descriptions of heaven and hell, which Jean Pierron graphically illustrated by painting a scene "which represents the deaths of the pious and the wicked." In 1668, a war captain who was about to go on a campaign, perhaps influenced by Pierron's painting, asked what he should say or do if death were imminent to ensure that he would go to heaven. Mohawks in extremis—not only warriors facing battle, but also, especially, adults on their deathbeds or parents about to lose a child—began to ponder the Christian alternative to their understanding of the world. A growing number opted for baptism, often at the last possible minute. In part their choice was a response to the widespread conviction that this was an era of singular misfortune. The Mohawks "were formerly one of the most flourishing Iroquois Nations, and have always, up to the present time, passed for one of the most valiant, and one of the proudest," explained François-Joseph le Mercier, superior-general of the Jesuit order in New France, in 1669.

That martial spirit, which occupied them in war, separated them so effectually from the Faith that it was thought that the Agnez [Mohawks] would be the last to submit to the Gospel. But God employed the arms of France to give their conversion a beginning; their courage weakened after their defeat; they are now, of all the Iroquois tribes, the one that gives the greatest hopes of its conversion to the Christian Faith.

By that year 151 residents of the Mohawk villages had been baptized, about half just before their deaths.[16]

The success of the Jesuit fathers profoundly disrupted the Mohawk communities—especially Caughnawaga, which became the mission's principal focus. Missionaries stressed that Christian faith and worship were incompatible with Iroquois beliefs and with the practices and festivals that structured traditional life. They challenged their followers to withdraw from local observances they deemed superstitious and to follow the one true God. As they won converts, they fractured towns, clans, and families. The Jesuit fathers reserved the highest praise for those who withdrew most completely from communal rituals and celebrations and who practiced prayer, catechism, and Christian exhortation. Caughnawaga had its own "fervent" Native catechist by the end of the decade. Though he and his fellow Christians were subjected to scoffing and insults from other members of the community, they bore it "nobly for the love of Jesus Christ."[17]

Gradually the mission enterprise began to appeal to some Iroquois leaders. For them, acceptance of Christianity appears to have been calculated to reverse Iroquois fortunes in war and bring a new source of power to bear on their enemies. After a devastating battle with the Susquehannocks in 1669, a sachem named Garakontié announced to Father Pierre Millet that the Onondagas "renounced the superstitions that [Millet] had ordered them to renounce, and pledged themselves to obey dreams no longer." This was no idle promise. Though the Onondagas did not abandon traditional practices en masse, Garakontié remained a committed Christian until his death, as did many of his supporters. In the same year a well-armed party of Mohegan warriors besieged Caughnawaga. The Mohawks won the battle that followed, but at a high cost: though the Mohegans lost some fifty warriors, the Mohawks lost forty of their own. As Pierron noted, "These wars weaken the Angierron [Mohawks] terribly; and even his victories, which always cost him bloodshed, contribute not a little to exhaust him." Following this costly battle a group of Mohawk headmen approached Pierron to inform him of their new interest in Christianity. A wave of conversions ensued.[18]

Several years later another Mohawk leader, who would come to be known as the "foundation-stone" of Mohawk Catholicism, followed suit. Born into a prominent family, Assendasé was an influential elder of "intelligence" and "experience." The Jesuit fathers had found him to be arrogant and treacherous in the early years of their mission. He was also closely connected with the traditional practices against which the fathers preached. Bruyas noted that "he derived considerable profit from the practice of superstitions" at Caughnawaga. Yet around 1673 he experienced a change of heart and sought Christian instruction and baptism. After he was baptized he gave a feast "at which he declared to all the guests that he had renounced dreams and the other superstitious customs" and "would never again be present at the meetings over which he was accustomed to preside when dreams were discussed."[19] It is tempting to debate whether such conversions were sincere or calculated for political advantage, but this is a false distinction. The headmen and their followers who sought Christian instruction and support desired the protection of a powerful god during a period of profound need, at the same time they assumed that cooperation with the missionaries would strengthen their alliance with New France and encourage its leaders to support them against their enemies.

The linkage between spiritual, material, and martial support was dramatized with particular clarity in the 1673 visit of Governor Louis de Buade, comte de Frontenac to Iroquoia. Frontenac sought to broker a peace between the Iroquois and their Algonquian and Ottawa enemies and to identify a good site for a French fort on Lake Ontario, on the northern edge of Iroquoia. Leaders from each of the Five Nations welcomed Frontenac and helped him locate a site at Cataraqui, on the St. Lawrence River near its outlet from the lake. In the years to come, Cataraqui would become an important center of gravity in Iroquoia that would draw much of the Iroquois trade toward Canada. An orator named Toronteshati, likely a Mohawk and previously pro-Dutch and anti-French, expressed joy on behalf of the assembled Iroquois at the prospect of a new French post in their midst. The enthusiasm was widespread, not only among the Senecas, Cayugas, and Onondagas in the west but also among the Mohawks and Oneidas, who had previously relied on a Dutch trading connection and had long been suspicious of French encroachments. But New Netherland was captured by England in 1664, and from that point forward the Fort Orange trading connection grew more attenuated and uncertain. Many of its trading partners were happy to have a strong, stable alliance with New France.[20]

In Mohawk country, joining forces with Jesuit missionaries came to blend more and more seamlessly with a desire for the stability that an alliance with New France seemed to promise. When a new mission community was founded far to the north, along the St. Lawrence River near Montreal, many Mohawks found it attractive. The mission originated when a party of Oneida Christians traveled north to Montreal in 1667. There they met a priest who had just been granted a tract of land at La Prairie, on the south bank of the St. Lawrence, and he invited them to stay. The offer was especially appealing to adopted captives among the Oneidas; within two years, a small mission community comprised mostly of former Eries, Hurons, and Susquehannocks had grown up at La Prairie. Soon the settlement drew the attention of the growing contingent of Christian converts in the Mohawk towns, where conflict between Christians and traditionalists was often fierce. The early 1670s brought a new plague of disease, drunkenness, and violent disorder to the Mohawk towns, especially Caughnawaga. Christian Mohawks were subjected to verbal and physical abuse. As favorable reports of La Prairie made their way back to Mohawk country, Christian families and kin groups considered relocating, while even traditionalist Mohawks began to see conversion as a way to escape their miseries.[21]

The community at La Prairie grew steadily during the 1670s. In 1673–1674 alone it received 180 newcomers, most of them Mohawks, bringing the local population to about three hundred. In 1676 the village moved a short distance upriver to better land alongside the Lachine Rapids. It was renamed Kahnawake, which means "at the rapids" and evoked the Mohawk Valley town of the same name.[22] By 1682 the population had grown to about six hundred. Daniel Richter estimates that, in all, Jesuits baptized approximately four thousand Iroquois between 1668 and 1679. Just over half were on the verge of death, so the number of surviving Catholic Iroquois was somewhat less than two thousand at a time when the total Confederacy population was about eighty-six hundred. Thus nearly a quarter of the Iroquois Confederacy converted to Catholicism in the 1670s; among the Mohawks the percentage seems to have been a little higher. Curiously, given the tensions that divided Mohawks and the other Iroquois nations from their captive populations, and the large number of captives who were among the Christians moving north, the former captives' ethnicities of origin quickly faded after their relocation, and the residents were known, and identified themselves, as Mohawks or Iroquois.[23]

Tejonihokarawa grew to adulthood in this era of violent confrontation, conversion, and emigration. We know nothing of his experiences in these years—his name had not yet entered the documentary record—but we can make some inferences. He was certainly among the three-quarters or so of Mohawks who chose not to follow the Jesuit fathers; given his youth in the late 1660s and early 1670s, this probably reflected the sentiments of his mother's Wolf clan relatives more than any independent judgment of his own. He would also have been too young to participate directly either in the last wars against the French in the mid-1660s or, probably, in the fight with the Mahicans and their allies in the late 1660s and early 1670s. But he must have seen male relatives—perhaps his father, uncles, or older brothers or cousins—go to war. Given the scale of Mohawk losses in these years, he would almost certainly have known and mourned some of those killed. And it is likely that he knew some who abandoned their Mohawk homeland in favor of the more peaceful and orderly villages at La Prairie and Kahnawake.

Whether he and his kin viewed the northward migration as an act of betrayal and abandonment, or as a sensible choice in a tumultuous age, we cannot know. We do know, however, that as Tejonihokarawa reached adulthood he became a key figure in the emerging anti-French, pro-English faction among the Mohawks. But not as a warrior: Tejonihokarawa may have accompanied a war party or two, but it was as a sachem and, equally important, as a convert to another brand of Christianity—Dutch Reformed Protestantism—that his influence came to be most strongly felt in Mohawk country.

Covenant Chain

The anti-French Iroquois enjoyed a brief renaissance beginning in the mid-1670s, when they forged the first links of a diplomatic relationship with the colony of New York known as the Covenant Chain. Their partner in this effort was Major Edmund Andros, who was appointed governor of New York when the English recaptured the colony from the Dutch in 1674. (It was originally conquered by England in 1664; the Dutch had briefly reclaimed it in 1673 during the Second Anglo-Dutch War.) Not yet forty years old at the time of his appointment and only recently commissioned a major in the English army, Andros brought a new level of energy and engagement to the interrelated problems of Indian relations, trade, and war. His initiative was a welcome antidote to the indecision and inattention that had plagued the first decade of New York's existence. Within a few years, Andros gave the anti-French faction in Iroquoia new grounds for hope and reordered Indian relations in New York. Under his leadership, the Covenant Chain emerged from unpromising beginnings, at a moment of desperation and chaos, and quickly became the structuring metaphor in imperial relations with the Iroquois.[24]

It is much harder to identify the Iroquois architects of the Covenant Chain. Indian records from New York are scattered and confused in the mid-1670s, and no single name or set of names emerges clearly from among the Indians involved in a series of key conferences. Even where names appear, they were often those of speakers chosen for their oratorical skills, not sachems. Thus it is difficult to determine who shaped the emerging relationship with Andros and the colony of New York. But there is no question that Iroquois leaders were central to Andros's success in the 1670s, and that the Mohawks, in particular, were prime movers in Covenant Chain diplomacy. In the spring of 1675, and again in the following year, Andros visited Mohawk country in an effort to resolve the conflict between the Mohawks and Mahicans and to draw the Mohawk interest away from New France. In 1676 Andros forbade the sale of gunpowder to any Indians except the Mohawks, a decision for which he won the praise of James, the Duke of York and future king of England, on the grounds that the "friendship" of the Mohawks was "necessary to be preserved."[25]

From Andros's early visits to Iroquoia emerged the essential elements of Covenant Chain diplomacy. The Iroquois had used the metaphor of a "chain of friendship" to describe their relationship with the Dutch in earlier years, so the image itself was not new, but the Covenant Chain was formalized in new ways. Building on the condolence rituals of the Iroquois League, Andros's Iroquois partners taught him a series of ceremonial practices through which they were able to exchange gifts, air grievances, and make requests of one another. These meetings originated in a time of dire need on both sides: many members of the Iroquois Confederacy, especially Mohawks, wanted to blunt the rise of French power and heal their fractured communities. For his part, Andros hoped to discover in the Iroquois connection a way to strengthen New York's hand against its

French rivals and extend his influence in the Anglo-American backcountry. Each found a willing partner, and through Covenant Chain diplomacy they were able to build sufficient trust and mutual confidence to address their most pressing needs. They began to meet regularly to "brighten" the chain by giving one another gifts and conferring on matters of shared concern.[26]

Andros helped to engineer three crucial Mohawk victories that together brought them a stunning reversal of fortune. The first came in the context of Metacom's, or King Philip's, War, which raged in New England through 1675 and much of 1676. Eventually this war caused the abandonment or ruin of more than half of all New England's towns, while many thousands of Algonquian-speaking Indians died in the fighting or were enslaved and shipped to England's West Indian colonies. Andros recognized in this conflict an opportunity for the Mohawks to assert their value as English allies and offered their services to the New England colonies. Though New England leaders mistrusted Andros's intentions and refused Mohawk aid, Mohawk warriors nevertheless chose to fight and, as it happened, decisively influenced the war's outcome. They conducted a series of raids against the New England Algonquians that helped to ensure the failure and defeat of Metacom's forces.[27]

The Mohawk role in Metacom's War set the stage for a related triumph: the end of the conflict with the Mahicans, who were closely allied with Metacom's New England Algonquians. At war's end, Andros invited the defeated and dispossessed Indians of New England, including the Mahicans, to move to Schaghticoke, a short distance north of Albany on the Hoosic River. There they fell under the joint protection of New York and the Iroquois Confederacy. By 1680 the Mahicans, recently a dangerous enemy to the Mohawks, recognized the Mohawks as their fathers and protectors and accepted a subordinate status on the eastern margin of Iroquoia. They never again directly challenged Iroquois influence and authority in the region.[28]

The third cardinal achievement of these years involved another war between Indians and colonists, this one in Maryland and Virginia. In 1675–1676, exactly coincident with Metacom's War, Bacon's Rebellion grew out of a frontier conflict between Virginians and Indians and, at its height, threatened the colony of Virginia with overthrow. The principal Indian victims of this fighting were the Susquehannocks, a formidable group who had dominated the lower Susquehanna Valley for many years but were nearly destroyed in a massacre inflicted by Bacon's followers. The Iroquois, with Andros's encouragement, offered refuge to the Susquehannocks. Some accepted adoption into Onondaga and Cayuga communities; others returned to the lower Susquehanna Valley and founded the village of Conestoga under Iroquois protection.[29]

The events of the late 1670s transformed Iroquois relations with neighboring Indians and English colonies alike. Schaghticoke and Conestoga became buffer communities through which the Iroquois managed their relations with other Indian groups to the east and the south and ensured that their core territories were protected from attack. At the same time, leaders of other English colonies sought to use the newly forged Covenant Chain to gain the Iroquois as partners in managing their own Indian affairs. Andros brokered meetings between the Iroquois nations and Colonel Henry Coursey, a spokesman for Lord Baltimore and representative of Maryland, in the summer of 1677, and did the same for Colonel William Kendall representing the government of Virginia in 1679. Both hoped to curb violent encounters between colonists and Indian warriors along their colonies' frontiers. Leaders from each of the Iroquois nations agreed to do what they could to pacify the Chesapeake backcountry. At about the same time, Andros responded to the fraud and abuse that plagued the Indian trade at Albany (the English town that supplanted Fort Orange) by imposing new regulations to ensure fair dealing in open, public places.[30]

These agreements and reforms brought a measure of stability to

Iroquoia, and with it a new confidence to challenge the French. Beginning in the late 1670s, Iroquois warriors reasserted themselves in the Great Lakes region. In part this was a response to the Iroquois' newfound security and renewed supply of arms from Albany; it was also a response to the continuing loss of population to disease, which culminated in a smallpox outbreak in 1679. The warriors were especially aggressive in the years immediately following the outbreak, both to the south—where they now fought against the traditional enemies of the recently adopted Susquehannocks—and to the west, where they resumed their attacks on the French-allied Indians of the Great Lakes. French reports of Iroquois hostilities in these years strain credulity. In 1682, one noted that an Iroquois war party brought seven hundred captives home from the Illinois country, while six hundred more were killed and eaten on the spot, "without counting those whom they burned along the road." Another account claimed nine hundred prisoners and three or four hundred dead. A third writer said the captives numbered a thousand. These assertions cannot be strictly true—no Indian war party of the seventeenth century was large enough to wreak such havoc—but they register the fear and horror with which French observers had come to regard Iroquois warriors. And if they contain even a grain of truth, they suggest the way that the culture of Iroquois warfare was spinning out of control in these years.[31]

As in the 1650s and 1660s, so again in the 1680s, confidence turned quickly to overconfidence and mourning war to something more like total war. And again, as Iroquoia overreached militarily it suffered growing misfortunes. Mounting deaths, escalating violence, a flood tide of captives far too numerous to assimilate: from the triumphs of the 1670s, Iroquoia descended quickly toward disaster. The crises of the mid-1680s were compounded by the deaths, in rapid succession, of nearly every sachem of note with whom the English had recently dealt. In 1688 a Mohawk spokesman named Sindachsegie informed Andros, who had just returned to Albany after a long absence, "The Sachems who spoke formerly with you, are dead, and we have not so much knowledge as they had."[32]

Where was Tejonihokarawa during these turbulent years? He was still in his teens when the first links of the Covenant Chain were forged and would have played no part in the councils that brought that alliance system into being. He may well have been a young warrior expected to prove himself in the campaigns of the late 1670s and 1680s. But as the decade progressed, there is good reason to think that Tejonihokarawa rose into the ranks of the Mohawk sachems and emerged, by 1688, as one of the new generation of leaders seeking to mark out a new path from the ruins of the old. It would have been about this time that he married Catharine, a daughter of the matron of the Turtle clan. By marrying Karanondo's daughter, Tejonihokarawa entered into the pre-eminent family of the Mohawks. At the time of their marriage, Tekari-hoken, the leading sachem of the Mohawk nation, was Catharine's brother; on his death, the title would pass to the son of her older sister. As I have already suggested, it was likely at about this time that Tejoni-hokarawa acquired his name, "open the door," and the new ceremonial role it seems to imply.[33]

It is possible that Edmund Andros was the first English visitor for whom Tejonihokarawa opened the door of the Iroquois longhouse, because in September 1688 Andros returned in glory to Albany. He had been away a long time. He had been recalled from the governorship of New York in 1681 to answer charges—unfounded, as it turned out—of fiscal malfeasance. Once he was absolved, Andros received an extraordinary new commission from his patron, formerly the Duke of York and proprietor of New York and, after 1685, the new monarch James II. It was James's ambition to consolidate the administration of Britain's confusing welter of American colonies into two or three rationalized and centralized administrative units. The first of these—and, as it happened, the only one he managed to establish—was the Dominion of New England, an amalgamated territory that embraced the former colonies of New York, East and West Jersey, Massachusetts Bay, Connecticut, Plymouth, and New Hampshire. When Andros arrived in Albany in the fall of 1688 with his new commission in hand, he was at the height of his powers. In his mid-fifties, he was now styled "His Excellency Sir Edmund Andros, Knight, Captain General and Governor in Chief of His Majesty's Territory and Dominion of New England."[34]

The Iroquois sachems who gathered in Albany to meet Andros were pleased to see an old familiar face. They called him "Father Corlaer," an honorary title that reflected the high esteem in which they held him. But they were mystified by his message. They expected Andros to brighten the Covenant Chain with gifts—including guns, powder, and lead—and offer support against their enemies. And they believed they needed support. Though the Iroquois had enjoyed a brief truce in their wars with New France, the French continued to hold many Iroquois captives, including the prominent Cayuga leader Ourehouare, who had been consigned along with more than two dozen other captives to slave in French galleys in the Mediterranean. They spent the winter of 1687–1688 so "penn[ed] up" by the governor of Canada that "we could not hunt." Then, in the spring, a band of Wyandots who claimed to be acting on the governor's orders had attacked a group of Iroquois traveling to Canada. In years past, Andros had been a champion of Iroquois warfare, and the reputation of the Confederacy had been dramatically enhanced as a result. The assembled headmen expected nothing less on this occasion. But Andros surprised them. Instead of nurturing their grievances, he urged the sachems to observe their truce with New France and its Indian allies "punctually" and avoid any further hostilities. This was hard for the Iroquois leaders to swallow. But although they hoped for Andros's support, they could do little without it. Reluctantly, the Mohawk spokesman Sindachsegie agreed: "If we meet any French in the woods lakes or creeks, we will treat them as friends; and the same we will do with the Indians that live beyond us."[35]

This meeting was a confusing blow to Iroquois hopes, but its message was short-lived. Andros's attitude embodied his sovereign's will: James II hoped to establish more amicable relations with Catholic France, and it was essential that the Indian policy of his newly created Dominion of New England reflect this desire. Thus the grievances of the Iroquois fell victim to the dynastic ambitions of the English monarch. But James's pro-Catholic sympathies got him into trouble at home. In the fall of 1688 he was deposed in the so-called Glorious Revolution by William of Orange, champion of the Protestant cause in the Netherlands, who promptly brought England into the "grand alliance" of European powers against France in 1689. Thus England entered into the War of the League of Augsburg in Europe. In America, the Dominion of New England, which had briefly united all of New England, New York, and the Jerseys under Andros's rule, dissolved. Andros, whose authoritarian and arbitrary efforts to impose Dominion rule had outraged the colonists of Massachusetts Bay, was thrown in jail in Boston. And the colonies found themselves embroiled in King William's War against New France.[36]

War in Europe raised the stakes of the conflict between New France and England's colonies on both sides. In a rapid reversal of Andros's message of restraint, New York officials gave Iroquois leaders "all encouragement imaginable to pursue the French vigorously," while Frontenac, the veteran governor of New France, prepared for an invasion of New York and Iroquoia. In the summer of 1689, anti-French Iroquois warriors besieged forts Frontenac and Niagara and destroyed the village of Lachine on Montreal Island, where they killed two dozen residents and took seventy or more prisoners. Meanwhile, though Frontenac's plan for a full-scale invasion fell apart, he mustered a raiding party that attacked the village of Schenectady in February 1690. Sixty inhabitants were killed, another twenty-seven were taken prisoner, and the town went up in flames. This attack was especially noteworthy because of the active involvement of warriors from Kahnawake: though they deliberately avoided killing their Iroquois kinsmen in the raid, their actions invited retaliation and marked them as enemies of the anti-French alliance. In response, New York and New England leaders planned a coordinated land and sea invasion of Canada for the summer of 1690.[37]

The prospect of a full-scale invasion of Canada would have mobilized warriors from every Iroquois village, but smallpox swept through the four western nations in 1690. Only the Mohawks were spared; thus, only they could provide warriors for the Canadian campaign. One group of Mohawks traveled to Wood Creek, near the southern end of Lake Champlain, where the invasion was being staged, by way of Albany. In Albany, in the summer of 1690, Tejonihokarawa and a small circle of fellow Mohawks paused on their way to battle to ask the Dominie Godfridius Dellius, the resident Dutch Reformed minister, to baptize them in the Christian faith.

Protestant Mohawks

Tejonihokarawa appeared at the Dutch Reformed church in Albany on July 11, 1690, where he was baptized along with two other Mohawk men, three women, and four children. They were an interrelated family group of great influence among the Mohawks. Their matriarch was Karanondo ("Lifter"), who took the baptismal name of Lydia. Her son Tekarihoken—the principal sachem of the Mohawks—was also baptized and took the Christian name Isaac. Karanondo's oldest surviving daughter, Kowajatense, and her husband, Swongara, were baptized as Rebecca and David, while Tejonihokarawa took the name Hendrick. His wife, Catharine, Kowajatense's younger sister, had been baptized earlier by a Jesuit father and was not rebaptized in Albany. (Their only known child, a daughter named Lysbet, was baptized five months later.) Also present were a prominent war captain named Lawrence and his wife, Maria, who may have been either a daughter or niece of Karanondo.

Like Catharine, Lawrence and Maria had already been baptized by Jesuits; now they brought their adopted son to be baptized while they themselves were admitted to communion in the Albany church. Another couple probably unrelated to Karanondo, Sionheja ("Lively"), now Rachel, and her husband Skanjodowanne ("Eagle's Beak"), now called Joseph, were also baptized that day, along with their four-year-old son Manasse.[38]

These baptisms marked an extraordinary triumph for the presiding minister, the dominie Godfridius Dellius, who had been serving in the Albany parish for seven years. Little in his early service had suggested that he might one day win the loyalty of such a prominent group of Mohawk converts. Called from Amsterdam in August 1683, he requested permission to return to the Netherlands two years later. His request denied, Dellius settled into his meager parish. His duties brought him from Albany to Schenectady, a remote village twenty-four miles northwest of Albany that lay close to Mohawk country. Connected to Albany by a "fine, sandy cart road through a woods of nothing but beautiful evergreens or fir trees," Schenectady lay on a flat plateau above the floodplain of the Mohawk River, its residents' wheat fields spread out below with their rich loam deposited by the river's periodic inundations. The "black sandy soil" could "hardly be exhausted": it was planted "year after year, without manure." It was the kind of frontier community in which contact between Indians and colonists was frequent. Perhaps it was in Schenectady that Dellius first met Lawrence and Joseph, two of his earliest Mohawk supporters. In the years to come both men visited his Albany home often.[39]

They would have had little to say to one another had it not been for Hilletie van Olinda, a half-Mohawk woman (probably of the Wolf clan) who served Dellius as an interpreter and became his loyal partner in the effort to bring Dutch Reformed Christianity to the Mohawks. Jasper Dankers, a devout Labadist who traveled through New York in 1679 and

1680, left a long and sympathetic account of Hilletie. She told him that she had been raised in her mother's Mohawk community. She looked enough like her Dutch father, though, that her appearance was strikingly different from that of her Mohawk family, and from a young age their Dutch neighbors had expressed interest in raising her. They treated her kindly and spoke to her "about God, and of Jesus Christ and the Christian religion." Her family responded to this attention by showering her with scorn, so she left them to live with a woman who taught her to read and write. She became an avid Christian and was baptized. She married a Schenectady tailor named Peter Danielse van Olinda and began to serve as a Mohawk interpreter. Before Hilletie applied herself to the task, earlier ministers had worked with translators who were generally Dutch traders and understood only a trade pidgin; no minister had previously had access to a skilled interpreter with a strong grasp of both Mohawk and Dutch languages who was interested in religious ideas.[40]

Together, Dellius and Hilletie began to make inroads into the anti-French Mohawk community. As with the early Jesuit conversions, Dellius was first successful with outsiders, for whom Christianity offered a stark alternative to Native practices and beliefs and for whom conversion was a profoundly personal choice. For Hilletie and her Mohawk nephew Wouter, Christianity was a faith of both power—the traditional measure of spiritual efficacy—and love, which they understood as an ideal almost too fragile and beautiful to be imagined. Wouter believed that the Christian God brought him success in hunting in two episodes that were central to his conversion experience and faith narrative; they proved the power of the Christian god in terms that Wouter's Mohawk friends and relatives clearly understood. But Hilletie and Wouter also saw in the ideal of Christian love an alternative to the coarse, earthly bonds of community they knew in Mohawk country and in Schenectady. It was a difficult ideal to fulfill; in Dankers, Hilletie thought she discovered its realization for the first time. "How glad am I that I am so fortunate; that God should permit me to behold such

Christians, whom I have so long desired to see, and to whom I may speak from the bottom of my heart without fear; and that there are such Christians in the world," she reportedly told Dankers.[41]

Wouter, too, was touched by the opportunity to meet individuals whom he could regard as true Christians.

I am like a person who has three knives or some other articles which are valuable, useful and necessary, but has lost the one he has most need of. . . . Thus I have forsaken my relatives, and all my friends, my nation and country, which is good, and that is one of the articles. Moreover, I have come among the Christians, and Dutch, and begun to know something of God, and that also is good, and that is the second one. But I am wanting something more than these, and without which they are of no service to me, namely a knowledge of the Dutch language, ability to enter into the grounds of Christianity, and become a good Christian.

Dankers and his companion encouraged Wouter in his quest for true faith by quoting one of the Beatitudes. "Blessed are they who hunger and thirst after righteousness, for they shall be satisfied." Wouter was overwhelmed by this response. "Oh, how I love people who speak so kindly and mildly, and know how to utter such sweet and beautiful comparisons. Oh, what love I have for them!"[42] Dankers's narrative presents the vocabulary of Christian love as the foundation for new modes of thought that had profound implications for Hilletie and Wouter, who abandoned their Mohawk roots to explore its potential more fully.

Beyond Hilletie and Wouter, Dellius began to reach into a larger group of Mohawks. It is difficult to know whether they found the Christian gospel to be as transformative as these first two converts apparently did. Hendrick and his wife's clan did not disavow their Mohawk ties in the same way Hilletie and Wouter did, and it is possible to argue that they embraced Christianity in a cynical or instrumental way, to strengthen their alliance with New York and stake a stronger claim to the colony's resources and support. But in 1690 Dellius had no special claim to authority in the colony of New York, and Albany officials would have promised their support to the Mohawks whether some of them chose to be baptized or not. More likely, as with the Iroquois who accepted the teachings of the Jesuit fathers in the 1660s and 1670s, anti-French Mohawks saw in Dellius's instruction a spiritual counterweight to the rise of French power and the decline of their own fortunes. Perhaps, like Hilletie and Wouter, they also found in the Christian message a profound ideal that they hoped to internalize and use to restructure their community relations.

But unlike those first two converts, Hendrick and his cohort hoped to reconcile Christian and Mohawk identities rather than reject their Mohawk roots. Like the Jesuits, Dellius offered support and fellowship to Mohawks who were concerned about the future of their communities. In contrast to the Jesuits' entry into Mohawk country, however, there was nothing coercive in Dellius's presence. Preaching in Albany and, occasionally, Schenectady—there is no evidence that Dellius ever visited a Mohawk village—he invited interested listeners to hear and consider his Christian message. In the course of a few years Dellius attracted a large proportion of the remaining Mohawks.[43]

In choosing to listen to Dellius, Hendrick and his fellow Mohawks set themselves on a journey that they and many others—including the second Hendrick, Hendrick Peters Theyanoguin—would struggle to follow for many years as they sought to discover a meaningful, authentic path through the rapidly changing landscape of Iroquoia.

Woeful war

In 1690 Albany, like the Mohawk castles, was a village surrounded by a stockade. Six gates allowed visitors points of entry. The original Dutch settlement consisted of a single street—Haendeler's, or Trader's, Street—running parallel to the river, along which were clustered two rows of houses. They pinched together at the ends in a way that reminded early visitors of the shape of a fish net. Between the street and the river lay the original Dutch fort, Fort Orange. The English abandoned this fort and built a new one, above the town and farther away from the river. By 1690 a second major street, later called State Street, intersected Haendeler's and ran up the hill toward the fort. With 150–200 houses and a population between five hundred and seven hundred, Albany was built around the cross that was formed by the intersection of its two major streets (Figure 6). At the center of this intersection, in the heart of the community, stood Dellius's church. Erected in 1656 to double as a blockhouse, the Dutch Reformed church was the town's most substantial building and home to its most important institution.[44]

Hendrick and his Mohawk companions might have been struck by the contrast between Albany and their own villages, whose population had declined from over seven thousand in the 1630s to perhaps twenty-eight hundred in 1650 to a little over a thousand by 1690. Albany had not yet outgrown the total number of Mohawks, but in 1690 it was larger than any single Mohawk village and growing at a healthy pace. Perhaps Hendrick and his group saw in the rise of Albany the promise of a strong ally in their long, grinding conflict with New France and the Great Lakes Algonquians. Or perhaps the party with whom Hendrick traveled to Albany in 1690 saw in its rise the obverse image of their own people's decline. They might have recognized, even as early as 1690, that the steadily growing hamlet of Dutch and English traders, artisans, farmers, and petty officials was beginning to eclipse its Native neighbors.

Did conflicting emotions afflict Hendrick and his friends as they sought baptism and contemplated their collective and individual futures? We cannot know how they understood their entry into Christian communion and fellowship. Perhaps they saw it as an opportunity to add another powerful god to their pantheon of protectors before they plunged into battle yet again. But on the basis of their later actions, there is reason to think that they understood it to be, in some more fundamental

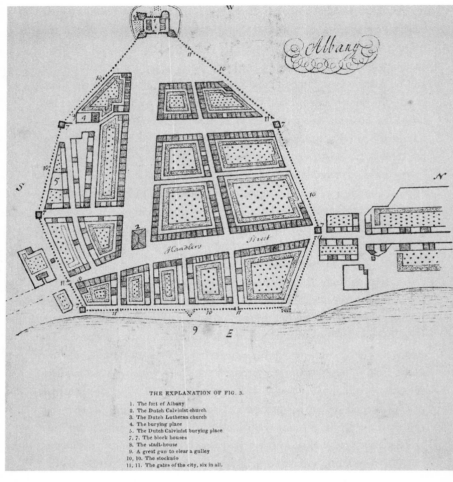

Albany

THE EXPLANATION OF FIG. 3.

1. The fort of Albany
2. The Dutch Calvinist church
3. The Dutch Lutheran church
4. The burying place
5. The Dutch Calvinist burying place
7, 7. The block houses
8. The stadt-house
9. A great gun to clear a gulley
10, 10. The stockade
11, 11. The gates of the city, six in all.

Figure 6. A map of Albany that shows the village's fort, outer palisade, and two major streets, with the Dutch Reformed church sited at their intersection. From John Miller, *A Description of the Province and City of New York . . . in the Year 1695* (London: T. Rodd, 1843). The Lionel Pincus and Princess Firyal Map Division, The New York Public Library, Astor, Lenox and Tilden Foundations.

way, a transformative moment in their spiritual and communal lives, one that might offer deliverance from the radical instability of Mohawk country, just as the migration to Kahnawake had brought their French-allied kindred a new measure of order and security. Likewise, there is no way of knowing whether Hendrick and the other Mohawk men who accompanied him—Isaac, David, Lawrence, and Joseph—intended to participate in the impending invasion of Canada. Lawrence was a war captain, and would surely have planned to fight. Hendrick may already have been a Mohawk sachem by this time, and Isaac was certainly one. Traditionally, scholars tell us, sachems—"peace chiefs"—did not fight. But if that is correct, the disastrous population decline of the late seventeenth century seems to have scrambled the traditional division of labor that separated warriors from sachems and brought all able-bodied men into the field, at least some of the time. Hendrick later claimed that he had participated in one or more raids on Canada. Given the intended scale of the 1690 invasion, it is likely that all five of the newly baptized men intended to fight.[45]

If they entertained high hopes for the invasion—the largest and most complex military venture that the English had attempted in North America—it failed to live up to their expectations. In fact, it failed altogether. The Massachusetts fleet never made it as far as Quebec; the colonies provided only a small fraction of their promised men-at-arms; and, as noted, the number of Iroquois warriors was dramatically reduced by a smallpox epidemic. So insufficient was the force that gathered at Wood Creek that the invasion was not even attempted. As a face-saving gesture, Johannes Schuyler (brother of Peter Schuyler, the mayor of Albany) led a small force of New York militia and Mohawk and Mahican warriors in a raid on La Prairie—the farming village near Montreal that was the first home of the Jesuit mission, which had since moved to Kahnawake—but hopes for a massive invasion of Canada were dashed.[46]

In the wake of this disappointment, the growing Christian faction of the English-allied Mohawks separated from their fellow Mohawks. Perhaps they sought an alternative to the incessant, destructive cycle of warfare that had plagued their people for so long and imposed such crushing burdens on their communities. Whatever motivated their decision, the Christian Mohawks who followed Dellius presented themselves as a distinct group for the first time in May 1691. They informed the governor that they intended to settle a new town, Tiononderoge, at the eastern edge of Mohawk country and asked that he arrange for a minister and chapel there.[47] The creation of Tiononderoge represented a further splintering of Mohawk society. Though the Turtle and Wolf clans predominated, the new community was defined primarily by its residents' attachment to Christianity, not their clan identity. In Tiononderoge they hoped to build a new kind of Mohawk settlement, akin to Kahnawake to the north, in which Protestant Christianity would modify traditional patterns of life.

But if the residents of Tiononderoge hoped to build a refuge from the destructive waves of violence breaking around them, they had not yet escaped the worst. War—and its constant companion, epidemic disease—steadily eroded Iroquois numbers. In 1690 and 1691 the Mohawks and Oneidas lost ninety warriors in battle. By December 1691 the Mohawks had only about 130 warriors left, and their misfortunes were about to intensify. In February 1693 a French force of some six hundred soldiers, militiamen, and allied Indians attacked Mohawk country and burned all three villages to the ground. Though most residents survived the attack and avoided captivity, not enough Mohawks remained to support three castles. After dispersing for a short time into a number of small hamlets, they organized themselves around two communities, which remained the principal towns in Mohawk country throughout the eighteenth century: the recently founded Tiononderoge, which now became the Mohawks' Lower Castle (so called because it lay lower, or farther east, along the Mohawk), which was rebuilt about eight miles from its original site; and Canajoharie, the Upper Castle, some twenty-four miles farther upriver.[48]

The failure of the 1690 invasion and the devastation that followed, which culminated in the destruction of the three Mohawk castles in February 1693, must have shaken the foundations of Mohawk society and led all its members, particularly those associated with Protestant Christianity who had made a new home in Tiononderoge, to wonder where their future lay. This is precisely the moment at which Hendrick's name begins to appear more regularly in the records of New York's Indian affairs and Albany's Dutch Reformed church. On December 23, 1692, Hendrick was admitted to full membership in the church. By June 1693—four months after French forces burned Mohawk country to the ground—Dellius claimed to have baptized some two hundred converts, though only fifty-three of their names are recorded.[49] The rise of this Christian faction gave Dellius unique influence among the Mohawks. But his influence was short-lived. Dellius's career as an Indian missionary came to an abrupt and unhappy end when he used that influence to betray the Mohawks to enrich himself and his Albany circle.

The Albany swindle

After his early success with leading members of the Turtle clan, in 1694 and 1695 Dellius baptized a number of prominent members of the Bear clan as well. Young adults, generally in their twenties, appear to be over-represented in Dellius's baptisms during the 1690s, suggesting that individuals like Hendrick who were rising into leadership roles in their clans and communities were especially likely to heed the dominie's call. Along-side these younger converts, Dellius also had success with a smaller number of key elders. We have already seen that the baptism of Karanondo, or Lydia, matron of the Turtle clan, was critical in Dellius's early success with her extended kin group (though we have no way of knowing whether it was her interest that drew her children along with her, or whether her children led and she followed in making this choice). In a similar way, the Bear clan family of Gideon Tonidoge constituted an important extended lineage whose members were baptized beginning in

1693. In addition to Gideon's five children—three with his first wife, Catrina, and two more with his second wife, Dorcas Sakkoherriho ("One Who Reenters the Bushes")—his grandchildren and great-grandchildren, numbering some twenty-five in all, were also baptized into the Christian Mohawk community. At the same time, Dellius continued to gain influence with key sachems, among them Rode ("Stupid") of the Turtle clan, Joseph Dehanochrakhas of the Bear clan, and Gideon Sharenhowaneh of the Wolf clan.[50]

Dellius's growing influence among the Mohawks was paralleled by his rise in colonial affairs. His name was increasingly linked with that of Peter Schuyler, who became Albany's first mayor in 1686 and remained its most powerful figure for decades, and a circle of former fur traders who had become prominent Albany merchants and citizens: Dirk Wesselse Ten Broeck, Evert Bancker, and Nicholas Bayard. In August 1696, Governor Richard Fletcher made Schuyler, Dellius, and Wesselse Ten Broeck New York's Indian commissioners in dealing with the Iroquois. The very substantial sum of £100 was "lodged in the hands of Mr. Dellius" to defray the expenses they would incur.[51]

As Dellius moved toward the center of the colony's Indian affairs, so too did the Christian Mohawks who were most closely associated with him. Hilletie began to act as an official interpreter for the colony, and Christian Mohawks became valuable informants by passing along intelligence from their French-allied relatives in Kahnawake and the other mission communities in the St. Lawrence Valley. In February 1697, Hendrick and Tjerk, a Mohawk whose daughters had been baptized by Dellius, traveled to Canada to return two prisoners to Governor Frontenac. Designated by the "governor of Man[h]atte[n]" for the role, the two messengers also delivered a belt to the governor on behalf of the Mohawk nation. Hendrick's star was on the rise, as were the reputations of Tjerk, Joseph, and the other young Christian Mohawk sachems.[52]

Yet Dellius's success made him a dangerous friend. Beginning in 1695, he and his Albany circle began angling for large grants of Mohawk land. With the permission of Governor Fletcher, Albany merchant Nicholas Bayard secured a deed to an extensive tract of land along Schoharie Creek near Tiononderoge. Soon Dellius and the others sought their own deeds to Mohawk country. In June 1696, Dellius convinced four of his recent converts—Rode, the Turtle clan sachem; Tjerk, who traveled to Canada with Hendrick as Dellius's emissary; Joseph, Bear clan sachem; and Gideon of the Wolf clan—to sign over to him a vast parcel of land, seventy miles long and twelve miles wide, surrounding the refugee town of Schaghticoke on the east bank of the Hudson River. In 1697, eight Mohawk sachems, including Hendrick and Joseph, signed away another enormous tract on the Mohawk River, fifty miles long and four miles wide, to Dellius, Schuyler, Wesselse Ten Broeck, Bancker, and William Pinhorne, a New York City merchant and member of the governor's council. Thus in three separate transactions, two involving Dellius, various Mohawk Christians signed away much of their land, thought to be worth £25,000 and including a fifty-mile swath cut from the heart of their territory on the Mohawk River.[53]

What were they thinking? According to a complaint signed by Hendrick and Joseph in the summer of 1698, the signatories were tricked by their Albany friends into believing that the deeds were only a formality through which the dominie, the mayor, and their allies would guarantee the protection of Mohawk land rights. The simplest explanation is perhaps also the most intuitively persuasive: manipulative colonists fooled credulous Mohawks, who unwittingly gave away nearly everything they owned. Certainly this seems to be the perspective eventually adopted by Sinnonquirese, the Mohawk spokesman who dramatically rejected one of the deeds on behalf of the Iroquois Confederacy by casting it into the Albany council fire in the summer of 1698.

Yet the view that the Christian Mohawks were the unwitting dupes of their duplicitous friends in Albany may not tell the whole story. It is worth remarking, for the sake of perspective, that the Iroquois had given land away to ensure its protection before. In 1684, the Confederacy supposedly delivered to then governor Thomas Dongan a deed for the lower Susquehanna Valley after they had wrested it from the control of the Susquehannocks. There is a particularly close parallel here to the deed given by the Mohawks to Dellius for the land around Schaghticoke, which, like the lower Susquehanna, had recently belonged to their enemies—in this case, the Mahicans—and was now home to a mixed refugee community.[54]

It is also possible that the Mohawks who signed these deeds believed their communities were in especially dire need of outside protection in 1695 and 1696. These were the final years of the War of the League of Augsburg; its North American analogue, King William's War, had gone from bad to worse for the anti-French Iroquois. Despite their long-standing hope that sustained support from New York and the New England colonies might finally tip the scales against their rivals to the north and west, Iroquois warriors once again received only halting aid from the English; and once again, their communities were pushed to the brink of collapse. English officials ignored the request of the Tiononderoge Christians for a minister and a fort. In the middle years of the decade, the Iroquois Confederacy sent emissaries to Canada to sue for peace, against the wishes of New York officials, even as raids and counterraids continued to plague the region—a clear indication that the anti-French Iroquois believed they were fighting in a losing cause. For his part, the governor of New France dealt with them dishonestly. While he agreed to peace in his meetings with Iroquois delegates, he continued to press his advantage in the war on Iroquoia. When New York's Governor Fletcher learned that the French had used the cover of peace negotiations to rebuild the fort at Cataraqui, he blamed his Iroquois allies. "Since I have had the honour to serve the Great King of England my Master in this Province," he reportedly told a delegation of ten Mohawk sachems, "all your misfortunes have been occasioned by your own Drunken, supine, Negligent & Careless humours." Even allowing for the evasions and hyperbole embodied in Fletcher's accusation, there is probably some truth to the view that the Iroquois, and particularly the Mohawks, were dispirited and increasingly ineffectual in protecting their own interests as the war dragged unsuccessfully on.[55]

The decision of a cohort of younger Mohawk leaders, supported by a few older sachems, to seek baptism and church membership during these same years may be a symptom of a growing rift between Christians and traditionalists that was affecting both village life and the council of sachems. Perhaps Rode, Tjerk, Joseph, and Gideon took a calculated risk on behalf of the growing population of Christian Mohawks in entrusting Mohawk lands to their friends in Albany. If so, they apparently acted against the wishes of another group of sachems, for whom the land deeds represented a betrayal of Mohawk interests. And perhaps Dellius understood his actions less as an outright betrayal than a canny hedging of bets: an attempt simultaneously to strengthen the hand of his Christian Mohawk friends in relation to the traditionalists among the Mohawk sachems, and to gain for himself and his friends valuable concessions that might one day enrich them all—particularly if the precipitous decline of Mohawk fortunes continued to the point that they could no longer maintain an independent claim to their land. This is not to exonerate Dellius. The deeds he helped secure were clearly self-serving. Yet it is not difficult to imagine that he could rationalize his actions in a way that made them seem a defensible, honorable, and just response to the crisis in Mohawk country.

This view of events helps to explain the circumstances under which the deeds finally came to light in the summer of 1698. The War of the League of Augsburg had come to an end in the previous year, but as always word traveled slowly to North America. Richard Coote, the first Earl of Bellomont, replaced Governor Fletcher in the spring of 1698 and sent Dellius and Peter Schuyler to Quebec to begin peace negotiations with Governor Frontenac. Yet Bellomont's confidence in Schuyler and Dellius soon evaporated as he settled into the governor's role. Fletcher had sided strongly with the colony's anti-Leislerians: those who had opposed Jacob Leisler, a German-born militia commander who took control of the city of New York and proclaimed himself governor in 1689, during the crisis caused by the Glorious Revolution in England. Leisler had the support of many rank-and-file New Yorkers, but prominent citizens of both English and Dutch background—including all of the colony's Dutch Reformed ministers—opposed Leisler's Rebellion because of its threat to order and good government. In Albany, Leisler's supporters never gained control. Mayor Peter Schuyler, Dominie Dellius, and their allies, with the timely support of a band of Mohawk warriors, held a small, armed force of Leisler's men at bay and then kept power until a new governor, Henry Sloughter, arrived from England with orders to try and execute the rebels.[56]

Governor Fletcher succeeded Sloughter and, like Sloughter, maintained close ties to the anti-Leisler faction in the colony. But Fletcher's administration was so notorious for misrule that Bellomont soon made friends among Fletcher's enemies and sought to undo much of what Fletcher had done. In Albany, this meant reversing the land grants Dellius had helped to engineer. As Bellomont sought to overturn the grants and involve himself in Indian affairs, he came to regard Dellius as his principal obstacle. Given to hyperbolic condemnations of his political enemies, Bellomont soon cast Dellius as an archfiend whose lies and prevarications endangered English interests with the Iroquois. He accepted and amplified every charge made against Dellius, including the improbable accusation that he was a crypto-Jesuit who was secretly plotting with French missionaries against the interests of New York.[57]

Bellomont's education in Albany politics began in May 1698, when

Schuyler and Dellius were in Montreal. While they were away, Hendrick and Joseph appeared before Bellomont in the city of New York to denounce the purchase made by Schuyler, Dellius, and their partners in the Mohawk Valley. (Dellius's supporters later claimed that his enemies had led Hendrick and Joseph to the governor.) In their deposition, the two Mohawks said they had not intended to sell their land when they signed the document, which was presented to them as a way of securing the land against the French in time of war. Schuyler, Dellius, and the others had claimed that the document only made them "guardians or trustees" of their property. Now convinced that they had signed the "false paper . . . contrary to our intent," they asked that the deed be "vacated and destroyed" and that "the memory of so great a Corruption may be rooted out from among us Christians lest our unconverted brethren may be discouraged by so ill a practice and example from entering into the Christian faith." Hendrick and Joseph then went one step farther: acknowledging that "we are subjects of the great King of England and have long ago surrendered ourselves and lands to the protection of our said great King," they requested "that your Lordship would be pleased to let us have a patent for our said land to hold of our said Great King: with a limitation that none of the English may enter upon our said lands whilst any of us or our posterity are in being; except that our great King shall see cause to erect a Castle or Fort there for the security of the subjects on the frontiers." In all the arguments that followed, the possibility of a patent that would guarantee Iroquois or Mohawk land rights was never raised again.[58]

In defending their actions, both Dellius and Fletcher (whose approval of this grant, along with several others, inspired Bellomont's wrath) argued that they had, in fact, intended to secure Mohawk land rights against the pressure of French incursions. Dellius further contended that the deed was supposed to have included parcels of land that were reserved to the Mohawks, but that Fletcher's attorney general had refused to include such parcels in the final version of the patent because he "judged it was against the King's dignity to grant a conditional patent." We should not place too much weight on Dellius's protestations of innocence: clearly, he and his allies had sought to prosper in the long run from their enormous grant. Yet it is nevertheless possible that Dellius saw himself as unjustly accused by Bellomont, and that he had believed he was protecting the interests of his Christian Mohawks in the short run by securing their land against both French incursion and, perhaps, more aggressive New York speculators.[59]

When Bellomont persuaded the New York Assembly to revoke the deeds and suspend Dellius from his pulpit, the dominie prepared to sail for Amsterdam to plead his case. He collected a sheaf of testimonials protesting his innocence and proclaiming his good character. They came from his New Albany congregation; the Dutch Reformed churches in Schenectady, Kingston, and New York; the merchants of New York; and the Dutch, French, and English church leaders in the city. He also carried with him a statement of recantation and apology from Hendrick and Joseph that was made just before Dellius's departure. "Uneasy in their minds about what they had testified against said Dominie Dellius," according to the document, they renounced their earlier statement. "We have not done it," they reportedly told justice of the peace Killiaen van Rensselaer and three Albany aldermen. "It was done by others, who led us as if by a cord."[60]

Soon Hendrick and Joseph recanted this statement as well. Caught in a fierce partisan battle between Albany's chief rivals for power, Hendrick and the circle of Christian Mohawks were pawns in a game played at another level, while their own interests fell by the wayside. Two days after Dellius left Albany, Hendrick was examined under oath by Hendrick Hanse, the new mayor of Albany, along with the sheriff and eight justices of the peace. Hendrick explained that he had visited Dellius on the day of his departure only after a group of influential clan matrons, including Hendrick's mother-in-law, Lydia, had repeatedly pleaded with him to reconcile with the dominie. Hilletie, Dellius's faithful and long-suffering interpreter, had orchestrated the meeting and translated Hendrick's words into English, which were then recorded in the apology that Dellius had carried to Amsterdam.

Under questioning by the mayor and justices, Hendrick testified that he had expressed regret at Dellius's departure, but denied that he had said he and Joseph were "led as with a cord" to ask Bellomont to revoke the 1697 land deed. Then Hendrick gave a full account of the occasion. While the partisan context of Hendrick's deposition gives good reason to question the strict accuracy of the document, it purports to reproduce a lengthy narrative in Hendrick's own voice. On June 8, 1699, according to his account,

> he came there [to Dellius's house] with two other Indians and sat in the kitchen drinking some beer. Then Mr. Dellius came to them with Hille[tie] the interpretess, who asked them if it did not grieve them the Dominies going away. He answered Yes, it did grieve him. Then Hille[tie] the interpretess said, "Whose fault is it that Mr. Dellius goes away?" Joseph the Indian would have answered but Hille[tie] took the word out of his mouth, saying, "Those base people that stir you up and draw you with a line are the cause of it." The said Hille[tie] said further to Hendrick the Indian, "Tell the Dominie Mr. Dellius that it is their fault that he goes away that have incited you against him." She said further, "Speak now, Mr. Dellius is going oversea, speak hard talk your best that he may return again to us in the spring for you are praying Indians." Hendrick replied, "I am alone; what can I do? If we were all together then we could speak but now we can say nothing."[61]

Though Hendrick refused to speak for all the Christian Mohawks without first consulting with them, he proceeded to have a direct exchange with Dellius. More than three hundred years later, the tortured feelings hanging in the kitchen air on that early summer day remain palpable. The conversation began when Dellius asked Hendrick, "Do you love me?"

> Hendrick answered yes, I ever loved you since we have been praying Indians, and did never think that we should have disturbed your mind. We have observed and minded our praying well and have fought well for the Country in the late war. Then Mr. Dellius stood up and shaked hands with Hendrick and said, "I have long expected you and forgave you the evil you have done me." Hendrick replied, "I expected you would have sent for me because you are the greater man, but you always sent for others, not for me." Mr. Dellius told him it is more proper that the youngest should come to the eldest, I expected you to come without sending for [you].[62]

Half-reconciled and still nurturing their grievances, Hendrick and Dellius parted.

Hendrick's nadir

With Dellius gone and the Christian Mohawks disgraced, Hendrick's reputation was at a low ebb. The war damaged Albany and nearly destroyed the nearby Mohawk communities. Between 1689 and 1698, the fur trade that was Albany's economic lifeline decayed dramatically, while the number of colonists in and around Albany declined by nearly a third, from just over 2,000 to 1,449. During the same period, the number of Mohawk men reportedly fell by more than half, from 270 to 110. With the arrival of peace, many of the remaining Mohawks once again looked favorably toward the mission communities in Canada where many of their kinsmen already lived. In 1700, Robert Livingston reported that two-thirds of the Mohawks had relocated to Canada. In a pointed critique of England's dilatory response to the Christian Mohawks' earlier requests for ministers and a fort, he noted that the Mohawks who had gone to Canada were "kindly received, being clothed from head to foot, and are secured in a Fort guarded with soldiers, & have Priests to instruct them." Even the Christian Mohawks who were most closely associated with the Albany leadership were tempted. Tjerk, who went to Canada with Hendrick in 1697, moved there after the war, while Hendrick reported that Brant, Jacob, and three other Christian Mohawks were prevented only with difficulty from following suit.[63]

Paradoxically, the migration of so many Mohawks to Canada may have helped to keep Christian sachems like Hendrick in leadership roles despite their recent humiliation. But their options were dramatically circumscribed. In the aftermath of the recently concluded war between France and England, the governors of both New France and New York pressured the Iroquois to strengthen their ties to the colonies. French officials—Frontenac until his death in 1698, followed by his successor, Louis-Hector de Callière—encouraged the League Iroquois to continue moving north to Canada and hoped to assert control over northern Iroquoia. In August 1700 Bellomont pretended, at last, to answer the Mohawks' long-standing request for a fort. His true interest was to stake a claim in the heart of Iroquois territory by locating the fort near Onondaga, far from the New York frontier and in the center of Iroquois territory. When he announced his intention at an Albany conference, the Iroquois spokesman, Sadekanaktie, an Onondaga who had long been associated with the English alliance, pointedly ignored the suggestion. But Bellomont pressed him to endorse the plan, and Sadekanaktie grudgingly concurred. He had little choice: he could not afford a dramatic breach of the alliance; he spoke, after all, for the pro-English faction that relied on Bellomont's goodwill for the gifts he brought to the conference and, more generally, to maintain their own status within the Iroquois Confederacy. But Iroquois patience was wearing thin. When Bellomont reported that the fort would be large enough to hold two hundred men and asked the Iroquois to supply a hundred warriors to man it during wartime, Sadekanaktie refused to commit. And when Bellomont pressed Sadekanaktie to name the sachems who would help locate a site for the fort, he put the governor off and promised instead that they would be identified later, when Bellomont's surveying party arrived in Onondaga.[64]

While Sadekanaktie bent to Bellomont's will but refused to do all that was asked of him, the Christian Mohawks played the role of even more pliable allies in Bellomont's scheme. At the end of the second day of the conference, after Sadekanaktie finished speaking and the sachems had withdrawn from the council chamber, the Christian Mohawks requested an audience with the governor. Hendrick spoke for them. He wanted to make a particular response to Bellomont's request that Iroquois leaders stop the migration to Canada. Hendrick reported on his success in convincing Brant, Jacob, and three others to stay. Then Brant stood and emphasized that he had been convinced of the error of his ways and that he looked forward to "further instruction in the true Protestant Religion." Even among a pro-English group representing the Iroquois council of sachems, the Christian Mohawks apparently desired to present themselves to Bellomont as the most eager and supportive of his Indian allies.[65]

On the last day of the conference, as Sadekanaktie was making his final summary statement on behalf of all the assembled sachems, Hendrick again addressed Bellomont, this time interrupting the proceedings in a way that must have rankled with Sadekanaktie and the rest of the Iroquois leaders. He intervened in a tense moment to offer unalloyed thanks to Bellomont. Sadekanaktie had just finished delivering an unusually pointed criticism of English policy in Iroquoia. He did it by quoting the Jesuit Father Bruyas, but the import of his remarks was clear. Bruyas, Sadekanaktie reported, had been critical of New York's management of the alliance. By seeking to prevent trade between the Iroquois and New France, Bellomont apparently intended to provoke another war. Moreover, unlike the governor of Canada, Bellomont kept

Iroquois leaders in the dark about the negotiations between the colonies, implying that he did not trust them. Most tellingly, Bruyas noted, "the Governor of Canada did not claim a right to their land as Corlaer [the governor of New York] did, he left them to their liberty; but Corlaer pretended a superiority over them."[66] In thinly veiled form, Sadekanaktie issued a direct challenge to Bellomont's behavior and intentions.

As his words hung in the air, Hendrick rose to speak. Recalling the controversial deeds that Schuyler, Dellius, and the Albany merchants had wrested from the Mohawks, Hendrick noted that Bellomont had promised to write to the king to invalidate the grants. Now the Mohawks had been informed that the deeds were indeed vacated. He acknowledged Bellomont's intervention with a gift of nine beaver pelts and thanks "in behalf of the Five Nations for your fatherly care in restoring our land to us again."[67] The record of the conference does not tell us how Hendrick's speech was received, either by the governor or by the Iroquois sachems. It appears, however, to have been an awkward sequel to Sadekanaktie's climactic challenge, one that blunted its implied criticism and let Bellomont off the hook. Hendrick continued to appear at subsequent conferences as a Mohawk sachem, so we can conclude that the breach of protocol, if that is what it was, was not unforgivable. But it suggests, at least, a tension between Christian Mohawks like Hendrick and Confederacy spokesmen like Sadekanaktie.

If Sadekanaktie and Hendrick disagreed about whether Bellomont coveted Iroquois land despite his repudiation of Fletcher's grants, subsequent events quickly demonstrated that Sadekanaktie's fears were well founded. In September 1700 Bellomont dispatched Colonel Wolfgang Romer, his military engineer, to Onondaga country along with the Indian trader Hendrick Hansen and Major Peter Van Brugh. Romer's party placed a series of demands on the Iroquois leaders they met along the way. They expected to be guided to Onondaga country, to be aided by the Onondaga sachems in selecting a site for the fort, and to be supplied with a canoe for the trip home so they could assess the suitability of a water route. But at every stage of their journey, Romer's party met with frustration. No Iroquois leader was willing to challenge their intentions directly; instead, through passive resistance they slowed the party's progress and disappointed their expectations. Upon his return, Romer reported unhappily to Bellomont that "the Indians entertained him coldly and rudely." No site was agreed on, and the plan for a fort in Onondaga country foundered.[68]

Bellomont's other initiative in the fall of 1700 was more successful, thanks largely to his influence with Hendrick and his fellow Christian Mohawks. Bellomont had been conscious since his arrival in New York that his colony might become an important supplier of naval timber to the Crown. Few resources were as important to the monarchies of western Europe as tall, straight, old-forest white pines, which served as mast timbers for the largest sailing ships of the early modern world. England had relied for too long on a somewhat troublesome trade with the Baltic states of northern Europe for its tall timber, and Portsmouth, New Hampshire, emerged in the seventeenth century as an important competitor in the trade. Bellomont hoped New York could enter the competition as well: a steady supply of tall New York timber would stand the colony in good stead with the Crown and strengthen his personal reputation at court.[69]

To accomplish this aim, Bellomont needed access to good stands of timber near the navigable waterways of the Mohawk and Hudson rivers. No place was more suitable to the purpose than the very parcels of land the Mohawks had recently deeded to their Albany supporters. (Indeed, one argument Dellius made in his own defense was that Bellomont had been infuriated by the Mohawk deeds because he coveted the same lands himself for the timber they could provide to the Crown.) In the fall of 1700, Bellomont contracted with two "honest substantial men" to cut twenty-four masts, ranging from thirty-five to forty inches in diameter. They were instructed to strike a bargain with the Mohawks for the timber. In his letter to the lords of the admiralty, Bellomont emphasized the importance of keeping the arrangement secret. "Those men that call themselves lawyers here," he warned, "are not of a principle to be trusted with any thing that's for the King's service, they being all disaffected to the government, and did they know this bargain and design of mine, they would . . . put notions in the Indians heads (who are the jealousest people on the earth) to make them either not consent to the Kings making use of the Woods at all, or consent, under an extravagant price."[70] His fear was directed especially at the Albany circle with whom he had placed himself at odds. If Schuyler and his allies caught wind of the plan, they would almost certainly attempt either to disrupt it or, as Bellomont predicted, profit from it.

Bellomont was fortunate to have a new supporter to whom he could turn. With Dellius gone, in an odd series of events the classis of Amsterdam sent two ministers, Johannes Lydius and Bernardus Freeman, to fill his place. Lydius's claim to the Albany pulpit was stronger, but Bellomont liked Freeman and encouraged him to take up the pulpit in Schenectady, where he could minister to the Christian Mohawks as well. With Freeman's help, Bellomont's agents in the woods signed an agreement with eleven "praying Mohawks and principal owners of the Mohawk country" that granted to the king a perpetual right to cut timber on their land. Hendrick, Joseph, and Brant were among the signers.[71]

Hendrick had his hand in one more event in the fall of 1700 that worked in Bellomont's favor and may have been orchestrated at his request. In a brief memorial submitted to Bellomont in October, Hendrick and another Christian Mohawk named Cornelius reported that five sachems, representing five western Abenaki villages, had asked to join with the Mohawks in the Covenant Chain. The Abenakis expressed their desire to "leave the Governor of Canada for the many cheats he has put upon us" and offered to allow the Iroquois Confederacy to absorb their territory in exchange for taking the Abenakis under their protection. The Mohawks responded favorably and informed the Abenakis that an alliance with the Mohawks meant an alliance with "Brother Corlaer," the governor of New York, as well. After a very brief exchange on both sides, the memorial ends with a nod to Protestant Christianity. "Now we leave off," the Mohawks told their visitors, "but [first] must tell you concerning our religion and how kind our Brother Corlaer is in causing us to be instructed in learning much exceeding the learning you receive in Canada; therefore we desire you to come and participate with us in our belief, so that thereby we may become one flesh and blood."[72]

The memorial is odd in several respects. It appears in the documentary record without any context; we cannot tell whether the Abenakis or the Mohawks initiated the meeting it describes. While it is possible that some of these Abenakis moved to Schaghticoke to come under Mohawk and New York protection, there is no evidence that their promise to cede their territory to the Mohawks had any meaningful effect. Nor is it possible to tell whether Bellomont had any hand in the proceedings. Whether he did or not, he soon claimed the outcome as his own. In a letter to the Board of Trade later in the fall, he wrote that he had set in motion a plan to draw these Abenakis to Schaghticoke to "strengthen our Indians and disappoint the French."[73] Whether Hendrick had actively sought out the Abenaki sachems on Bellomont's behalf or had given him an unanticipated but welcome gift, the effect was the same. By the fall of 1700, Hendrick and his circle seemed to identify with Bellomont and the Covenant Chain even more strongly than they did with the Confederacy council in Onondaga.

Neutrality

As Hendrick and the Christian Mohawks lurched toward the English alliance, the Iroquois Confederacy wrestled with the need to find a balance between French and English interests. Canada and its Indian allies had pressured the Iroquois relentlessly for more than a decade. Even af-

ter the Treaty of Ryswick in 1697 and the peace settlement between New
York and New France in the following year, Canadian officials continued to supply arms to their numerous Indian allies in the Great Lakes.
In 1699 a party of Ojibwa warriors attacked a group of Seneca hunters
near their home village; Ojibwa tradition suggests that they inflicted a
series of defeats on Iroquois hunters in this period. In the following
year, a combined force of Ottawa, Illinois, and Miami warriors defeated
another hunting party and killed more than fifty Onondaga and Seneca
men. All the while, Callière, the new governor of New France, pressed
the Iroquois to move north into the St. Lawrence Valley and to permit
him to rebuild and reoccupy Fort Frontenac, built at Cataraqui in 1673
and abandoned at the height of Iroquois hostilities in 1689. In 1701, with
the governor's blessing, Antoine de la Mothe, Sieur de Cadillac, built a
new French post, Fort Ponchartrain, at Detroit, where the Iroquois
feared their western enemies would gain additional support.[74]

Diplomatic ties to New York and New France had become indispensable to the Iroquois, but the pressure of Canada and its Native allies, counterposed by intermittent but inadequate support from the
English colony, threatened to destroy Iroquoia. As the governors of
New France and New York each pressed forward with ambitious fort-
building projects designed to secure a foothold in Iroquois territory,
Confederacy leaders searched for a way to maintain both alliances while
not selling out their interests or losing control of their territory. The
principal Iroquois leader identified with this challenge was Teganissorens, the Onondaga sachem and orator. New Yorker Cadwallader
Colden described him as "tall and well made" and noted that he had "a
great fluency in speaking, and a graceful Elocution, that would have
pleased in any Part of the World." In 1701, Teganissorens prevailed over
both Francophiles and Anglophiles within the Confederacy and helped
to engineer a pair of settlements intended to keep the Iroquois' European neighbors at bay.[75]

In seeking a balanced settlement, Teganissorens and his supporters contended with pro-English Mohawks on one side and a pro-French faction led by the Onondaga orator Aradgi on the other. In mid-1700, Aradgi and his followers believed that the best course for the Confederacy was an unconditional surrender to New France and its Indian allies. They contended that the Iroquois were too weak to resist any longer, and that the English were nothing but untrustworthy spies. In the summer of 1700, as Sadekanaktie scolded Governor Bellomont while Hendrick and the Christian Mohawks sought to blunt his message, another party of Iroquois sachems traveled north to Montreal to negotiate the terms of a settlement with New France. To do so without Bellomont's approval was, in his eyes, a violation of the terms of the Covenant Chain; he had long insisted that the Iroquois must not deal with the French directly, but must allow New York to negotiate with New France on their behalf. But communication and travel between Iroquoia and Canada had been frequent since the end of hostilities in 1698, and, given New York's inability to protect Iroquois interests, there was no support among the Iroquois for the idea that they should defer to Bellomont in such negotiations. The pro-French faction was gaining ground in Onondaga, and many sachems were growing openly contemptuous of English authority. The Mohawks, however, were especially reluctant to defy the governor's wishes. Though each of the other four nations of the Iroquois was represented in Montreal in the summer of 1700, no Mohawks were in attendance.[76]

The Covenant Chain, and the Mohawks who identified with it most strongly, received another blow in March 1701 when Governor Bellomont died. (The cause of death was severe gout, but tradition holds that he was done in by the rigors of governing three colonies—New York, Massachusetts, and New Hampshire—simultaneously.) His lieutenant governor, John Nanfan, was attending to personal business in Barbados at the time of Bellomont's death and did not arrive in New York until late May. Once present, he served capably for a year until Bellomont's successor, Edward Hyde, third Earl of Clarendon and Lord

Cornbury, arrived in the colony. But Nanfan had neither detailed knowledge of New York's affairs nor strong connections among its leading figures. Bellomont's death created a vacuum of power in Indian relations that allowed the Albany circle to reassert itself but left the colony without a strong hand or clear vision. For the Iroquois, Bellomont's passing was a mixed blessing. They lost a governor who had come to know the colony's Indian affairs reasonably well, and who had taken the Covenant Chain seriously as one key to the colony's defenses. Yet they were also freed from the growing pressure he had placed on Iroquois resources and loyalty. Nearly all of Bellomont's plans died with him: the effort to persuade the Crown to vacate Fletcher's grants; the timber scheme; the Onondaga fort; the attempt to settle Abenakis at Schaghticoke. Though Nanfan shared Bellomont's wish to maintain an effective alliance with the Iroquois, he was on uncertain footing in the spring and summer of 1701 and approached the Confederacy with more caution and hesitation than a governor of New York had displayed in many years.[77]

In the absence of leadership from the governor's office, Albany's Indian commissioners sent two delegates, Captain Johannes Bleeker, Jr., and David Schuyler, to Onondaga in early June. Their principal intent was to discover the substance of the Confederacy's negotiations with New France. What they found alarmed them. Messengers and sachems were coming and going from Montreal, and the Iroquois council was in turmoil. While they were in Onondaga, a French party arrived. Led by Paul le Moyne de Maricourt, a Montreal resident who had frequent contact with the Iroquois at Kahnawake, spoke Mohawk, and was considered a member of the Onondaga nation, and Jacques Bruyas, who had served as a missionary to the Oneidas and the Mohawks, the party's purpose was to summon the Iroquois sachems to Montreal for a conference with Callière. Though the Iroquois enthusiastically welcomed Maricourt's party—a reflection of the pro-French faction's growing influence—the Frenchmen's aggressive and domineering manner soon changed the mood.

Speaking on Governor Callière's behalf, Maricourt demanded the return of prisoners (and forcibly rounded up a few before departing); announced the construction of Fort Ponchartrain at Detroit, which Teganissorens and the other neutralist sachems considered an infringement on Iroquois lands; and continued to press the Iroquois to welcome a Jesuit priest among them.[78]

The assembled sachems were "much confused . . . and extreamly divided" as they discussed Callière's propositions, but Maricourt and his party had overplayed their hand and thereby strengthened the resolve of the sachems who sought neutrality. After three days of sleepless deliberation, Teganissorens replied to Maricourt's propositions and his English auditors at the same time. "You both tell us to be Christians," he began. "You both make us mad. We know not what side to choose, but I will speak no more of praying or Christianity. . . . We are sorry we cannot pray, but now we are come to this conclusion: those that sells their goods cheapest whether English or French, of them we will have a Minister. Our Sachems are going some to Albany, some to Canada. In the meantime we will consider of it till winter." Angry at being challenged in his attempt to carry away prisoners and insulted by the tenor of Teganissorens's response, Maricourt returned to Montreal to report to his governor.[79]

With neutralist sentiment again on the rise in Onondaga, the stage was set for two major diplomatic councils that have together been labeled the Iroquois' "Grand Settlement" of 1701. One, held in Montreal in July and August, brought representatives of more than thirty French-allied Indian nations from the Great Lakes and St. Lawrence Valley together with some two hundred Iroquois. As in the previous summer, no Mohawks were in attendance, though four Mohawks arrived several days after the conclusion of the conference to ratify its outcome. Though the gathering of more than a thousand Indians and dozens of French officials nearly collapsed when the Iroquois failed to bring captives to exchange, in the end a peace agreement between the Iroquois and the western Indians was ratified. For the future, the Iroquois promised to remain neutral in any conflicts between England and France and gained trading rights at Detroit and Fort Frontenac. The other diplomatic council, held in Albany in July, brought together representatives of each of the Five Nations with Lieutenant Governor Nanfan, Peter Schuyler, and the mayor and aldermen of Albany. In a pointed dramatization of his neutral stance, Teganissorens attended neither conference, though his fellow neutralists were well represented. Hendrick was among the Mohawk delegates in Albany.[80]

Bellomont's absence made the neutralists' task at Albany an easy one. Nanfan was eager to win the sachems' approval and support, and he pressed for little. Though he knew all about the recent extensive negotiations between the Confederacy and New France, he did not try to interfere; he only asked to be kept informed of important developments. He hoped that the Iroquois would soon agree to a workable peace with the western Indians, and he expressed pleasure that the Confederacy had refused Callière's offer of a Jesuit priest to live among them. Surprised that the Iroquois would permit the French to build a fort at Detroit, Nanfan told the sachems that he was about to rebuild the forts at Albany and Schenectady "to defend you from the attempts of an enemy." The Albany fort, he noted, would be "made so large to harbor all your wives and children upon occasion where you may freely make your retreat and be supplied with provisions and other necessities." Yet he made no mention of Bellomont's plan to build a new outpost near Onondaga.[81]

Two Anglophile sachems, Sadekanaktie and a Mohawk named Onucheranorum, spoke for the Confederacy. They flattered Nanfan and assured him of the Confederacy's faithfulness to the English alliance. From their perspective, the conference must have been an unqualified success. The points on which Bellomont had grown increasingly insistent—

that the Confederacy not negotiate directly with the French, and that the English be allowed to build a fort in the heart of Iroquoia—and that inspired fears of an English conspiracy against Iroquois interests had evaporated without a trace. In their place, Nanfan expressed concern for the Iroquois' western interests. It is unclear whether the conference's most concrete outcome was agreed on in advance or grew out of circumstances as the difference between Nanfan and his predecessor became clear. But in the end, the assembled sachems—six Mohawks, including Hendrick, three Oneidas, five Onondagas, three Cayugas, and three Senecas—signed a deed granting the king of England their western hunting grounds. The deed includes a narrative outlining the Iroquois claim to the land, the war against the French-allied confederation of Indians who challenged the Confederacy's possession of it, and standard language assigning ownership of the land to King William and his heirs "for ever."[82]

This is a surprising outcome of a conference so well known among historians as the beginning of a new Iroquois policy of neutrality toward French and English interests. It has been argued that the Iroquois lacked any clear title to the territory in question, and that their goal was to invite English protection against French encroachments and create an incentive to negotiate a clear boundary between the land claims of New France and New York. Yet the deed clearly spells out the claim that the Iroquois had conquered and controlled the territory: "we had been sixty years sole masters and owners of the said land enjoying peaceable hunting." Whether or not the Iroquois thought they had anything to gain from a clear boundary between French and English possessions, the sachems assembled at Albany repeated a practice in which the Iroquois had engaged at least two times previously: once in the 1680s when Confederacy leaders signed away their lands on the Susquehanna River to Governor Dongan, and again in the 1690s when a group of Mohawk sachems had deeded large tracts of land to Dellius and his circle.[83]

Perhaps the best way to understand the two treaty conferences of

1701 is not to lump them together as a single "grand settlement," but instead to recognize that the Iroquois faced an asymmetrical problem in their relations with the French and English crowns. The French had grown too powerful, while the English had proven themselves too weak. Thus, while Teganissorens and his neutralist supporters were concerned to distance themselves from the looming threat of French power to the north, they pressed the English to assert themselves more forcefully in the northern borderlands. Though this was part of a neutralist strategy for creating a stable balance of power in Iroquoia, it also affirmed the efforts of Anglophiles like Hendrick to strengthen the Covenant Chain. Historians who have looked back at this settlement from the perspective of the later eighteenth century, when the balance of power between English and French interests in the Northeast had shifted dramatically, have not always understood that in 1701, the English had never demonstrated in a sustained way that they could make their presence felt in the region.

Soon enough, the Iroquois would prefer to feel it less. But in 1701, the Albany conference offered a counterweight to French influence in Iroquoia, at the same time that it validated the efforts of Hendrick's circle to create a closer tie to New York.

2   Odyssey

In April 1710 Hendrick was half a world away from Tiononderoge and Albany, receiving a vivid lesson in Britain's power, splendor, and squalor. On April 28, after a meeting with the Board of the Society for the Propagation of the Gospel in Foreign Parts, he passed through the Moorgate in London's city wall to visit Bethlehem Hospital, the insane asylum known as Bedlam, where he joined the spectators who came to gawk at the inmates. Afterward he crossed Moorfields and wound his way through the narrow streets of working-class London to visit the workhouse off Bishopsgate Street. The Christian Mohawks Brant and John and a Mahican named Nicholas accompanied him, as did Peter and Abraham Schuyler and, in all likelihood, an English major named David Pigeon. Their impressions of the day went unrecorded, but a newspaper reported that the residents of this poor neighborhood, inhabited by apprentices and laborers and made up of hovels, small shops, manufactories, and brothels, were "thronging to see" the American natives. As they passed by, a "poor woman with child" reached out to try to kiss one of the Indians' hands. His "Indian Majesty," having been alerted to her effort, "permitted" the kiss "and afterwards gave her a half guinea to buy her some blankets."[1]

Nine days earlier, on April 19, 1710, the four Indians had an audience with Queen Anne. They were presented to her as the "four Indian kings" of Iroquoia, a designation that helps to explain the crowd's reaction in Bishopsgate and the poor woman's effort to kiss one of their hands. Hendrick Tejonihokarawa was identified in London as "Tee Yee Neen Ho Ga Row, Emperour of the Six Nations." Brant—the same man Hendrick had persuaded with some difficulty not to defect to Canada in 1700—was known among the Mohawks as Thowariage until he acquired the name Sagayenkwaraton, a name that was also held by a Seneca war chief later in the eighteenth century. Translated as "Vanishing Smoke," the name may refer to its holder's role in carrying a smoldering ember from one village to another to light a council fire. In London, Brant/Sagayenkwaraton was presented as "Sa Ga Yean Qua Rash Tow, King of the Maquas." The third Mohawk, John (the only one of the four who was not baptized by Dellius), was a member of the Wolf clan who came from the village of Canajoharie. In London John/Onigoheriago was called "On Nee Yeath Tow no Riow, King of Granajah Hore." The final member of the party was a Mahican named Etowaucum, a war captain who had led an English-allied party against French Canada in 1691. His Christian name was Nicholas; in London he was called "E Tow O Koam, King of the River Nation."[2]

Hendrick's audience with the queen must have been sweet vindication for a frustrating twenty-year relationship. He had repeatedly staked his reputation on the English alliance, often against the better judgment of his fellow Mohawk sachems and in the face of substantial evidence that England would never seriously challenge French power in Iroquoia. The persistence of his loyalty reflects his abiding resentment of the French challenge to Iroquois sovereignty, which was nurtured in his deeply anti-Catholic brand of Protestant Christianity. His confidence in his Albany connections was repeatedly disappointed, but he never abandoned them. The trip to London repaid Hendrick for the debacles of the 1690s, when his confidence in Dellius, Schuyler, and Bellomont was repeatedly misplaced.

If the visit was, in one sense, a culmination of past events, it also served as a new beginning, one that turned Britain's attention more fully toward Iroquoia and brought in its wake resources for which pro-English Mohawks had long pleaded.[3] As the visit initiated a new phase in the Anglo-Iroquois alliance, it also marked a new stage in Hendrick's precarious career. Neither fully a sachem of the Mohawks nor fully a convert to British ways, the London trip cemented his role as a go-between who would often be called on to mediate between Mohawk and British interests and who often expressed his frustration with Mohawk and British friends alike. Like go-betweens everywhere, Hendrick was frequently needed but rarely trusted. His behavior periodically annoyed or infuriated those around him. But even as he alienated British and Mohawk leaders, his efforts helped establish ties between them and forge a complex, durable alliance between the Iroquois Confederacy and the fledgling British Empire.

"Great veneration"

The trip of the "four Indian kings" to London grew out of a period of confused but improving relations between New York and its Iroquois neighbors. After Bellomont's death and Nanfan's brief term of service, Edward Hyde, Viscount Cornbury, arrived in the colony in 1702 to take up the governor's office. He found New York to be as divided as ever, and he struggled to find his way through the welter of disputes and animosities that energized the colony's Leislerian and anti-Leislerian factions. Though he did not ignore Indian relations altogether, there was little to demand his immediate attention in Iroquoia. After years of declining trade, the Albany merchants were happy to see their prospects improve after 1701. For a time, few pressures were placed on the Anglo-Iroquois alliance. This is surprising, since war between England and France—the War of the Spanish Succession, known in the English colonies as Queen Anne's War—resumed in 1702. But the French and English chose to respect Iroquois neutrality, and the war's principal actions in North America came along the New England frontier and in the southern colonies. While Canada and New York jockeyed for position in Iroquoia, neither immediately pressed the Iroquois to fight.

Instead, Iroquois neutralists held both colonies at arm's length while the colonies sought to insinuate themselves into the good graces—and into the villages—of the Five Nations. In the winter of 1701–1702, following the Montreal and Albany agreements of the previous summer, Nanfan dispatched emissaries to the four most distant Iroquois nations to gauge Iroquois neutrality and the French inclination to respect it. At a council with Iroquois leaders in the following summer, Lord Cornbury noted with displeasure the arrival of French priests in Seneca, Cayuga, and Onondaga villages (though, of course, the presence of English observers suggests that New Yorkers were ambivalent about respecting Iroquois neutrality as well). Yet he had little to fear. In contrast to the era of mass conversions in the 1670s, the Iroquois now treated French and English visitors alike as guests with whom they wanted to maintain friendly relations but avoid entanglements. As an Onondaga Indian said to Bleeker and Schuyler in the fall of 1701, "Brother Corlaer, you have ministers for us. . . . We won't have them now. . . . You [and the French] both have made us drunk with all your noise of praying. We must first come to ourselves again."[4] In the first years of the new century, affairs among the four western nations were firmly in the hands of neutralists who sought friendship and trade but resolutely refused spiritual instruction and political domination.

Mohawk country presented a partial exception to this picture. The Christian Mohawks continued to maintain close relations with Bernardus Freeman at Schenectady and Johannes Lydius in Albany. Lydius held Dellius's old pulpit in Albany, while Freeman's Schenectady posting placed him closer to Tiononderoge than any previous minister had been. Each of these ministers seems to have exerted considerable influence. By the early eighteenth century, the Protestant Mohawks had developed their own distinctive variant of Dutch Reformed Christianity. One element of Mohawk theology was a pronounced anti-Catholicism, nurtured by decades of contestation with their fellow Iroquois who had moved to the St. Lawrence mission towns or accepted Jesuit ministrations in their home villages. A second strand of Protestant Mohawk identity was a strong attachment to prayer, which they understood as the cornerstone of their faith. Unreceptive to the ceremonies and hierarchy of high-church Anglicans, which reminded them too much of the "popery" they had learned to despise, the Christian Mohawks found the theological emphases of Lydius and Freeman to be congenial. Freeman performed especially important services for the Mohawks during his five years in Schenectady when he collaborated with the interpreter Lawrence Claessen van der Volgen to translate two key texts into the Mohawk language (Figure 7). One was a catalog of Catholic errors; the other was a large portion of the English Book of Common Prayer, which became the central text of Mohawk worship. Freeman reported that the Christian Mohawks developed a "great veneration" for English liturgy.[5]

Trade, too, bound the Mohawks to Albany more closely than it did the other Iroquois nations. After the disasters of the 1690s, the Albany trade revived and expanded during the first decade of the eighteenth century. Indians from as far away as the Illinois country made exploratory trips to Albany, while Catholic Mohawks from Kahnawake and the other mission communities in the St. Lawrence Valley initiated a covert trade for English goods, especially cloth, whose reputation was eclipsing that of French merchandise in this era. The Mohawks of Tiononderoge and Canajoharie were middlemen in this activity; they carried merchandise west from Albany, helped visitors establish connections with Albany merchants, and gained prestige and commissions in return. Thus, while neutralists were ascendant in Onondaga, the Mo-hawk castles continued to lean toward Albany—and to guide others to its trading houses.[6]

"Glorious enterprise"

Lord Cornbury responded to the arms-length policy of the Iroquois neutralists by pushing for a military alliance with more vigor than any English governor had since Edmund Andros. He was not simply hoping for improved relations with the Five Nations. His ambition was greater: he began to formulate a plan to conquer Canada. In a twist of logic that does not give a modern observer much confidence in Cornbury's administrative acuity, he reasoned that the conquest of Canada would reduce English expenses in the northern borderlands. Cornbury was neither the first nor the last politician to think that war might be cheaper than peace, but in promoting an invasion of Canada as a way to reduce the cost of presents to the Iroquois Confederacy, he was making an especially dubious leap.

He explained his reasoning in a letter to the Board of Trade written in September 1702. Having met with representatives of the Five Nations and Mahicans in Albany during the summer, Cornbury was reflecting on his experiences and impressions. Hendrick had been there, as had the seasoned, pro-English Mohawk orator and sachem Sinnonquirese, but neither had had much to say. The four western nations were represented especially well, and neutralists dominated the proceedings. Though the Mohawk spokesman Onucheranorum emphasized that "our Covenant Chain is so strong that the Thunder and Lightning cannot break" it, Cornbury heard plenty to make him wonder whether storm clouds were on the horizon. Onucheranorum pointedly reminded Cornbury that the Iroquois had received "but little assistance" from the English during the 1690s, when Iroquoia had nearly broken. They had "lost many of our people but see none of our brethren either to assist us or to revenge the blood of those we had lost by the French." The neutralists drove home

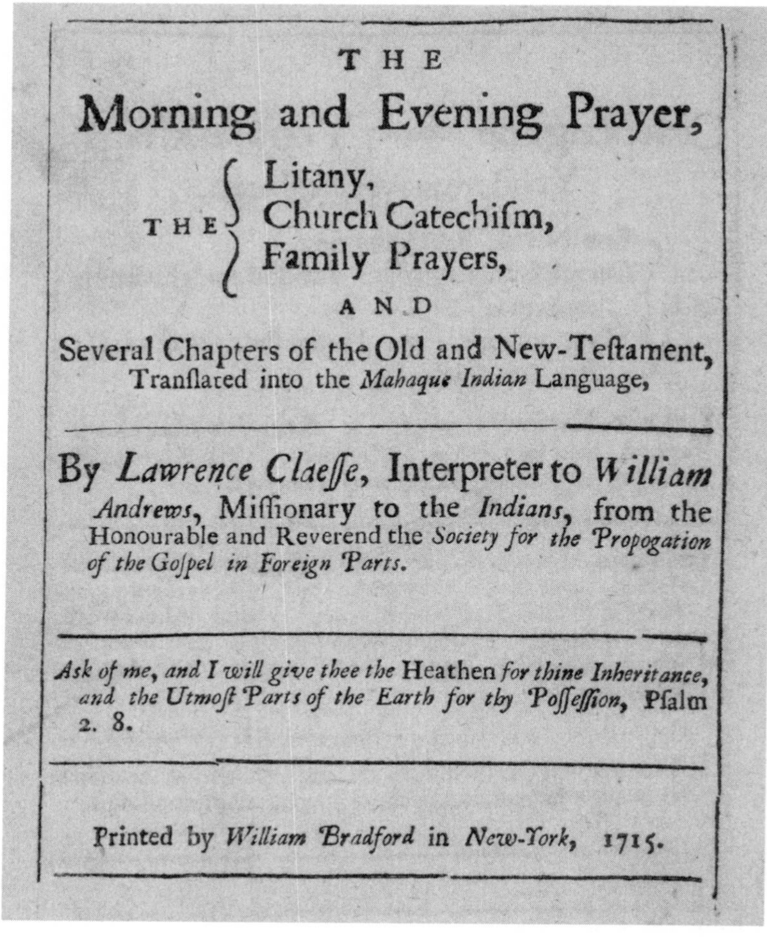

THE

Morning and Evening Prayer,

THE ⎧ Litany,
⎨ Church Catechifm,
⎩ Family Prayers,

A N D

Several Chapters of the Old and New-Teftament,
Tranflated into the *Mahaque Indian* Language,

By *Lawrence Claeſſe*, Interpreter to *William Andrews*, Miffionary to the *Indians*, from the Honourable and Reverend the *Society for the Propogation of the Goſpel in Foreign Parts.*

Ask of me, and I will give thee the Heathen *for thine Inheritance, and the Utmoſt Parts of the Earth for thy Poſſeſſion,* Pfalm 2. 8.

Printed by *William Bradford* in *New-York,* 1715.

Figure 7. Title page of the Anglican Prayer Book in English (above) and Mohawk (right) (New York, 1715). Several years after Lawrence Classen translated this text into Mohawk, it was printed in this dual-language edition under the auspices of the Society for the Propagation of the Gospel. Courtesy of the John Carter Brown Library at Brown University.

N E
Orhoengene neoni Yogaraskhagh
Yondereanayendaghkwa,

N E
- Ene Niyoh Raodeweyena,
- Onoghfadogeaghtige Yondadderighwanon-doentha,
- Siyagonnoghfode Enyondereanayendagh-kwagge,

Yotkade Kapitelhogough ne Karighwadaghkwe-agh Agayea neoni Ate Teftament, neoni Niyadegari-wagge, ne *Kanninggahoga Siniye wenoteagh.*

Tehoenwenadenyough *Lawrance Claeffe*, Rowenagaradatsk *William Andrews*, Ronwanha-ugh *Ongwehoemwighne* Rodirighhoeni Raddiyadanorough neoni Ahoenwadi-gonuyofthagge Thoderighwawaakhogk ne Wahooni Agarighhowanha Niyoh Raodeweyena Niyadegogh-whenjage.

Eghtferaggwas Eghtjeeagh ne ongwehoonwe, neoni ne fiyodoghwhenjooktannighhoegh etho ahadyeandough.

the point that they were determined to maintain relations with both Canada and New York, and there was little Cornbury could do about it. Indian hunters preferred to trade in Canada because merchandise was cheaper and elk and moose skins were valued more highly; "moreover your weights are too heavy . . . and we are oftentimes not fairly dealt with by the Traders." The assembled sachems also reminded Cornbury of unfulfilled promises of forts and other forms of support to help protect Iroquois lands.[7]

Cornbury's tone was conciliatory. He promised to satisfy their concerns and discouraged contact with the French. And to demonstrate his good intentions, he heaped presents on the assembled delegates. The Five Nations received a hundred guns, fifteen hundred pounds of lead, six hundred pounds of gunpowder, twenty-five hundred flints, 150 knives, and eighty hatchets; strouds, duffels, and blankets; a hundred pairs of stockings and fifteen laced hats; fifteen brass kettles, two hundred loaves of bread, and five live cattle; twelve casks of beer, a hundred gallons of rum, a cask of pipes, and a cask of spun tobacco. (The only public statement made by Sinnonquirese at the 1702 conference immediately followed the presentation of this gift, when he rose to request that the rum be put away until the assembled parties had finished their work, "since they are now just begun and if their People should fall a drinking they would be unfit for business." The rum, in fifty two-gallon kegs, was "lodged in Mr. Livingston's cellar" until the end of the conference.) Two days later, Cornbury presented a smaller version of the same gift to the assembled Mahicans, including twenty guns, two hundred pounds of powder, seventy loaves of bread, and thirteen kegs of rum.

Despite his effort to put a positive face on the proceedings, Cornbury found events in Albany tiresome. It must have been a long, hot summer. He asked that the conference begin on June 25, but when he learned that the Iroquois and Mahican delegations would not arrive until July 10 he delayed his own arrival until July 5. It was not until July 15 that the Iroquois group made its first appearance; the Mahicans followed on July 17.

Most of the business was conducted in the first week, but the conferences dragged wearily on. Cornbury met with a group of Mohawks on July 23; then a small delegation of River Indians on July 28; then with Hendrick and Joseph on August 9; then again with a group of Mahicans on August 13 and 15; and finally with the prominent sachem Teganisorrens and two other Onondagas on August 17 and 19. Apparently he learned his lesson: he never again spent the summer in Albany.[8]

By the time he wrote to the Board of Trade in September, Cornbury's mood had grown reflective and pessimistic. Beaten down by the uncertainty and expense of Indian affairs, he thought war might simplify things. The gifts that served to brighten the Covenant Chain placed a "very great charge" on his shoulders, "and yet I do not see any possibility of saving of it as long as the French are possessed of Canada, because if you once give over giving them Presents they will immediately go away to the French." Even the generous gifts and conciliatory messages of the recently concluded conference guaranteed little; he had just heard that the Senecas, Cayugas, and Onondagas were all welcoming priests into their villages. In the end, only one solution eased Cornbury's fears. "I think the only way of securing this whole Continent," he wrote, "would be to drive the French out of Canada." With fifteen hundred English troops and eight frigates joined with the combined forces of the northern colonies, "the thing may be done with ease." In the kind of wishful thinking characteristic of such proposals, Cornbury estimated that the Iroquois "send more goods from Canada in one year to Europe than we do in ten"; thus "the duties upon the Peltry alone in a very short time would reimburse the charge." Once completed, the conquest of Canada would cast the fortunes of England's colonies in a new light.

Then the constant charge of presents to the Indians will cease, for then the Indians must depend upon you for what they want, so you may do with them as you shall think fit: And the people of these Provinces will apply themselves to the improvement without fear of being Scalped whereas now they are in perpetual fears and alarms.

While the War of the Spanish Succession tore Europe apart and ravaged the New England frontier, the seed Cornbury planted lay dormant. But it germinated several years later through the efforts of an opportunistic young New Yorker, Samuel Vetch, who had crossed the Atlantic from his Edinburgh home in 1698 to assist in the Darien colony, which was supposed to tap the riches of Central America for Scottish interests. When it failed, the starving survivors made their way to New York. Vetch quickly endeared himself to Margaret Livingston, the oldest daughter of one of the city's most prominent merchants. They were married in 1700, and Vetch cemented his reputation as a man on the rise. In the summer of 1708, he presented a memorial to the Board of Trade in which he proposed that Great Britain undertake the "glorious enterprise" of conquering Canada. Astonishingly, it received careful attention and, eventually, approval. Vetch was commissioned a colonel and, with Francis Nicholson, a career soldier who had served as governor of New York, Virginia, and Maryland, raised a force of some four thousand provincial volunteers. With the help of Albany's Indian commissioners, they persuaded more than five hundred Iroquois and Mahican warriors to join them. They planned a coordinated land and sea campaign. The Iroquois gathered at the newly constructed Fort Anne, on Wood Creek at the southern end of Lake Champlain, along with companies from New York, New Jersey, and Connecticut, to prepare for an overland march. Troops from Massachusetts, New Hampshire, and Rhode Island waited in Boston for the royal fleet, whose arrival would signal the moment of departure for both prongs of the attack.[9]

But the fleet never came. Months later, in October, Vetch and Nicholson learned that the queen had chosen to divert her naval resources to the peninsular campaign. No one had bothered to inform the American commanders, and their forces melted away through a long, dispiriting summer. The colonies had taken their commitment much more seriously than the queen—Massachusetts alone spent more than £30,000 on the aborted expedition, and the total colonial expenditure exceeded £46,000—and a Congress of Governors quickly gathered to consider ways to salvage the plan. The governors decided to send Nicholson to London to plead their case, and they suggested that "a Sachim, of each Tribe of ye five Nations at their Election be Procured to Attend him in his Voyage." In the end, Nicholson sailed first and made preliminary arrangements. Four Indians followed a short time later, accompanied by Colonel Peter Schuyler; his cousin Captain Abraham Schuyler, who would serve as interpreter for the Indians; and Major David Pigeon, chosen as an aide to the colonel for his familiarity with English society and protocol.[10]

Peter Schuyler had risen from his origins as an Albany trader to become, by 1710, one of the leading citizens of the colony. Unlike his dominie and business partner Godfridius Dellius, Schuyler emerged unscathed from the questionable land deals of the 1690s. He served as mayor of Albany from 1686 to 1694, on the Governor's Council from 1692 until 1720, and twice—first in 1709 and again in 1719–1720—as acting governor of New York. Judgments of his character were mixed. Cadwallader Colden, a prominent Scots-Irish physician who later played an important role in New York politics and Indian affairs, hated the influence of the Albany merchants. He knew Schuyler as an aged but formidable figure and complained of his "sullen Dutch manner." But Anne Grant, who lived in Albany later in the eighteenth century and had a close relationship with Schuyler's descendants, judged him more favorably. "[T]he powerful influence, that his knowledge of nature and of character, his sound judgment and unstained integrity, had obtained over both parties," she wrote, "made him the bond by which the aborigines were united with the colonists." Throughout his career, Schuyler remained close to his Albany roots and his contacts among the Christian Mohawks. He spoke their language and understood Covenant Chain protocols. For their part, the Five Nations, especially the Mohawks, considered him a trustworthy ally. They called him Quider, the Mohawk version of his last name, which soon became an honorific title used to refer generally to the Albany government. They dealt with him whenever they could and trusted his judgment in both commercial and political affairs.[11]

Schuyler's involvement was crucial to the recruitment of an Iroquois delegation. Unlike the colonial governors, the Five Nations had nothing obvious to gain from the London trip, and the original plan to find a representative from each nation went nowhere. Instead, all four Indians were recruited from nearby communities with long-standing ties to Albany. Hendrick and Brant came from Tiononderoge and had impeccable credentials as Christian Anglophiles. Onigoheriago/John was baptized in Hendrick's Albany church in 1701 and likely knew both Schuyler and his fellow Christian Mohawks well. Etowaucum, who was probably from Schaghticoke and who was baptized as Nicholas, participated in an English-led raid on Canada in 1691 that Schuyler had led. The fact that Schuyler recruited all four delegates so near at hand may suggest how badly the governors' reputation was damaged by the previous summer's failure, or it may simply reflect a desire on Schuyler's part to travel with a close-knit group of trusted allies. In addition to their pro-English sympathies and their ties to the Albany trade, all four also had strong Christian loyalties. Schuyler and Nicholson hoped to win support for another invasion of Canada; the Christian Indians also intended to plead for missionaries and defensive support.[12]

Queen and court

What did it mean for Hendrick to cross the Atlantic for the first time at the age of fifty to visit the burgeoning metropolis of London? He was no stranger to travel, but an ocean voyage was an unusual experience.

The prospect of spending a month or more at sea must have inspired uncertainty and fear. To agree to the trip would have required a leap of faith. Even for an Anglo-American colonist, whose whole life was a manifestation of Britain's seafaring traditions, the prospect of an Atlantic crossing could be daunting. For a Mohawk, whose native experience of waterborne travel was limited to the canoe, the decision to cross the ocean would have required both courage and a determination to see what was on the other side. The weeks at sea must have seemed alternately terrifying and tedious.

The American delegation left Boston on the last day of February and arrived in Portsmouth on April 2; within a week they were in London. Hendrick was no newcomer to European settlements and the people who inhabited them. He had spent considerable time in Schenectady and Albany, where he had enjoyed the hospitality of each town's leading citizens. He had traveled to New York City, a rapidly growing seaport of more than five thousand inhabitants, and Boston, Anglo-America's largest community with a population of nearly eight thousand. But these visits did nothing to prepare him for London, which had burst its bounds in the previous generation to become Europe's fastest growing city. Since 1650 its population had doubled, from some 350,000 to 700,000 at the turn of the century. It had been pushing beyond its walls for some time, but the Great Fire of 1666, which destroyed nearly all of the old city, was a tremendous spur to expansion and reconstruction. When Hendrick and his traveling companions arrived, London was an ancient city embarked on its greatest era of development.

The delegation had the good fortune to enter London at a moment when they were politically useful. It is not hard to imagine events unfolding quite differently: the queen had, after all, spoiled the previous summer's Canada campaign and might have regarded the Americans'

presence as an inconvenience or an embarrassment. Her leading ministers had been focused for a decade on heroic, exhausting, and all-
consuming continental campaigns; most would have considered the
interests of New York and Massachusetts insignificant by comparison.

But Queen Anne was on the verge of making momentous changes in
her government, and the Indians' visit gave her a perfect vehicle to justify and dramatize her choice. The War of the Spanish Succession had
brought a series of victories to Marlborough and the Whig ministry,
but their cost was mounting. Queen Anne was beginning to listen to
Tory advisors who advocated a "blue-water" policy that emphasized
naval power over land forces, and colonial expeditions in place of
Britain's staggeringly expensive commitments in Europe. On April 15,
only four days before she would meet Hendrick, Schuyler, and their
party, the queen began to distance herself from the Whigs by dismiss-
ing the earl of Kent from the post of lord chamberlain. Her turn from
Whig policy, which culminated in August with the dismissal of the earl
of Godolphin as lord treasurer, created an opening for the Tories, who
had been shut out of power for years. Both Queen Anne and the blue-
water Tories recognized in the Americans' visit a useful symbol of their
alternative strategy, and as a result they were fêted and fawned over
without mercy throughout their stay.[13]

It is not clear when or by whom Hendrick, Brant, John, and
Nicholas began to be called the "four Indian kings," but once established the association with royalty was unshakeable. Hendrick was
styled "Emperour of the Six Nations," Brant became "King of the
Maquas [Mohawks]," John was "king of Ganajoh Hore [Canajoharie],"
and Nicholas was called "King of the River Nation [Mahicans]." (It
was apparently because the Mahican Nicholas was along that the Iroquois were called the Six Nations during this trip, nearly a decade before
the Tuscaroras became the sixth nation of the Iroquois Confederacy.)
They lodged in a "handsom[e] Apartment" in the Two Crowns and
Cushions, a comfortable house on King Street in Covent Garden. Carved

out of the grounds adjacent to the Earl of Bedford's London town-house in the 1630s, Covent Garden was the first in a long series of fashionable West End developments. It featured stylish Italianate architecture, a piazza and church designed by Inigo Jones, and a market where its residents could find fresh fruits and vegetables. By 1710 Covent Garden had been eclipsed by a series of later, more lavish West End neighborhoods, but it remained a bustling center of city life. It was home to London's two principal theaters, the Covent Garden Theatre and the Theatre Royal in Drury Lane, and a mix of coffeehouses, taverns, and respectable tradesmen's establishments.[14]

The owner of the Two Crowns and Cushions, Thomas Arne, was an upholsterer and undertaker whose household had a singular impact on the city's cultural life. His son Thomas Augustine, an infant at the time of the four kings' visit, later went to Eton to study law but was drawn instead to musical composition. He became one of eighteenth-century Britain's most successful composers, and his "Rule, Britannia" was perhaps the era's most famous song (as the *Dictionary of National Biography* notes with some pride, it is "perhaps the finest national song possessed by any nation"). In 1730, Arne again hosted a Native American delegation when a group of seven Cherokees, accompanied by Alexander Cuming, arrived in town, lost their lodgings, and needed a place to stay. He quickly volunteered the Two Crowns and Cushions. Clearly, Arne enjoyed the attention such visitors brought. In 1710 he was a young man with good prospects, and the opportunity to play host to the American delegation brought him and his upholstery business to the attention of people of wealth and influence throughout the city.[15]

Upon their arrival, Hendrick and his Indian companions visited the "dressers of the playhouse" to be outfitted appropriately for their audience with the queen. At the beginning of the eighteenth century,

Britons were much more preoccupied with events in Europe and the Mediterranean than they were with North America, and Ottoman Turks were more familiar as exotic outsiders than American Indians. In attempting to invent an air of royal splendor for the four Indian kings, the playhouse dressers turned Hendrick and his companions into an Oriental fantasy. They wore "black undercloth[e]s after the English manner." Then, "instead of a blanket, they had each a scarlet-in-grain cloth mantle, edged with gold, thrown over all their other garments." Each scarlet mantle was "bound with a Gold Galloon." In place of shoes, the Indian kings wore "yellow slippers." Their "Hair [was] ty'd short up, and a Cap something the Nature of a Turbant [was placed] upon their heads."[16] The slippers and turbans, in particular, signal the dressers' desire to invoke images of the Orient. Nicholson and Schuyler went along with it; perhaps they felt it would be inappropriate for the four kings to appear at court dressed as Englishmen yet also considered their native costumes to lack the luxury and splendor associated with royalty. So the playhouse dressers improvised to create an air of magnificence and mystery for Hendrick and his companions. How the Indians felt about it is impossible to say.[17]

On April 19, two royal coaches drew up outside the Two Crowns and Cushions, and Sir Charles Lodowick Cotterell, Queen Anne's master of the ceremonies, conducted the four Indian "kings," Nicholson, the Schuylers, and Major Pigeon to the Court of St. James. They were announced by Charles Talbot, the first Duke of Shrewsbury and the newly appointed lord chamberlain of the royal household, who led them into the queen's presence.[18]

"A more than ordinary solemnity attended the audience they had of her Majesty," according to a contemporary account. This may have been a throwaway line, but it probably contains an element of truth. The "kings" and the queen may have been uncertain and uncomfortable with each other. Hendrick, who had waited a long time for this kind of validation, was perhaps especially awestruck and grave. The queen was still in mourning for her husband, Prince George of Denmark; his death a year and a half earlier was an event from which she would never recover. A contemporary visitor noted that the rooms of the palace were "large and handsome" but "entirely bare on account of the mourning for Prince George. . . . There were still hangings everywhere—even the stairs outside being draped with black flannel, while inside in the apartments there was black cloth. . . . All the paintings have been taken to Hampton Court and Windsor."[19] In her prolonged mourning, it was as if the queen had retreated behind a curtain to shield herself from the cruelties of her life.

The Indians' speech, read by Major Pigeon, emphasized their commitment to the British cause and pleaded for the queen's support in America. "We have undertaken a long and tedious Voyage, which none of our Predecessors could ever be prevail'd upon to undertake," the speech began.

> The Motive that induc'd us was, that we might see our *Great Queen*, and relate to Her those Things we thought absolutely necessary, for the Good of Her, and us, Her Allies, on the other side of the Great Water.
>
> We doubt not but our *Great Queen*, has been acquainted with our long and tedious War, in Conjunction with Her Children . . . against her Enemies the *French*, and that we have been as a strong Wall for their Security, even to the Loss of our best Men.

This was a fair characterization of the disastrous battles of the 1690s. "The kings were mightily rejoiced," Pigeon continued, when they learned of the previous summer's plan to invade Canada. They "hung up the *Kettle*, and took up the *Hatchet*"; they "joined . . . in . . . building Forts, Store-Houses, Canows, and Battows"; they "waited long in Expectation of the Fleet from *England*." With the invasion's failure, they worried that the French, "who hitherto had dreaded us, should now think us unable to make War against them." If the queen would renew her commitment to the Canadian initiative, the Iroquois could enjoy "*Free Hunting*, and a great Trade with our *Great Queen's* Children." But if "our Great Queen should not be mindful of us, we must, with our Families, forsake our Country, and seek other Habitations, or stand Neuter; either of which will be much against our Inclinations."

The speech concluded with a petition of long-standing interest to Hendrick. "Since we have been in Alliance with our Great Queen's Children," Pigeon continued, "we have had some Knowledge of the Saviour of the World; and have often been importuned by the *French*, both by the Insinuations of their Priests, and by Presents, to come over to their interest, but have always esteem'd them *Men of Falshood:* But if our *Great Queen* will be pleas'd to send over some Persons to instruct us, they shall find a most hearty Welcome."[20]

We can imagine the four kings standing in costume before the queen—perhaps feeling awkward or ridiculous—while Pigeon read their speech. When he made the case for a renewed invasion, Hendrick stepped forward to present belts of wampum to solemnize their commitment to the alliance. At the conclusion of the speech, the kings gave Queen Anne "Neck-Laces, Bracelets of Shells, and other Curiosities of their Country, much valuable for the finess of Work." The queen, in turn, "promis'd them Her Assistance, and order'd 200 Guineas to be given them." It was spent on gifts that awaited them when they set sail for Boston in mid-May. She ordered the lord chamberlain to entertain the kings at her expense during their stay and asked "that they be shewn what is remarkable here." Then the American delegation was conducted back to the Two Crowns and Cushions, where they met with a group of American merchants.[21]

Queen Anne did not want the visit of the four Indian kings to be quickly forgotten. In an unusual gesture, she arranged to have them sit for state portraits by the painter John Verelst, who received a commission of £100 plus fees for his efforts. The paintings were soon hung in a small room in Kensington Palace, off a larger one that contained portraits of fourteen English admirals. These paintings have become enduring icons of the Anglo-Indian encounter. They are remarkable in large part because Verelst tried to present the kings in the way an English gentleman would have been painted: he focused carefully on their faces and forms, he posed their bodies in conventional ways, and he produced very human images that command the viewer's attention. Though Verelst surrounded the kings with the exotic trappings of their American identities, when we view the paintings everything extraneous fades into the background and we encounter men—strangely dressed, heavily tattooed, but immediately, obviously, and profoundly human—standing at the threshold between two very different worlds and seeking, through their efforts, to bridge them.[22]

City and country

During the next two weeks, the four kings embarked on an exhausting round of visits and entertainments. Their time in England combined statecraft, tourism, and improvised spectacle. On the day after their audience with the queen the group sailed to Greenwich, where they saw the Woolwich dockyards and the new sailors' hospital. Though the hospital was still incomplete, "no royal palace could be more sumptuous." Next to the hospital was a park; atop a high hill stood the residence and observatory of John Flamsteed, "an ugly little fellow of about sixty years of age" who was the founder of the royal observatory and England's first astronomer royal. They toured the observatory and admired his collection of "Mathematical Instruments," then boarded one of the queen's yachts to dine with some of the lords commissioners of the admiralty, by whom they were "nobly treated." The next day they saw the banqueting house and chapel at Whitehall Palace.[23]

Throughout the trip, the four Indian kings were "magnificently entertain'd by several of the Nobility." The Duke of Ormonde was conspicuous among the political opportunists who associated with the kings. He hosted a dinner in their honor, and on April 25 he met them in Hyde Park to review four troops of the Life Guards. A contemporary report indicated that Hendrick and his associates were deeply impressed by the guards. "What then must be the Commander, if those that are under his Obedience, make so August and Noble an Appearance?" they were reported to have asked their host. A subordinate and rival of the Duke of Marlborough, Ormonde saw his stock as a military leader rise under the new Tory ministry until, in January 1712, he succeeded Marlborough as captain-general of the Land Forces, England's supreme military office. Matthew Aylmer, admiral and commander of the Royal Fleet, sent his yacht to collect the kings and bring them aboard his flagship the *Royal Sovereign*, where he hosted a shipboard dinner in their honor. They met with the Board of Trade several times. Following church services at St. James' Chapel on April 30, where they heard the lord bishop of London preach, they attended a lavish dinner sponsored by the bishop and then visited the Duke of Montagu's magnificent Bloomsbury townhouse (Figure 8).[24]

The archbishop of Canterbury instructed the governing board of the Society for the Propagation of the Gospel (SPG) to consider the kings' request for missionaries, and on April 28 they appeared before the board. The visit profoundly affected the society—so much so that the board adopted a fundamental change in its mission. Previously, its principal goal had been to establish churches among English colonists. Now the board decided that "a stop [should] be put to sending any more Missionaries among the Christians." Instead, the Society's first duty should be to convert "Heathens and Infidels." The board formulated a plan to send two missionaries to Iroquoia with a salary of £150 each (more than Dellius ever dreamed of), along with a translator to facilitate their work. They would also arrange to build the long-awaited chapel and fort. The missionaries were expected to begin translating the

MONTAGUE HOUSE,

Figure 8. Following a dinner sponsored by the bishop of London, the four Indian kings were entertained by the Duke of Montagu in his Bloomsbury townhouse, later the first home of the British Museum. The north view of Montagu House and gardens, engraved by James Simon, 1714. © Trustees of the British Museum.

Bible, along with prayers and catechisms, into Iroquoian languages to be printed and distributed among the Indians. All of this was explained to the four kings during their visit to the board. This visit must have encouraged and gratified Hendrick, who had been pleading for missionaries and military protection for many years. At the conclusion of their audience, the board of the SPG presented each of the kings with a quarto Bible and a Book of Common Prayer, "bound handsomely in red Turkey Leather." Later, in a social event that confirmed their connection to the SPG and the Church of England, the archbishop entertained the four kings in his home.[25]

Beyond their official engagements, the American delegation—like tourists in every age—took in the sights, sounds, and sensations of Britain's most magnificent city. Crowds followed them everywhere. Joseph Addison recalled that "when the four *Indian* Kings were in this Country about a Twelvemonth ago, I often mix'd with the Rabble and followed them a whole Day together, being wonderfully struck with the Sight of every thing that is new or uncommon." They were the objects of a fierce competition among purveyors of entertainment. On April 24, the Queen's Theatre in the Haymarket—the largest and finest in the city—staged a performance of *Macbeth* intended "For the Entertainment of the Four INDIAN KINGS lately arriv'd." It worked: three of the four kings (one, probably Brant, having taken ill) saw the play that night. The Theatre Royal in Drury Lane quickly followed suit, as did Punch's Theatre, which staged an operatic revue of the previous year's military campaign with puppets. Another performance, offered "at the Desire of several Ladies of Quality," included an evening of "Vocal and Instrumental Musick." The kings were also encouraged to enjoy "the Royal Sport of Cock-fighting" at the Cockpit Royal in Cartwright

Street near St. James' Park, and on May 3 they were invited to "A Tryal of Skill to be fought at the Bear-Garden in Hockley in the Hole" between "John Parkes from Coventry, and Thomas Hesgate a Barkshire-Man, at these following Weapons, viz. Back-Sword, Sword and Dagger, Sword and Buckler, Single Falchon, Case of Falchons, and Quarter-Staff."[26]

This might seem an unlikely combination of entertainments, but if the experiences of other foreign travelers of the day are any indication, the American delegation may have attended all of them. Gentlemen and commoners rubbed elbows at the theater, the cockpit (site of "a sport peculiar to the English"), and the bear garden alike. Peers of the realm likely dominated the cockpit near St. James'; "can you believe," one contemporary visitor asked, "that here several hundred pounds sterling is sometimes bet on the head of a cock?" At Hockley-in-the-Hole, the kings may have seen fierce, bloody combat. Two accounts from the early eighteenth century describe combatants who received horrifying gashes, only to have them hastily sewn up so the contest could go forward. The theatre, too, could be a raucous place. According to one account, when the kings attended a play the mob in the upper gallery refused to let it proceed until they had seen them. "[T]hey came to see the Kings, 'and since we have paid our Money, the Kings we will have.'" The theatre manager brought chairs onto the stage, and Hendrick and his companions occupied them until the crowd was satisfied.[27]

The kings toured the city among throngs of people. They reportedly visited St. Paul's Cathedral, the rooms of the Royal Society at Gresham College, the Tower of London, Exchange Place, and Guildhall. They passed through the city's wall at Moorgate to visit Bethlehem Hospital, or Bedlam, one of the city's finest buildings and most popular attractions. Designed by Robert Hooke after the Great Fire of 1666, Bedlam was modeled on the Tuileries Palace. "The gateway," wrote César de Saussure, "is superb, and above it on each side is a statue representing a chained lunatic"—a reference to Caius Gabriel Cibber's famous statues of melancholy and raving madness. Inside,

> [a] long, wide gallery, running the whole length of the building, gives access to a large number of little cells, where the insane of all kinds are shut in, and where they can be viewed through small hatches. Those who are not dangerous walk in the gallery. On the second floor, there is another corridor with cells of a similar type, where most of the occupants are kept chained. Several of them are terrible to behold. Usually, on holidays, a great number of people of both sexes from the small traders and lower classes make it their amusement to come and see these objects worthy of pity, many of whom nevertheless give cause for mirth.[28]

From Bedlam the four kings' entourage crossed Moorfields (a "charming spot . . . planted with trees and . . . most agreeable") and walked the short distance up Bishopsgate to Half-Moon Alley. (It was along this route that the poor woman tried to kiss one of the four kings' hands and received half a guinea for her troubles.) The group had come to visit the London Workhouse, built by the London Corporation of the Poor in 1699, where destitute children worked off the cost of their upkeep by spinning, sewing, and knitting for ten hours a day. Two additional hours were set aside for instruction. In another part of the building, the more dangerous inmates—"vagabonds, sturdy beggars, pilfering and other vagrants, lewd, idle and disorderly persons"—had "such relief as is proper for them, and are employ'd in beating hemp, picking oakum, or washing linen." It is difficult to know how Hendrick, the other Indians, and the gentlemen who accompanied them would have viewed the hospital and workhouse. Despite the harsh conditions, both were seen as important institutions of Christian charity and uplift. They would have stirred a complex mix of emotions even in visitors inured to life in London; Hendrick, Brant, John, and Nicholas saw things that day they had neither seen nor imagined before.[29]

The strongest impression Hendrick and his companions left on the British public came through three sets of portraits painted during their visit. One pamphleteer offered a physical description of the kings that could just as easily have been based on a close examination of the Verelst set as on personal observation:

> As to the Persons of these Princes, they are well form'd, being of a Stature neither too high nor too low, but all within an Inch or two of six Foot; their Habits are robust, and their Limbs muscular and well-shap'd; they are of brown Complexions, their Hair black and long, their Visages are very awful and majestick, and their Features regular enough, though something of the austere and sullen; and the Marks with which they disfigure their Faces, do not seem to carry so much Terror as Regard with them.

In the paintings, Hendrick's image stands out among the four (Figure 1). The other three wear something like a short toga, with bare legs and moccasin-like slippers (probably the same slippers provided to them by the dressers of the playhouse). Hendrick is clothed in English shoes, stockings, breeches, and overcoat. In contrast to the elaborate tattooing of the others' faces (and of Brant's neck and chest), Hendrick bears only a single, irregular oval scar on his left cheek. (There is nothing in the historical record to indicate how he got it.) Alone among the four, Hendrick appears as if he might pass for an Englishman on a London street. While the other three kings hold weapons, Hendrick is pictured with a wampum belt: a symbol of communication, diplomacy, and public memory, and an instrument of peace (Figure 9).[30]

Tee Yee Neen Ho Ga Row Emperour of the Six Nations

Verelst pinx.   I. Simon Fec.   Sold at the Rainbow and Dove the corner of Ivy bridge in the Strand

From the three portrait sets—by Verelst, Bernard Lens, Jr. (Figure 10), and John Faber, Sr.—engravings soon followed. Some made elegant prints, sold by subscription and suitable for framing and display in London's finest households. Others were cruder but likely to be pinned up on a wall. Some were simple woodcuts that accompanied ballads or texts of the speech (Figure 11). The proliferation of pictures, pamphlets, and ballads suggests that the four kings were more than a fleeting phenomenon. Though the purpose of the trip soon faded in public memory, the idea of four Indian kings lingered, with its vague and exotic evocation of the possibilities of empire. As one contemporary chronicler concluded, the visit of the four Indian kings "made a great noise through the whole kingdom. The mob followed them wherever they went, and small prints of them were sold among the people."[31]

Hendrick's transformation

No one in the group kept a journal, and Hendrick's impressions are lost to history—not a single word survives to characterize his reactions. Probably they ranged widely; he may have been awed by the magnificence of St. James and Montagu House, humbled by his audience with the queen and the governing board of the SPG, delighted by the theater, engrossed by the scene at Hockley-in-the-Hole, and moved by the plight of Bedlam's inmates. The city's teeming multitudes, its extremes of wealth and poverty, the overwhelming stench of raw sewage in the Fleet Ditch, the glorious symmetry of Inigo Jones's Covent Garden

---

Figure 9. *Tee Yee Neen Ho Ga Row, Emperour of the Six Nations*, mezzotint, by John Simon after a portrait painted by John Verelst (London, 1710). First sold by subscription, this fine engraving and its three companions would have been framed and hung. They went through at least three editions. William Andrews, the first SPG missionary to the Mohawks, carried fifty-one copies of each mezzotint with him to New York. Courtesy of the John Carter Brown Library at Brown University.

Tee Yee Neen Ho Ga Row.
Emperour of the six Nations.

Sa Ga Yean Qua Rah Tow.
King of the Maquas.

Oh Nee Yeath Tow No Riow.
King of Ganajoh hore.

E Tow Oh Koam.
King of the River Nation.

The Four Indian Kings.

Done after the Original Painings.

piazza—all these features of London life and many more must have left indelible impressions. But if the trip was full of powerful reactions and emotional highs and lows, there is no indication of that in the printed descriptions of the four kings. "They are Men of good Presence," according to one account, "and those who have convers'd with them, say, That they have an exquisite Sense, and a quick Apprehension." "According to the Custom of their Country, these Princes do not know what it is to cocker and make much of themselves," another author wrote.[32] In a sense, these impressions tell us little; the writers were probably not speaking at first hand, and their descriptions sound more polite than accurate. Yet in another sense, they confirm that Hendrick and his fellow Indians played their roles well. Placed in a wide variety of scenes and settings, exposed to the exacting standards of behavior that attended royal audiences and noble entertainments, we know at least that they avoided any disastrous embarrassment. They apparently carried off a series of extraordinarily difficult performances with grace and skill.

Though Hendrick may have been little more than an exotic curiosity to many Londoners, the trip was surely the defining moment of his adult life. His identity as a Christian anglophile became a passport to the cosmopolitan world of English gentlemen. Welcomed in the Palace of St. James and the highest circles of London society, he joined fellow Christians in observing the charitable efforts at the Bishopsgate workhouse, mixed with crowds on the city's streets, observed genteel and popular entertainments, and was a noteworthy sensation wherever he went. He returned from the trip with a new confidence in his political

---

Figure 10. *The Four Indian Kings,* by Bernard Lens, Sr. (1659–1725) after Bernard Lens, Jr. (1682–1740), 1710, mezzotint, 13 ½″ x 9 ⅞″. This well-executed engraving places the busts of all four Indian kings economically on a single sheet. A moderately expensive mezzotint, it was also worthy of framing. Courtesy of the Albany Institute of History & Art, gift of the Estate of Cornelia Cogswell (Mrs. Henry M.) Sage, 1972.65.7.

Tee Yee Neen Ho Ga Row, Emperour of the six Nations.

Sa Ga Yean Qua Rah Tow, King of the Maquas.

E Tow oh Kaom, King of the River Nation.

Oh Nee Yeath Tow no Riow, King of Ganajoh Hoie.

THE FOUR INDIAN KINGS SPEECH to her Majesty on the 20th of April. Translated into verse by T.S. With their Efigies taken from the Life and Curiously Engrav'd by S.N 1710.

Great Queen

A tedious Voy'ge from near Canada
On that vast continent America
(A Voy'ge our predecessors ne'er did make
Nor could prevail'd with be to undertake)
We undertook with pleasing hopes that wee
Britania's Queen our Great Allie might see
In all her Splendid Ray's of Majesty
And take this Happy Juncture to Declare
What things we Judge most necesary are
And most expedient In our country's war
When Anadagarjaux said You did Intend
For to Reduce Canada, Fleets to Send
We were Rejoyc'd at that most wellcom news
And hop'd't wou'd prove more than a bare amuse
Then we in token of our friendship hung
The Kettle up and Songs of transport Sung
And likewise we Did up the Hatchet take
Thereby to Shew our Best Defence We'd make
With one consent as soon as that was done
We Joyn'd our Brothers Queder Schuyler Nicholson
In makeing and Provideing Forts Cannows
Store-houses Fences Barracks and Battows
Whilst Anadiasia Coll'nell Vetch at Boston
Rais'd Such an Army France cou'd never Boast on

Then Long we waited for the the English Fleet
At who's arival Victory more compleat
Than ever yet By Art or Arms was Gain'd
We do perswade our Selves had been obtain'd
But being disapointed for that Season
By bus'nes of Import our Great Queens Reason
Extreamly Sorrowfull it did us make
And Soon obleag'd us, this Long Voy'ge to take
In Sincerity of the Nations whence we come
Great Queen we do present these Belts of Wampum
And as we Joyntly ask we hope you will
As heretofore be mindfull of Us Still
Or else we must from our own Kingdoms fly
Stand Nuter: or live Mean, Ingloriously
All which Is much Against Our Inclination
All which Is Unbecoming our High Station
Since we with you have In Alyance Been
With you Great Queen and with your Children
Some Knowledge of A Saviour we have had
And of farther Instruction Should be Glad
If you'd So Gracious be Great Queen to Send
Us Parsons to Instruct Us to that end
We now close All In hope that you will Grant
These and all Such like favours which we want

Printed and Sold by Sutton Nicholls against the Angel in Aldersgate Street LONDON.

judgments. He had won recognition and approval at the highest levels of British society and had received, at long last, promises for meaningful support that would soon be fulfilled.

His confidence carried with it a new willingness to challenge authority when it suited him to do so—and it mattered little to him whether it was the authority of the Mohawk sachems, the Confederacy Council, or the British Empire. In the last phase of his career, Hendrick was more assertive, quicker to press his interests, and more willing to offend those around him in defense of principle. For the first time in his long public life, Hendrick followed his judgments where they led him, without regard for consequences or their effect on his reputation. His more assertive behavior challenged Iroquois norms of leadership and led to a disastrous falling out with Robert Hunter, governor of New York. Hendrick's statements and actions caused offense and anger. Yet seen from the distance of three hundred years, we can also sense, as he passed fifty years of age, Hendrick finally coming into his own.

On May 3 the American delegation left London to visit Hampton Court and Windsor Palace and then proceeded to Portsmouth, their port of embarkation, where a lavish store of gifts from the queen awaited them. They carried home as large a quantity of trade goods as had ever been dispensed at Albany, including fabrics, brass kettles, lead bars, four hundred pounds of gunpowder, ten pounds of vermilion, six

---

Figure 11. *The Four Indian Kings Speech to her Majesty . . . Translated into verse,* author (T. S.) unknown. Engraved by Sutton Nicholls (London, 1710). This inexpensive knockoff of the Lens mezzotint is accompanied by a rhymed version of the four kings' speech to the queen. Some owners might have framed it; others might have tacked it up on a wall as an inexpensive reminder of the four kings' visit. © Trustees of the British Museum.

kinds of knives, mirrors, scissors, tobacco boxes, necklaces, razors, combs, and mouth harps. Each of the kings also received a more personal gift: a hat, gun, and sword, a pair of pistols, a trunk, a picture of the queen, and a "Magick Lanthorn with Pictures." On May 19, fair winds finally allowed Hendrick and his companions to leave England behind them. Sailing on the *Dragon*, a man-of-war accompanying a merchant fleet, they entered Boston Harbor on July 15.[33]

Three weeks later, the four kings led a delegation of Iroquois and Mahican Indians to welcome Robert Hunter, the new governor of New York, when he arrived in Albany to convene an Indian conference. Hendrick and his fellow travelers would have worn the hats and swords that were gifts from the queen, new marks of their high status. When Hunter came ashore, "they heartily congratulated his safe arrival, and thankt God that he had been so mercifull to send him safe to them . . . and presented him with a black otter [pelt]." They went on to request particular favors from the governor in anticipation of the conference, including a prohibition of strong drink and the provision of wagons to carry "the old Sachims" from Schenectady to Albany. Finally, they "prayed that during their Stay provisions may be ordered more largely, for the allowance they had had hitherto before his Excellency[']s arrivall was very Scrimp." Hunter assured them that they would be "taken care of and victualled as well as ever they had been formerly."[34] The request for more generous gifts was satisfied, but it presaged a concern Hendrick would voice repeatedly in years to come: that the power and riches he had seen in London were not sufficiently in evidence in Mohawk country.

Inglorious enterprise

For now, though, the alliance was more promising than it had ever been. Hunter's message to the assembled Iroquois representatives confirmed that the queen had approved both of the principal requests the four kings had made. A fort, chapel, and missionary program would soon come to Mohawk country. In the meantime another massive invasion of Canada was being planned for the summer of 1711, and Hunter asked for the warriors' support. The 1709 invasion, undertaken with great energy and seriousness in the colonies, had been all but ignored in London. This time things were different. In 1711, Britain mobilized the largest military force assembled for any undertaking in North America prior to the Seven Years' War. Under the command of Admiral Sir Hovenden Walker and Brigadier General John Hill, a force of more than nine thousand British troops massed on Noddles Island in Boston Harbor (a huge offshore island that is now connected to the city by tunnels and comprises part of East Boston, home to Logan Airport) as ships, arms, and supplies were painstakingly assembled. Walker attended to a thousand details. He shuttled back and forth between port town and soldiers' camp, arranged for ships to be fitted out, waited impatiently for supplies and additional support, and even haggled with Boston's merchants over the exchange rate between Massachusetts currency and pounds sterling. (The merchants wanted £1.20 Massachusetts to trade for £1 sterling, which struck Walker and his fellow officers as outrageous; eventually, in a generous compromise, Walker agreed to a rate of £1.30 Massachusetts currency for £1 sterling.)[35]

Dignitaries and curious visitors flocked to the island. Nicholson was in and around Boston throughout July, reviewing the troops along with General Hill and periodically introducing parties of Indians to Walker and Hill. On July 22, Nicholson brought several Mohawk sachems to meet Walker; on the following day they visited the island, reviewed the troops, and were entertained aboard the *Humber*. Walker wrote that the Mohawks were "surprised and amazed, as well as pleased" by the scale of the planned invasion. Walker served the sachems wine and entertained them with music and sailors' dances. The Mohawks danced and sang too, "in a very different Manner to any thing ever seen in *Europe.*" A soldier in the camp remembered the visit in his memoirs. He recalled that "the *Indian* king" came to review the troops.

[W]e all should have like to have a full View of him, but to prevent our Curiosity, he had a Vail that covered his Face, and his Secretary was painted with Reddle, and had a Crow-Quill stuck in his Hair bare headed. I thought they made but a very shocking Appearance. As soon as he passed our Regiment, our Orders were to follow him along the Line, and our Officers by way of Compliment went Front and Rear with him. That gave the *Indian* King a great deal of Satisfaction, and the Sight of him pleased us much.[36]

One of the Mohawks—almost certainly Hendrick—delivered a long speech. He said they had long awaited the expedition that was now in preparation, had "almost despaired" of ever seeing it come to fruition, and were now "much rejoiced that the Queen had taken such care of them." Walker, who recorded these events, noted that the speaker "deliver'd himself with much Gravity and Sagacity, and to me they seem'd to be a People of Thought and Understanding, Sincere and void of Levity." In response Walker expressed the hope that "now an End would be put to all their Wars, and a lasting Peace ensue." They drank a toast to success, prosperity, and an "Understanding and Friendship between the Queen and their Nations" that would last forever. Walker met again with the Mohawks the following day and wrote afterward, "they are a People worth keeping in the British Interest, and might be made very useful Subjects to the Crown, if right Methods were taken, being able, upon Occasion, to bring a pretty good force into the Field." He gave them a present (which Nicholson had prepared for him) and sent them on their way.[37]

As in 1709, this was a two-pronged invasion. A massive flotilla set out from Boston under Walker's command: fourteen line-of-battle ships, the largest of which had crews of 520 men and carried eighty guns; four frigates; thirty-three transports and supply ships, with a train of eight additional ships. Another six ships, five brigantines, and two sloops transported the Massachusetts troops. A second force, including seven hundred Iroquois warriors and nearly a thousand Indians in all, gathered at Fort Anne on Wood Creek under Nicholson's command. Just before they set out, disastrous news reached Nicholson. As the fleet had been making its way up the St. Lawrence River, it had become enveloped in fog. Its pilots became disoriented, and near midnight on August 21 the fleet ran into the rocks on the river's north shore. Eight transports were lost, and some nine hundred troops, with uncounted women and children, perished. In a hasty council of war, Walker and his captains concluded "that by Reason of the Ignorance of the said Pilots it is wholly Impracticable to go up the River of St. Lawrence," and they reversed course and headed back downriver. After briefly considering whether to carry out the second part of their mission—to attack the French settlement of Placentia in Newfoundland—Walker, Hill, and their officers concluded that they were inadequately supplied even for this relatively modest task, and instead they sailed for home.[38]

The failed campaign echoed through British public life for years. Walker was disgraced. Deprived of his half-pay by the lords of the Admiralty, he moved to Carolina, then Barbados, in search of a livelihood. A pamphlet war hashed over the wisdom of the campaign and the details of its failure, which prompted Walker to publish his own self-justifying account in 1720. Not until the Seven Years' War did Britain again commit substantial military resources to a campaign in North America. And in 1760, a year after the fall of Quebec, in a quiet coda to Walker's tortured career, detailed directions for piloting the St. Lawrence were finally published in London.[39]

Nicholson, Hunter, and Schuyler inherited the task of placating the Iroquois. In October a group of Iroquois sachems visited Schuyler's house in Albany, where Nicholson gave them a series of presents to reaffirm the alliance. The gifts were more symbolic than substantive—

presumably Nicholson's treasury had all but run dry—but in a departure from the normal way of offering gifts, he carefully explained each one. The sachems received a Queen Anne guinea to remind them of her; an Oxford almanac cut on the page that described the four kings' appearance at court; a walking cane with an amber head, to remind them of Nicholson; a "Multiplying Glass to represent to them the Fraud of the French in making a few things seem to be many"; a pair of pocket brass musquetoons and one long gun, "to show the French how well they are armed"; and two barrels of beer "to Drink the Queen[']s health." The sachems thanked Nicholson politely but had little to say. A week later they met with Governor Hunter. Hendrick spoke for them. He expressed his thanks to the queen, Nicholson, and Hunter, and he gave Hunter a letter to the archbishop of Canterbury expressing their "wants." Then, shrouded in bitter disappointment, the sachems turned their backs on Albany and returned home.[40]

Decades later, the Swedish botanist Peter Kalm was traveling through New York and came upon the charred remains of Fort Anne. He asked why it had been put to the torch only a short time after it was built. He happened to be in the company of a veteran of the 1711 campaign who knew the answer. When Nicholson received word that the fleet had run aground and abandoned its mission, he was "so enraged, that he endeavoured to tear his wig, but it being too strong for him, he flung it to the ground, and trampled on it, crying out *Roguery, treachery.* He then set fire to the fort, and returned." Having twice failed to serve its intended purpose, Fort Anne was left to burn.[41]

Fort and chapel
Despite the failed invasion, Hendrick did his best to put a positive face on the Mohawks' relations with New York. No one was more disap-

pointed by the collapse of this enterprise than he was. For years he had placed his faith in the English alliance, despite abundant evidence that it would not live up to expectations; the trip to London had encouraged a high opinion of English power, a view that the preparations for the 1711 invasion seemed to confirm; now, inexplicably, he was right back where he started. In public, Hendrick continued to profess his confidence in the alliance. But behind the scenes he pressured church and colony officials to recognize and protect Mohawk interests, and in doing so he ran afoul of powerful men, especially Governor Hunter, who did everything he could to destroy Hendrick's reputation.

In 1712 a fort, chapel, and missionary were installed in Mohawk country. Fort Hunter was built on the south bank of the Mohawk River, east of Schoharie Creek and opposite Tiononderoge. A square log structure, it measured 150 feet on a side and twelve feet in height and was supported by a force of twenty men. Inside its walls was soon built a log chapel. Queen Anne, for whom the chapel was named, provided a seven-piece silver communion service, a large Bible, and a purple altar cloth. In November 1712 its first missionary, the Reverend William Andrews, took up his post. Hendrick immediately met with Andrews to welcome him to Mohawk country and offer whatever assistance he could.[42]

In welcoming the missionary for whom he had so long pleaded, however, Hendrick had to contend with powerful voices of opposition among the Mohawks. The invasion's failure encouraged rumors of conspiracy, and the new fort and chapel became a focus of discontent. Thus, Hendrick and his fellow Christian Mohawks conveyed to Andrews the worry that this new presence in Mohawk country may lead to more clandestine land sales, or that the Mohawks might be expected to contribute a tenth of their property to the support of the mission. Among the most hostile to Andrews was Tagnaynaut, a Mohawk headman, who openly challenged Andrews on several occasions.[43]

Andrews soon took up his duties, and for a time he met with considerable success. He conducted weekly worship services, performed baptisms, and opened a school for Mohawk children. As the first Mohawk missionary to speak English, Andrews needed two interpreters: Lawrence Claessen, to translate Mohawk to Dutch, and John Oliver, to translate Dutch into English. About a hundred of Tiononderoge's 360 residents regularly attended worship. Infants were routinely baptized, and for a short time Andrews's school attracted several dozen Mohawk students. He made no sharp break with the customs of Dellius and his successors; he preserved many of their liturgical practices, and like the dominies he did not interfere in his congregants' community or daily lives. During its first three years, his mission seemed to flourish.[44]

Near the end of 1716, however, Andrews's fortunes turned for the worse. Beyond Tiononderoge, the other Iroquois communities resisted his influence. A smallpox epidemic in Tiononderoge led that community, too, to return to "their Old Heathenish practices." Former Christians in the village stopped coming to church, baptizing their children, and solemnizing their marriages. Their recalcitrance exasperated Andrews. In 1719, the SPG decided to abandon the mission, and the unhappy Andrews sailed for home. Assessing his accomplishments at the end of his mission, he concluded wistfully, "Heathen they are and heathen they will still be!" It was nine years before another representative of the SPG came to Mohawk country.[45]

Schoharie lands

As Hendrick and his fellow Mohawks absorbed the failure of the 1711 invasion and observed Andrews's arrival, they were also being drawn into another land controversy. Governor Hunter was at its center. Initially it developed around an odyssey of thirteen thousand refugees from the Palatinate region on the upper Rhine River. Displaced by war and famine, they were offered refuge in England by Queen Anne. Arriving in London in waves during the summer of 1709, the so-called Palatines camped in army tents in the fields of Blackheath and Camberwell. They soon became a source of public concern, and during the winter the government considered various resettlement plans. One involved sending several thousand refugees to the pine forests of New York, where they could be employed in the manufacture of naval stores—the pitch, tar, and resin that helped to preserve rope and wood from the punishing effects of seawater. The plan took shape as Nicholson and Schuyler were laying the groundwork for Hendrick's visit to London. In the spring of 1710, eight days after the four Indian kings disembarked at Portsmouth, some three thousand Palatines set sail on nine ships for the colony of New York.[46]

Robert Hunter was the prime mover in the resettlement effort. Appointed governor of New York in September, he was instrumental in laying the final plans. The ship that carried him to his new post was one of those transporting the refugees. His first priority was to identify a promising tract of land where the Palatines could set to work, making pitch and tar for the benefit of the British navy and the profit of the men who organized their efforts—preeminently Hunter himself. The new governor quickly identified the Bayard grant as a likely site. This was the large tract of land along the Schoharie River that the Albany trader Nicholas Bayard had purchased in 1695—the first of the three purchases (and the only one that did not involve Dellius) that had caused a political firestorm and had since been vacated by the New York Assembly. Hunter knew that the grant had been invalidated, but hoped to pressure the Schoharie Mohawks into ceding the land all over again.[47]

In early July, Hunter met with a group of Mohawk sachems to arrange for a survey of the Bayard tract. No doubt puzzled—and perhaps horrified—by the new governor's attempt to revive the discredited grant, they responded cautiously. They informed Hunter that the grant had been rejected, but also emphasized that they did not want to offend the queen. They asked that the survey wait until their delegation returned from London, presumably on the assumption that Hendrick and the others might have made some agreement that bore on the Palatine resettlement.[48]

A week later, despite the eminent good sense of their original position, a Mohawk delegation approved the survey. One wonders what pressures might have been brought to bear on the Schoharie residents between the two meetings. A short time later, Hunter investigated the Bayard grant closely enough to discover that it lacked the sandy soil and dense stands of pine best suited to produce naval stores. He diverted the Palatine resettlement to a more suitable tract of land at Livingston Manor on the Hudson River, some forty miles south of Albany. Nevertheless, Hunter pressed his newly won concession from the Mohawks and ordered that the Bayard tract, which was unsuitable for pitch pine but ideal for farming, should still be surveyed.[49]

Events had proceeded to this point when Hendrick and his party returned from London. In a speech delivered to Hunter in late August, Hendrick—flush with the success of his transatlantic voyage and believing that the Mohawk alliance now bore the imprimatur of royal approval—promised to cede whatever land the colony needed. But he wanted to handle such arrangements in a new way. He asked that "none of their land might be clandestinely bought from any of them for that would breed a faction and disturbance among them." The Bayard grant had been just such a purchase. Instead, Hendrick wanted land dealings to be conducted publicly between the sachems and the Crown.[50] In arguing for such public land concessions overseen by the Crown, Hendrick anticipated by several decades a recommendation that would be championed by imperial reformers who hoped to impose order on the chaotic borderlands of Anglo-America around midcentury. He also challenged the precedent from the 1690s of private land sales to trusted individuals. The controversial sales of that decade initiated a larger pattern that spanned the colonial era. Perhaps they reflect a long-standing Native American strategy to protect community lands by granting or selling them to trusted colonists; or perhaps they belong to a consistent pattern of fraud, perpetrated by erstwhile friends of Indians in combination with powerful men in the colonies. In either case, the result became all too familiar: Indians granting or selling large tracts of land, often to trusted associates, to protect the integrity of their communities.

Influenced by his exposure to imperial authority, Hendrick thought he saw a new and better way to protect Mohawk land. Instead of relying on trusted local allies like Albany's traders and Indian commissioners, who often pretended to have the Mohawks' best interests at heart but acted out of local and personal interests that could be antithetical to those of Indian communities, Hendrick wanted to put the impartial authority and benevolence of the monarch to work in Iroquoia. Yet however confidently Hendrick championed this new approach to land sales, he was working against powerful traditions and interests in Iroquoia and New York alike. His plea fell on deaf ears all around. Mohawks who had not seen London, sailed on a British warship, or met the queen had little sense of the tangible power of this abstract, distant force, while New Yorkers—both Governor Hunter and the Albany commissioners and traders—preferred the freedom and opportunity they enjoyed when power was exercised locally.

Here the matter rested, with the status of the Bayard grant unclear, as preparations for the invasion of Canada went forward. With its failure a year later, Hendrick's hope for close cooperation between the Mohawks and the Crown gave way to chaotic, ad hoc land sales and strong resistance—led by Hendrick—against the colony's efforts to extend its claims in Mohawk country. In August 1711, as the fleet sailed toward disaster, a group of Mohawks made a private sale to the Schenectady merchant Adam Vrooman. A year later, the Tiononderoge Mohawks met with a group of Palatines who were furious at the mismanagement and failure of the naval stores operation on Livingston Manor. In response to their overtures, the Mohawks agreed to take in a teenager named Conrad Weiser to learn their language and customs. (Weiser learned well; as an adult, he played a critical mediating role in Anglo-Indian relations along the New York and Pennsylvania frontiers.) In the spring of 1713, 150 Palatine families moved to the upper Schoharie with the Mohawks' blessing.[51]

Yet even as the Tiononderoge Mohawks acceded to these sales, Hendrick tried to frustrate Governor Hunter's efforts to claim Mohawk land. In the ongoing negotiation over the Bayard grant—once vacated by the colonial Assembly, now reactivated by Hunter—Hendrick tried everything to block the sale. According to Hunter's account, Hendrick first persuaded his fellow Tiononderoge Mohawks that the governor's payment was inadequate. When Hunter responded by augmenting his gift, the community decided that they were satisfied with the proposed cession. Hendrick was designated to speak for them in a council with Governor Hunter. But instead of expressing the will of his fellow Mohawks, Hendrick could not reconcile himself to the land deal and railed against it. The others were aghast; to speak his own mind instead of representing the wishes of his community in such a setting was an almost unimaginable breach of protocol. According to Hunter, as soon as the Mohawks left the council the others "fell upon him and [would have] . . . torn him to peices but for the interposition of some soldiers and my servants." Having dealt with Hendrick, the rest of the group then returned and completed the sale of the Schoharie lands.[52]

The fact that we have this episode only from the pen of Governor Hunter raises essential questions about its truthfulness. The larger purpose of the letter containing this story, which was written to the Board of Trade, was to discredit the Iroquois Confederacy as a political force and to diminish Hendrick's reputation in London. Hunter characterized Hendrick as a man of little influence, "a very turbulent, subtile fellow, who since his return has given us more trouble than all the other Indians beside." He scornfully suggested that Hendrick was "full of his Imperial power" when he tried, without success, to block the land transfer—a mocking reference to his presentation in England as "Emperour of the Six Nations." The larger point of the letter was to stress that the Iroquois tradition of decentralized government made the Confederacy unthreatening to British interests. However, if Britain made the mistake of designating "princes" among them, as the organizers of the London trip had tried to do, and "should these Princes assume or acquire an authority in any measure proportion'd to that of European Potentates, from that minute our quiet and safety must depend upon their caprice." To prevent such an occurrence, Hunter took every opportunity to disparage Hendrick's influence and judgment. Two days before he wrote this letter, in another he contended that Hendrick had tried to turn the Christian Mohawks against Andrews by warning them that he would demand a tenth of their property to support his mission. Though Hendrick had communicated this concern to Andrews, there is little doubt that he was voicing the fears of others in his community. Hendrick had always championed the idea of a British mission in Iroquoia; in raising the possibility of a tithe, he offered Andrews and his patrons an opportunity to dispel the concern.[53]

The land sale that Hendrick tried unsuccessfully to block cleared the way for Samuel Bayard, son of the original grantee, to reassert his right to the land. Having done so, he promptly sold his interest to an Albany partnership comprised of Myndert Schuyler, Peter van Brugh, Robert Livingston, Jr., John Schuyler, and Henry Wileman. In November 1714, Hunter granted them a patent, and they proceeded to survey the tract.[54]

Eclipse

Sometime in 1716—at about the same time that Tiononderoge turned against Andrews—Hendrick was suspended from his role as a Mohawk sachem. No surviving documents shed light on his suspension, and we can only speculate as to its cause. One possible reading of events is that Hendrick's intransigence in the controversy over the Bayard tract signaled a larger change in his character and public actions, one his fellow Mohawks found increasingly difficult to swallow. Unlike many Native American polities, neither the Iroquois Confederacy nor its constituent nations were chiefdoms—that is, they were not dominated by a single, powerful leader—and historians have generally emphasized the importance of consensus in their decision-making. Sachems were expected to follow the rules. When they came together, they deliberated until they reached a shared understanding. In public councils, Iroquois spokesmen were constrained to articulate that consensus; they could not deviate from the message, or even respond to new questions or concerns, without additional consultation. Hendrick had already shown some tendency to stray from the script at diplomatic conferences, as he did in contradicting Sadekanaktie and defending Governor Bellomont in the summer of 1700. After his return from London, Hendrick's independence was even more apparent. Perhaps Hunter's characterization of Hendrick— "full of his Imperial power"—did not entirely miss the mark.

But there is strong evidence to suggest that Hendrick was suspended as a sachem not because of conflicts with his fellow Mohawks but because his personal relationship with Hunter had deteriorated beyond repair. Perhaps the Mohawks did not object to his style of leadership: they may have valued the presence of a seasoned sachem who would stand up to an imperious royal governor. His London experience gave him unique authority, and he was not afraid to speak his mind. Hunter's attempts to slander Hendrick and destroy his public reputation suggest how much his independence enraged the governor.

Though we lack the documents to explain Hendrick's suspension in 1716, we know the circumstances surrounding his reinstatement in 1720. In the intervening four years, Hendrick remained in the background. But when Hunter left the colony in 1720, with Indian relations seriously frayed, Peter Schuyler immediately organized a conference in Albany to mend fences with the Mohawks and their fellow Iroquois. At that meeting, Hendrick rose to register a complaint about yet another "clandestine" sale of Mohawk land, this time to a Captain Scot. On the following day, Schuyler asked Albany's commissioners for Indian affairs to receive Hendrick once again as a sachem. It is striking that Schuyler did not direct his request to the Mohawk delegation, who apparently already regarded Hendrick in this light. The fact that the request was directed to the commissioners suggests that his suspension had been an act of the colony, not the Mohawks. With Hunter's departure, Hendrick could be welcomed back into the colony's public councils with its Indian neighbors.[55]

The Albany commissioners quickly accepted Schuyler's request. Thus Hendrick resumed his role as a central figure in the Mohawks' alliance with New York, and he did so at a critical time. Not only were the Albany Commissioners once again concerned about a growing French threat in the New York–Canada borderlands, but the representatives of several other British colonies would soon ask the Iroquois Confederacy to undertake new responsibilities on their behalf. The Anglo-Iroquois alliance was about to enter a new and more expansive phase.

Backcountry crises

During the second decade of the eighteenth century, Britain's colonial administrators faced growing crises in three separate regions, all with links to the Iroquois Confederacy. The first was to the south, where the expanding frontiers of Virginia and Pennsylvania were increasingly threatened by the activities of Iroquois warriors, who traveled regularly to the Virginia and Carolina backcountry after 1712 to fight against their southern enemies. The "warriors' path" that ran along the Susquehanna River and then bent south through the Great Valley of Virginia to the Carolina piedmont carried streams of warriors south throughout the decade. With colonial settlement pressing westward along much of this path, conflicts between Indians and colonists in western Pennsylvania and Virginia had begun to arise with alarming frequency.[56]

These violent encounters produced a flurry of correspondence among the governors of Virginia, Pennsylvania, and New York that spilled over to both the Lords of Trade in London and confederacy leaders in Iroquoia. Governor Alexander Spotswood of Virginia warned that if things failed to improve, the backcountry would soon be engulfed in war. Though he would seek to forestall disaster,

> a Governour of Virginia has to steer between Scylla and Charybdis, either an Indian or a Civil War, for the famous insurrection in this Colony called Bacon's Rebellion, was occasioned purely by the Governour and Council refusing to let the People go out against the Indians, who at that time annoyed the Frontiers, and it seems as if the same Humour was again arising in Virginia.

Pennsylvania's Governor William Keith wondered why the Iroquois had turned their aggression from the French-allied Indians of the Great Lakes region toward the Indians allied to Carolina and Virginia along the eastern seaboard. Perhaps, he suggested, this was a French plot; even if it was not, it should be a source of concern to the British colonies.[57]

At the same time, New York leaders—including Schuyler in Albany and Hunter's successor, William Burnet, who arrived in the colony in September 1720—had concerns of their own that were focused to the west. French traders had just rebuilt an outpost at Niagara that threatened to draw the trade of Iroquoia away from Albany. Albany traders worried they were about to lose their livelihoods, while the colony's political leaders feared that trade would lead to a military alliance that would threaten the colony's frontiers.[58]

The third center of concern was to the northeast, where New York and Massachusetts officials were convinced that the French were stirring up their Indian allies against the straggling, undefended settlements on the Maine frontier. Massachusetts Bay had been at war intermittently for many years with the Wabanaki Confederacy, which was composed of Penobscot, Mi'kmaq, Maliseet, eastern Abenaki, and Passamaquoddy Indians and occupied much of modern-day Maine, New Brunswick, and Nova Scotia. In New England, the Wabanakis were known as the Eastern Indians. Jesuit missionaries had been active in the region since the early seventeenth century, and in 1646 established a mission village at Norridgewock. This settlement had become a key staging ground for attacks against the English colonists who had moved north to the Maine frontier and, in so doing, encroached on Wabanaki lands. Beginning in the 1680s, those local conflicts were bound up with the larger contest between France and England for control of the Northeast.[59] The 1713 Treaty of Utrecht was supposed to have ended hostilities between France and Britain in North America, but by decade's end conditions on the Maine frontier were once again deteriorating, and British administrators had reason to believe that officials and missionaries in New France were at least partly to blame.

The solution to all three problems seemed to lie in Albany. In August 1722, governors Burnet, Keith, and Spotswood converged on the trading village to seek something new in Anglo-Iroquois relations: a coordinated agreement that might establish an enlarged sphere of intercolonial cooperation in Indian affairs. Though Andros briefly attempted something similar, his efforts had been short-lived; for most of the span of England's involvement in North America, individual colonies had pursued Indian relations independently, often to one another's detriment. Now the governors of New York, Pennsylvania, and Maryland hoped to combine their efforts and enlist the Iroquois Confederacy as a partner. The careers of the three governors could themselves be read as evidence of new opportunities in an integrated, expanding empire. All three were Scots who had risen through the army to become career colonial administrators.[60] They had made their peace with the union of the English and Scottish crowns in 1707 and capitalized on their access to English avenues of power to gain office. Now they hoped to enlist

Iroquois leaders as fellow architects of an expansive new vision for Anglo-Iroquois affairs. It was a vision that placed considerable pressure on Confederacy leaders to manage the behavior of their warriors and regulate the activities of their Indian neighbors, but as in the days of Andros, it also promised substantial rewards to those who would shoulder its responsibilities.

The tone of the 1722 conference was set when Governor Burnet had a preliminary meeting with representatives of each of the Five Nations at the end of August. He told them that he would be renewing the Covenant Chain not for New York only, but in the name of "my great & good Master ye King of Great Britain & your loving Father" on behalf of all Britain's colonies in North America. He referred to this enlarged chain of friendship as "the General Covenant Chain," which he hoped to brighten so well "that it will shine with new Lustre as long as the sun & moon shall endure."[61]

Seventeen days later, on September 13, 1722, the three governors and Albany's Indian commissioners opened the proceedings. Each governor spoke separately with the Iroquois representatives to air his own concerns. The Iroquois who were present are unidentified in the record. Either they were carefully coached ahead of time or the record of the meeting was sanitized, because they could not have been more compliant with the governors' wishes. They acceded to every demand and—in sharp contrast to the regular meetings of previous decades—raised no additional concerns of their own.[62]

Governor Burnet highlighted the violence on the Maine frontier and the problem of illicit trade with Canada. He asked the Iroquois to send representatives to Boston, where Massachusetts officials would accompany them northward to Maine to treat with the Wabanakis. In response, an Iroquois spokesman assured Burnet, "We have pitched upon an Indian of each nation to go to Boston."[63] (One of these was Hendrick, now about sixty-two years old; the trip to Maine would be his last major public act.) Governor Keith raised concerns about violence between Iroquois warriors and recently settled colonists in the Pennsylvania backcountry. Spotswood was especially petulant and demanding. He berated the Iroquois representatives for not keeping previous agreements with Virginia; he insisted that in the future the Confederacy sachems ensure that all Iroquois and Iroquois-allied warriors remain west of the Blue Ridge as they traveled the warriors' path; he asked that any runaway slaves encountered by Iroquois warriors be delivered back to the colony. The stridency of his demands echoes through the pages of the transcript.

The responses of the Iroquois spokesmen at the 1722 conference seem to reflect a change of heart, if not leadership, in their ranks. During the 1690s, strong neutralists like Sadekanaktie had checked the overeager voices of Anglophiles like Hendrick in public conferences, challenging New York's weakness and inconstancy and arguing for stronger support. More recently, Hendrick himself had emerged as a powerful advocate of Mohawk interests in the face of colonial pressures and in opposition to a governor's wishes. No such counterbalancing voice was heard in Albany in 1722. Compliance was the order of the day.

Yet these spokesmen knew there was a limit to what they could promise or explain. Asked about the intentions of their warriors, they replied to Governor Burnet, "You say that you are informed that there was a warlike Preparation making among the Five Nations which we acknowledge to be true but we know not as yet ourselves where they intend to go." With Britain and France currently at peace, New York officials had pleaded with the Confederacy for several years to ensure that their warriors neither fought *against* the French-allied Indians to the west nor *with* them in any raids they might conduct against their enemies, for fear that either course of action might upset the precarious transatlantic peace. Now Burnet and Spotswood also insisted that their warriors curtail activities to the south. The Albany spokesmen acknowledged the request and promised to do what they could:

> We take notice that you thanked us for not suffering any of our Indians to go a Warring with the French Indians of Canada, we resolve to do the same for the future & disuade any of our People to join with the French Indians to go to War, & if any of the French Indians should happen to come through our Country to go a warring we will endeavor to stop them, but if they cannot be persuaded then we will warn them not to go over the Great Ridge of Mountains that surround Virginia, nor pass over the Great River called Potowmack.[64]

Anyone who understood the centrality of war to Iroquois culture knew how difficult it would be to fulfill these promises.

In another way, too, the governors misunderstood the basis of Iroquois power. Though British administrators liked to think of the Iroquois Confederacy as a single polity, each of the three problem areas the governors were concerned about in 1722 was the province of a different faction within the Confederacy. Events at Niagara primarily involved Senecas and Cayugas, the two westernmost nations in the Confederacy. The Senecas, Onondagas, and Cayugas had authority over the Susquehanna Valley and the warriors' path to the south. Relations with the Wabanakis were conducted through the Mohawks, who had warred with them periodically during the seventeenth century and who were acknowledged, by the 1720s, as fathers to the Wabanakis. By asking the Confederacy to address these three areas of concern at once, the colonial governors were not mobilizing a single, centralized body to engage in a coordinated action; rather, they were calling on every leadership faction within the Confederacy to act in their interests simultaneously—something that had never happened before, and that the Confederacy council had always resisted in the past.

The 1722 Albany agreement was a landmark in Anglo-Iroquois relations. For the governors, it reflected a new vision of Britain's American empire. Previously the colonies had been, for all intents and purposes, a jumble of competing and uncoordinated enterprises. Burnet, Keith, and Spotswood sought to forge instead a unified sphere of imperial dominion. Among the Iroquois, too, the agreement marked a significant departure from earlier practice and involved considerable risk for Confederacy leaders. Since 1701, the Confederacy council had held both British and French colonies at arm's length. Though some Iroquois leaders, especially among the western nations, continued to hold back, a majority of sachems were apparently willing to embrace a modification of the Covenant Chain that would give them preeminent status among the Indian nations in the Anglo-American backcountry. To act on their vision of a unified sphere of imperial authority, the governors were willing to delegate to the Iroquois council authority for managing Indian affairs from Maine to the Carolina piedmont. At Albany in 1722, Confederacy leaders accepted the challenge.

It was not immediately clear whether this was a position of strength or weakness. The Iroquois spokesmen who convened at Albany in the summer of 1722 made a series of concessions to their British allies that are astonishing in retrospect. It is almost certain that they faced stiff opposition from Francophile and neutralist factions in Onondaga and Seneca country. But the prospect of a new, expanded alliance with Britain meant larger presents and more power. The chief complaint of the Iroquois against the British alliance had always been that it was unreliable and inconstant—the crises of the 1690s and the failed invasions of 1709 and 1711 stood as persistent reminders of British weakness. If things were about to change, then perhaps the Anglophile gambit made sense at last.

Boston and Maine

Within a few weeks of the Albany conference, Hendrick was part of a delegation of seven Mohawk, Mahican, and Schaghticoke sachems who traveled to Boston, along with Colonel Schuyler, at the invitation of the Massachusetts Governor's Council. An unidentified member of the party died at the Royal Exchange Tavern in King Street shortly after their arrival. Following an elaborate state funeral, the remaining sachems boarded a sloop commanded by John Alden, together with a group of Massachusetts commissioners of Indian affairs, and sailed to Casco Bay on the colony's Maine frontier. The on-again, off-again war between Massachusetts Bay and the Wabanakis was heating up again in the isolated maritime communities along the northeastern coast. In July 1722, the raids and counterraids began to accelerate. Indian parties descended on homesteads, stole and killed cattle, and destroyed property. The town of Brunswick, a fortified settlement on Casco Bay, was set afire, and a man was killed. A local militia company killed eighteen Indians in retaliation. On several occasions, Indians captured fishing boats. Men were being mobilized in coastal communities from Massachusetts to Nova Scotia to assist in the crisis. Rumors reached Boston that the town of Annapolis Royal, Nova Scotia, had been burned to the ground, while the crew of a Rhode Island sloop reported that they had seen a corpse in the water along the Maine coast, headless, its hands and feet bound.[65]

The Massachusetts commissioners, accompanied by a Colonel Walton and Lieutenant Joshua Moody, thus sailed at a moment of extreme anxiety. Knowing that the Mohawks and Wabanakis were traditional enemies, and that the Mohawks could claim authority over the Wabanakis by right of conquest, the colony hoped to use Hendrick and his fellow sachems as a source of leverage against them. Arriving at the town of Falmouth in Casco Bay on October 12, they took two rooms at a local inn and prepared to send a party inland to Norridgewock with an invitation for the Wabanakis to come to Falmouth for a conference. This plan surprised Hendrick and his fellow sachems, who expected to travel to the Wabanakis' council fire themselves, but they agreed to the arrangement. A captive Abenaki named Abraham would lead the group, and one of the Iroquois sachems, an Indian named Tagayonout, would accompany him.[66]

After the messengers departed, the Massachusetts commissioners laid out their grievances before the rest of the group. They contended that the Wabanakis had repeatedly broken treaty agreements, and they blamed their difficulties on the influence of Jesuit priests. After listening to these presentations for several days, Hendrick and the other sachems conferred among themselves. Then, in an unprecedented gesture, they met again with the Massachusetts commissioners so Hendrick could rehearse his speech to the Wabanakis and see if it met with their approval.

The surviving text of the speech is damaged and partly illegible, but some of its elements are clear. Hendrick intended to begin by reminding the Wabanakis that they had previously asked to be members of the Iroquois Covenant Chain—in Hendrick's terms, to "thrust their Arm into the Golden Chain of Amity and Friendship between the Nations"— and had accordingly been designated as children to the Iroquois, a designation they had accepted. Now, however, the Wabanakis had "Twisted and wrung your Arm cant keep it still can't hold it still as we do and always have done." Hendrick exhorted the Wabanakis to hold their arm still.

The details of the exhortation can be recovered only in fragments. Hendrick emphasized that the Iroquois brought with them "a Sun to enlighten you in all your ways"—presumably a reference to the elements of Covenant Chain diplomacy that were borrowed from the Iroquois League's rituals of condolence. These rituals eased the anguish associated with warfare, which otherwise caused warriors to lose their reason and retaliate in grief. Covenant Chain ritual, according to Hendrick, "Clarifies the sight" and "strengthens the mind and inward man." In an effort to bring closure to the long war between Massachusetts Bay and the Wabanakis, the Iroquois delegation intended to "gather up all the old Bones and lay them upon the Dead and they shall be seen no more." The Massachusetts commissioners asked Hendrick to explain his sun metaphor. "[W]hen any nation or people are Engaged in a War," he replied, "they are in darkness and they now designed to give them light, that is make peace for them."

The commissioners accepted the content of the speech, but they urged Hendrick to place the blame for Wabanaki hostilities more squarely on "the Priests that are among the Indians who are the Cause of all our disturbances." Given Hendrick's own experience with the French and his fierce anti-Catholicism, this was, in all likelihood, a congenial suggestion.

Yet the apparent accord in these preliminary meetings between the sachems and the commissioners soon gave way to a sharp disagreement. The party that had been sent to find representatives of the Wabanakis while Hendrick and the commissioners discussed his speech returned to Casco Bay empty-handed. They had arrived in Norridgewock but found it abandoned, a note on the door of the church imploring them not to burn it and threatening revenge if they did; and so they returned to Falmouth.[67]

This brought confusion and rancor to the proceedings. The Massachusetts commissioners, hoping to salvage the trip, suggested that the whole party might travel farther into Wabanaki territory to see if they could find suitable representatives and hold the conference elsewhere. This suggestion infuriated the Iroquois delegation. Such an arrangement might have made sense to the Massachusetts commissioners, for whom diplomacy with Indians was always a more or less improvised affair, but for the Iroquois sachems it was an unconscionable breach of protocol. Hendrick replied angrily, "We would not have you Treat us like Children and talk of sending us elsewhere." Events had reached an awkward, insurmountable impasse, and the entire group returned to Boston, the Maine odyssey having come to nothing.

For the Massachusetts commissioners, the failure of the Maine mission offered further proof of the Wabanakis' treachery, and—in accord with their understanding of the alliance they shared with the Iroquois

Confederacy—they began to lobby Iroquois leaders to go to war against them. There is a certain logic to this expectation, since, as the Wabanakis were members of the Covenant Chain, their ongoing conflict with the colony seemed to violate the wishes and policy of the Confederacy council. But from Hendrick's perspective, the expectation that the Iroquois could be dragged in to fight Massachusetts's battles was based on a profound misunderstanding of the situation. It assumed that the colony could dictate to the Confederacy—that Massachusetts Bay could treat the Iroquois "like Children." In Albany, the commissioners for Indian affairs feared that if the Iroquois were drawn into the conflict, it might broaden the scope of the war and endanger New York's frontiers. They advised Hendrick and the other emissaries to Massachusetts to resist the commissioners' pressure.[68]

Hendrick clearly recognized the importance of maintaining the Iroquois role as father to the Wabanakis and not acceding to the will of the colony. He understood how important it was to prevent the colony from transforming the Confederacy from mediator into mercenary. Other Mohawks, however, were tempted. The headman Aaron, for example, was willing to accept the substantial gifts offered by Massachusetts Bay in exchange for going to war against the Wabanakis. But Hendrick, and the confederacy council with him, refused to take that step. Instead they encouraged Massachusetts Bay's representatives to "take a Coal of fire from Albany" and "kindle a fire where you think fit in your Government for us to meet the Chief of the Eastern Indians." In late July a messenger from Canada pleaded the Wabanakis' case to the Mohawks and encouraged them to break with the Massachusetts commissioners. Hendrick turned him away, saying that the Mohawks would listen to the Wabanakis' concerns in Boston at the meeting to be arranged by the commissioners.[69]

The Wabanakis refused to attend the Boston meeting, and the fighting dragged on for four more years before they finally admitted defeat and accepted the colony's terms. Throughout, the Mohawks and the Iroquois council steadfastly followed the lead of Hendrick and the other sachems who argued against mobilizing for war.[70] This was a critical step in defining the newly reshaped Anglo-Iroquois alliance. By agreeing to act as mediators but not warriors, the Confederacy steered clear of another catastrophe like the one had that visited their communities in the 1690s. Though Hendrick and the Iroquois were willing to help Massachusetts make peace with its enemies, they left the burden of war squarely on the shoulders of the colony.

The land under their feet

The 1722 mission to Maine was not the end of Hendrick's career, but it was the last time he traveled beyond Albany in service to the alliance. In the subsequent decade, his final public appearances concerned affairs close to home. As in the 1690s, the colony began to put pressure on Tiononderoge lands; and as in that earlier period, the individuals most dangerous to Mohawk interests were the ones they thought were their closest allies. And Hendrick was, once again, at the center of things. Beginning in 1730, when Hendrick was perhaps seventy years old, a circle of men at the highest level of colonial affairs began angling for control of Tiononderoge's territory. In so doing, they triggered one of the largest and most sustained land bonanzas in British North America. Hendrick must have been in the dark about what was happening around him, but he and the other sachems of Tiononderoge facilitated events. One of his last public acts was to scratch his wolf totem on a piece of paper that signed over nearly every acre of land the Tiononderoge Mohawks could call their own to King George II and his heirs and successors forever.

The controversy began in 1730, when the corporation of Albany tried to exercise a right granted in its charter to buy one thousand acres of prime farmland from the Mohawks near Tiononderoge. The Mohawks were apparently persuaded to sign a deed to the land, but then concluded that the town had cheated them and began a sustained protest. Three years later, Hendrick and six other sachems stood before Governor William Cosby and several members of his council to denounce the deed. The mayor and corporation of Albany, they complained, "insinuated to us that if we did not put our lowland at Tiononderoge under their protection that some other people would attempt to take it from us. . . . [B]y these & other Deceitfull & Indirect ways and means they did prevail on us to Sign a Deed." Then, according to the official record of the meeting, they demanded to see the deed itself. When the governor produced it, the sachems "Burnt the same in the presence of this Board."[71]

To this point, we have a clear and credible story. But this is only the most visible, public face of a series of events murky in their details and troubling in their implications. In July 1730, within a few months of Albany's attempt to purchase one thousand acres, Captain Walter Butler, the commanding officer at Fort Hunter, and five partners petitioned the governor for the right to purchase twelve thousand acres at Tiononderoge. (Since the massive land transfers of the 1690s, the Crown had ruled that no individual could claim more than two thousand acres in a single grant. Thus, a grant of twelve thousand acres required six beneficiaries.) The mayor of Albany learned of the petition and sped downriver in a canoe to lodge a protest with Governor John Montgomerie, who denied Butler's request. Butler, however, was a patient man. A year later, with a group of petitioners that had grown to fifteen, Butler sought permission to purchase thirty thousand acres. By expanding their circle of prospective purchasers to include men of political influence, Butler and his associates improved the petition's chances. This time, the council—whose members now had ties to the petitioners— recommended that the governor approve the request, and early indications were that Montgomerie would do so. He died suddenly, however, before taking action. Rip Van Dam, a Dutchman with strong Albany ties, became acting governor and rejected the petition.[72]

Butler and his associates bided their time until Van Dam's replacement,

William Cosby, arrived in the colony. The group of petitioners, and the size of the purchase, expanded once again. Now a consortium of forty-three petitioners sought a grant of eighty-six thousand acres. Nearly all those named on the petition were straw men—individuals who would convey their shares to one of a handful of wealthy and powerful men for a small price after the initial transaction was completed. Often, the straw men were servants or tenants of one of the grant's real beneficiaries. In this case, the prime movers of the sale included George Clarke, James DeLancey, Archibald Kennedy, and Francis Harrison, all members of the governor's council. To push forward their interests, the purchasers guaranteed the new governor a one-third share in the grant, and also provided for his two sons and his brother-in-law. Cosby approved the petition.[73]

The next challenge was to gain Mohawk approval for the sale. To that end, Governor Cosby invited a delegation of Iroquois sachems to Albany, ostensibly for a conference that would brighten the Covenant Chain. During five days—from September 7 to 12, 1733—Cosby and the sachems discussed nothing in particular. It is striking, in fact, how little they had to say to one another in public. Privately, however, Cosby had two specific ends in mind: to invalidate the Albany deed and to pave the way for a vast land transfer to Captain Butler. On the last day of the proceedings, Hendrick and six other sachems appeared privately before Cosby, Clarke, Harrison, and Philip Livingston. This was the meeting at which Hendrick denounced the Albany deed and then burned it before the governor's eyes. The burning of the deed takes on a new significance when we know that three of the four Britons in the room had a stake in Mohawk land that competed directly with Albany's claim.[74]

The same council minutes that record this protest include another set of remarks that cannot be easily reconciled with the sachems' anger over the Albany deed. Hendrick purportedly began the meeting by thanking Governor Cosby for returning Captain Butler to his post at

Fort Hunter. "[F]or the affection we share for him," Hendrick is supposed to have said, "we have given him our Woodland at and about Fort Hunter and we desire you will Order it to be Survey'd for him and that we may be present when the survey is made . . . and that when it is Surveyed that you will grant him a patent for it."[75] Nothing is less likely than the possibility that Hendrick would have delivered such remarks, however welcome they would have been for the three men present who had so much to gain from the deed to Captain Butler. This can only be understood as a fabrication, inserted into the record of the meeting to cover for the apparent contradiction between the sachems' protest against the Albany deed and their willingness to make a much larger sale to Captain Butler.

That sale was completed six days later. Its details only compound the mystery surrounding the secret transaction. On September 18, a group of ten Mohawks, including Hendrick, representing each of the three clans, met with Captain Butler at Fort Hunter. William Printeys served as interpreter. For merchandise worth £368 New York currency, they agreed to transfer "an hundred fifty thousand acres more or less" to the king. Though ten Mohawks are named on the deed, only three signed: Johannes, Thomas, and Hendrick, one from each clan. Hendrick's familiar wolf totem appears, upside down, at the bottom of the paper.[76]

Puzzles abound. First: since Butler had a patent for only 86,000 acres of Mohawk land, why did he prepare a deed for 150,000 acres? Perhaps he felt that, with Cosby securely in his camp, it was worth pressing for every acre he could. Another puzzle is why Hendrick and his fellow Mohawks, having protested so vigorously against the thousand-acre grant to Albany, would have acquiesced in this massive land transfer to the Crown. One possible explanation is that this is another example of Mohawks seeking to protect their claims to lands by granting them to the Crown, as they had done when they granted much of the Susquehanna Valley to Governor Dongan in 1684, and when they placed their hunting grounds near Lake Ontario under the king's protection in 1701. But those cases were very different from this one. Each involved lands far from the Iroquois homeland; in both cases, the grant to the Crown helped establish their own claim to disputed territory. The 1733 deed, by contrast, granted nearly every acre of land in the vicinity of Tiononderoge. It left the Mohawks of that village destitute.

Why did Hendrick and his fellow sachems, given all their unhappy experiences with shady land deals, ever agree to put quill to parchment when they met with colonial officials? Hendrick repeatedly fought to hold onto Mohawk land, and twice repudiated documents that he had signed. New York officials were shameless in their attempts to acquire Mohawk lands, and the pressure rarely let up. Nevertheless, even as Hendrick renounced some land transfers, he approved others—though none as massive as the 150,000-acre grant to Captain William Butler in the fall of 1733. Could he have believed, in this case, that a deed to the Crown would protect Mohawk lands? It is not out of the question, but Hendrick had already publicly rejected that kind of logic twice before: when he repudiated the sale of lands to Dominie Dellius in 1698, and again when he rejected the Albany deed less than a week earlier. It is hard to believe that he would reject the claim that the Albany deed for one thousand acres would protect Mohawk interests, but then turn around six days later and sign a deed for 150,000 acres according to the same logic. It is much more likely that he did not know what he was signing—that, in some fundamental way, the contents of the deed were misrepresented to him.

But if that is the case, then what, one wonders, did he think the paper meant? Did he and the other sachems trust Butler so fully that they harbored no suspicions? Or perhaps a pile of merchandise worth £368 New York currency, however paltry it seems to us, meant too much to its recipients to pass up. In the end, none of these explanations seems fully persuasive. The greatest puzzle of all is also the one that most resists a satisfactory solution.

A year later, Hendrick affirmed his role in the burning of the Albany deed in a petition to King George II. The petition stated that the Tiononderoge Mohawks had been resisting the sale to Albany for forty years, that they had been deceived when they signed the deed, and that the sachems had unanimously agreed to repudiate and burn it. The first name affixed to the petition is "Teononhogerawey [Tejoniho-karawa], Sachem in Chief" of Tiononderoge. (In a break with past practice, the sachems signed the petition by writing initials next to their names rather than drawing clan totems. Hendrick signed with the letter "T.")[77]

But the Albany deed meant little alongside the bonanza in Mohawk lands that resulted from the Butler sale. By February 1735 Cadwallader Colden, the colony's surveyor general, had laid off the first twenty-eight thousand acres of the grant, and individual claims began to be filed. By year's end, forty-three thousand acres had been claimed south of the Mohawk River between Tiononderoge and Schenectady. In the same year, six Mohawks styling themselves the "sole and absolute proprietors of the Mohawks Country" sold Butler another thirty-six thousand acres in exchange for £107 New York currency. A year later, Butler conveyed his share of that parcel to James DeLancey, Jacob Glen, John Lindesay, and Paschal Nelson for £100. Governor Cosby died in 1736 and was succeeded in office by his former councilor George Clarke. Perhaps to curry favor with the new governor, in June 1737 DeLancey, Glen, Lindesay, and Nelson sold the lands included in the thirty-six-thousand-acre grant that had not already been laid out on their behalf to the new governor for £50.[78]

It would take a long time for the full scope of these events to become apparent. But in the span of a few short years, Hendrick and a handful of Tiononderoge Mohawks had unwittingly signed away nearly every acre they could claim—everything but the land beneath their feet.

End of days

Hendrick was growing old. In 1720 he became a grandfather when his only daughter, Lysbet, gave birth to her first son, who was christened Ezras. Two more followed: Seth in 1722 and Thomas in 1724. The joy of new life was tempered with grief when Hendrick's wife, Catharine, died sometime in these same years as she approached the age of sixty. Hendrick soon married her widowed sister, Rebecca, with whom he spent the last decade of his life. Despite all of his appearances in the public record, we know nothing about Hendrick's family life. He continued to be active in church affairs, both at Fort Hunter and in Albany, if his periodic appearances as a baptismal sponsor are any indication. He and his family seem to have survived the smallpox outbreak that afflicted Iroquoia in 1733. He is last mentioned in the records of the Albany commissioners in April, 1735, when he would have been about seventy-five years old. His death, whenever it occurred, went unremarked.[79]

Hendrick's legacy was immense. Along with Catharine's family, he was one of the mainstays of early Mohawk Protestantism. He was also, despite his periodic conflicts with Governor Hunter and the Albany commissioners, the bedrock of the Anglo-Iroquois connection. The alliance was, at bottom, profoundly personal. It rested on the ties that Hendrick and a small circle of associates built with key figures in Albany, including Dellius and Schuyler, and through them, with leading men in the colony of New York and the British Empire. Among the Iroquois, Hendrick's long-suffering efforts on behalf of the British alliance seemed finally to be bearing useful fruit as his life came to a close—even as the alliance began to generate unprecedented pressures on Iroquois resources. Among the British, Hendrick played a key role in the reconfiguration of Iroquois identity that was under way in the minds of imperial officials.

The visit of the four Indian kings to London initiated the change, and Hendrick, in particular, stood as an enduring symbol of Indian civility. In the famous Verelst portraits, Hendrick in several respects stands alone: he wears European clothing, he is without tattoos, and he holds a symbol of diplomacy and peace. His is a humane and civil visage. As British administrators began to argue for strengthening the Iroquois alliance and using it as a model in their relations with other Indian nations, we might imagine that Hendrick's example, above all, shaped their understanding of the potential value of such relationships.

3 Hendrick's War

A decade after Hendrick Tejonihokarawa's final appearance in the public record, in the fall of 1745, Hendrick Peters Theyanoguin made an inauspicious entrance onto the public stage in Albany. The occasion was a grand council. The War of the Austrian Succession raged in Europe, ending the long, uneasy truce between Britain and France that had persisted since 1713, and hostilities had begun to spill over into the Canada–New England borderlands. New York's governor, George Clinton, arrived in Albany in early October with four members of his council, where they were joined by commissioners representing the governments of Massachusetts Bay, Connecticut, and Pennsylvania. Anticipating a major public event, members of five of the six Iroquois nations arrived in force: 464 men, women, and children streamed into town. Only the Senecas, who "had been visited with an epidemical disease"— and who, perhaps not coincidentally, continued to maintain close ties with French Canada—were unrepresented.[1]

Clinton and the commissioners had high expectations for this conference. The Wabanakis were once again attacking the Maine frontier. They had killed several colonists, slaughtered livestock, and put houses and a sawmill to the torch. Though the Iroquois Confederacy had avoided war with the Wabanakis in the 1720s, they had agreed in the summer of 1744 to retaliate if the French-allied Indians killed any British colonists. Now, a year later, Clinton argued that the recent outrages demanded a response. "The Six Nations were formerly esteemed powerful," Clinton said, goading the assembled sachems,

> and your neighboring Tribes stood in fear of you; but now the French and their Indians by the little regard they have to your threatenings, or to the covenants they have made with you, do declare that they think you do not intend to perform what you have threatened, or that they do not fear your displeasure. . . . It is high time for us and you to exert ourselves and vindicate our honour.[2]

Yet even as Clinton spurred the Six Nations to action, he was aware of discontent among the Mohawks. For months, he had heard that the Mohawks were "uneasy" and "dissatisfyed." Almost a year earlier they had heard the rumor that New York was conspiring to destroy them, and it had proven unusually persistent and hard to dispel. So on the evening before the Albany conference convened, Clinton met privately with thirty-three of the principal Iroquois sachems to take the measure of the Mohawks' unhappiness. He began by asking whether his message, assuring the Iroquois that the rumor was baseless, had been received and understood. The Onondaga sachem Canassatego replied that they did receive it, but said nothing more. Finally, after a long, uncomfortable pause, Hendrick broke the silence.[3]

Though Hendrick had previously appeared before the Albany commissioners as a Canajoharie sachem, this was the first time he had addressed the governor. Already a middle-aged man, he was nevertheless new to the spokesman's role. If the surviving account of the speech is accurate, it was a less than stellar performance. The other sachems seemed uncomfortable with his remarks, but no one interrupted. Hendrick began by reporting that word had come out of Seneca country a year earlier, in the fall of 1744, that the British and French were conspiring together to destroy the Six Nations. He then spun a tale of fear and confusion that his audience was hard pressed to follow. He "run on for above an hour," according to the official record of the meeting, "in an harangue which the Interpreter could make little or nothing of, and at which the rest of the Indians seemed . . . to be ashamed." When he finally reached the end, "as neither head nor tail could be made" of the speech, the room fell silent. Finally, Canassatego suggested that the matter "required sober consideration," and the group adjourned for the night.[4]

The next night they gathered again, and this time Hendrick began the conversation. Clinton and his councilors wanted to know who had started the rumor of a conspiracy between New York and Canada against the Iroquois. Hendrick told them that it was Andries van Patten, a Dutchman who lived near Schenectady. With his female slave acting as interpreter, van Patten had told Johannes, a Mohawk who was lodging with him, that "the people of Albany had a design to destroy the Mohawks." Though Clinton was quick to reassure the Mohawks that the rumor was groundless, Hendrick argued that van Patten's warning fit a larger pattern. Two Indian towns had been "cut off" near New York; now, the Mohawks worried, "[t]hey were become the property of the Albany people, they were their dogs." Soon the Mohawks would be like the Mahicans: the Albanians "get all their lands and we shall soon become as poor as they."

Hendrick's "harangue" wove concerns that had long plagued the first Hendrick—the problem of clandestine land sales and the piecemeal dispossession of the Mohawks—together with an improbable conspiracy theory. Even if Clinton could dispel the possibility that New Yorkers and French Canadians were conspiring together, he could not deny the larger truth that lay everywhere before the Mohawks' eyes. Lands that had once belonged to the Mohawks were being steadily absorbed by colonial expansion. The first Hendrick, who had lived in Tiononderoge, had been on the front line of this pattern. Now the second Hendrick, who came from Canajoharie, the Mohawks' "upper castle," spoke for a community that was experiencing the same worry a decade later. His concerns were intensified by the renewal of imperial warfare, a prospect that seemed to threaten all of Iroquoia with destruction.

The career of the second Hendrick echoed that of his predecessor. In the 1690s, the first Hendrick and his fellow Christian Anglophiles observed the near annihilation of their communities. Hendrick Tejonihokarawa's public utterances in those years were similarly marked by confusion—in his case, confusion over his role in land grants to Godfridius Dellius, Peter Schuyler, and their friends. In 1709, and again in 1711, he risked everything to support two failed invasions of Canada. Only after 1711 did he acquire the independence necessary to see the interests of his community clearly. Then he learned how to use imperial levers to counterbalance local power relations between Albany and Tiononderoge, and personal alliances in Albany to shelter himself from the wrath of imperial officials like Hunter. In 1745, the second Hendrick was still unable to recognize the difference between local and imperial forces; pressure from Albany implied a dark conspiracy in New York and Montreal that could be traced to London and Paris. He and the Canajoharie Mohawks had been insulated from contact with Albany and Schenectady, and had passed three decades without experiencing war between France and Britain. As a result, they understood neither the fissures that ran through Anglo-American interests in New York and the Northeast nor the powerfully distorting vortex of global warfare.

Hendrick Peters Theyanoguin soon received a thorough education in these subjects. The impending war would make him a feared figure in Canada and a man of consequence in the New York borderlands. He would gain transatlantic fame—ironically, given the reaction to his Albany harangue—as the most forceful and eloquent orator the Mohawks had ever produced. He would win praise for his confident bearing and genteel comportment. And he would learn to exploit the divide between Albany and empire in ways that even Hendrick Tejonihokarawa had not quite managed to do.

Origins of the Iroquois myth

By 1745, Britain's colonial governors, lords of trade, and knowledgeable political commentators had come to place great weight on the Covenant Chain, and great faith in the Iroquois Confederacy as a partner in extending and stabilizing the authority of the British Empire. In part this was a result of Hendrick Tejonihokarawa's powerful, protean image, which forced Britons to reconsider their views of America's natives. When the "four Indian kings" visited London in 1710, printers and entrepreneurs generated a flurry of pamphlets to satisfy the curious, but the literary tradition that shaped them was a shallow one, grounded in the fantastic and the grotesque. Most included descriptions of the Iroquois and their environs that were hastily assembled from earlier accounts. The resulting texts partook liberally of what might be called an ethnography of wonders. They dwelled longest on the strangest and most fantastic details, they were concerned only minimally with narrative coherence or consistency of fact, and they revealed no curiosity about the historical experiences of the people they presumed to describe.[5]

In all these qualities, the ephemeral texts that appeared in 1710 shared much in common with the literature of travel, exploration, and ethnography that dominated the English print market around the turn of the century.[6] Take, for example, an anonymous pamphlet entitled *The Four Kings of Canada*. It begins by offering its readers a specious account of the origin of the name "Canada": "The *Spaniards*," it claims, "were the first who discover'd Canada; but at their first Arrival, having found nothing considerable in it, they abandon'd the Country, and call'd it *il Capo di Nada*, that is, a Cape of nothing. Hence, by Corruption, sprung the word *Canada*; which is now us'd in all Maps." It then describes two unlikely species of fish. One, found in the "River Canada," was "call'd by the Inhabitants *Cadhothins*, having heads resembling the Heads of Hares, and Bodies as white as Snow." The other, in Lake Champlain, was "the strange Fish call'd *Chaousarou*, generally ten Foot long, with Heads like Sharks, and two Rows of Teeth in their Mouths, their skins full of strong Scales, which are sufficient Shields against Swords and Lances."[7]

Having introduced the reader to some of the country's most peculiar aquatic life, the pamphlet proceeds to describe its human inhabitants. "The Natives of this Country anoint their Bodies with Oil, or Bear's Grease," it notes. "In the Summer they go naked, and in Winter mantle themselves in Fur, &c. Their Warlike Accoutrements are Darts, Clubs, Shields, Guns and Spears now, and their Diet *Indian* Corn, fresh and salt Fish, Venison, Buffalo's, and Beaver-Flesh, wiping their Hands or Fingers, when greasy, on their Heads." Even where the account is essentially accurate, it seeks to invoke the strange and unfamiliar. It also shares with many such texts the tendency to overgeneralize and to make the Indians it describes both timeless and uniform in character. "The *Indians* are inconstant in their Tempers, crafty, timorous, but quick of Apprehension, and very ingenious in their Way," its author claims; "they were more barbarous and cruel formerly, 'till acquainted with the Europeans, and were great Eaters of human Flesh, as formerly the Heathen *Irish* were."[8]

This pamphlet, with its etymological inaccuracy, its fascination with the improbably grotesque, its mixing of details from geographical, natural, and human realms, and its ethnographic timelessness, reflects the limits of both the assumptions of most popular writers and the information that was available to them. As late as 1710, English writers could draw on only a handful of texts for their accounts of Native American life. The early contact period generated several key books—notably those by Thomas Harriot, John Smith, and William Wood—that offered informed ethnographic impressions of Indians. But after their publication, a long hiatus in English-language works ensued. The principal addition to this literature in the last half of the seventeenth century was the strange work of John Josselyn, who offered a strikingly idiosyncratic reading of New England's Indians. Josselyn recapitulated many of the qualities of early texts of wonder; it is from him that the author of *Four Kings* drew his judgment that the Indians were "inconstant, crafty, timorous" and that they were cannibals. French travelers wrote several of the best accounts of Native Americans published in the seventeenth and early eighteenth centuries. When they were available in translation, English writers freely plagiarized them.[9]

ℍ

The impressions created in 1710 by the four kings, and especially by Hendrick, could not be reconciled with the crude, recycled stereotypes of the pamphleteers. The London visit caused Britons of all ranks, from the Board of Trade and the archbishop of Canterbury to the merchant community and the ranks of ordinary laborers, to reconsider their views of American Indians. To confirm and cement their impressions, and to take the Iroquois seriously as allies and partners, they needed a more thoughtful and less fantastic account of their history and culture. The English-language literature on Indians took a dramatic turn with the publication of Cadwallader Colden's *History of the Five Indian Nations* in 1727. Colden was an Edinburgh-trained physician and polymath who came to New York under the patronage of Governor Hunter and by the 1720s had become the colony's surveyor general and a member of the governor's council. He was the first English-language writer to historicize Indian experience and to treat Indians as comprehensible actors rather than mysterious exotics.

Though he did not eschew ethnography—nor did he resist the temptation to borrow material from French writers—Colden was primarily concerned to relate the history of the Iroquois' involvement in colonial warfare from the 1660s to the 1680s. This intention shaped his text in important ways. He resisted the common impulse to begin his account of the Five Nations with vague or fantastic generalizations. Instead, like Herodotus, who introduced his histories of the Greeks by narrating the origins of their wars with the Phoenicians, Colden located the genesis of the Iroquois as a people of historical significance in their conflicts with the Algonquins (whom Colden calls the Adirondacks). By introducing the Iroquois to the reader in the midst of a struggle for survival, Colden immediately evoked a sympathetic response and establishes a justification for later reprisals and hostilities.[10]

This beginning foreshadows a larger intention in Colden's work to make the Iroquois familiar and comprehensible to his readers. Instead of emphasizing their difference from European norms, Colden stressed that the Iroquois were much like Europeans had been at an earlier stage of social development. "As I am fond to think that the present state of the Indian Nations exactly shows the most Ancient and Original Condition of almost every Nation," Colden wrote in his introduction, "so I believe, here we may with more certainty see the Original Form of all Government, than in the most curious Speculations of the Learned." He regarded the Iroquois Confederacy as a league of nations analogous to the United Provinces, in which states participated as equals "without any superiority of any one over the other." Each individual nation of the Confederacy was an "absolute Republick by its self." Colden saw in the Iroquois a primitive virtue that generated ferocity and judiciousness in equal measure. The power of their leaders rested on consent rather than force; their "Authority . . . is gained by and consists wholly in the Opinion the rest of the Nation have of their wisdom and integrity. . . . Honour and Esteem are their Principal Rewards, as Shame & being Despised are their Punishments." For Colden, all these qualities offered evidence that Iroquois government "still remains under Original Simplicity, free from those complicated Contrivances which have become necessary to those Nations where Deceit and Cunning have increased as much as their Knowledge and Wisdom."[11]

In his discussion of Iroquois polities, Colden thus presents the Five

Nations as both forebears and exemplars to his Anglo-American audience. It is noteworthy, in the first place, that he refers to Iroquois "nations" rather than "tribes." While a tribe might be regarded as a forerunner to a nation, and thus consistent with his claim that the Iroquois illustrated the "the most Ancient and Original Condition of almost every Nation," tribalism also carried implications that might have seemed unpromising to an Anglo-American audience. A tribe, in eighteenth-century thought, was a warlike assemblage of primitives professing common loyalty to a charismatic chief, akin to the ancient Picts of Great Britain. Iroquois leaders, by contrast, won their authority by "wisdom and integrity," as in the city-states of Greece or Rome's ancient republic. By describing each individual nation of the Iroquois as an "absolute Republick" and the Confederacy as a league of equal states, Colden invoked the kind of decentralized federalism that other Scots, drawing on the political philosophy of Francis Hutcheson, would soon champion as a model for the British Empire and, later, for the American confederation.[12]

Just as Colden explained Iroquois polities through analogy with ancient republics, he assumed that Iroquois culture held up a mirror to the distant past. "We are fond of searching into Remote Antiquity," he wrote, "to know the Manners of our Earliest Progenitors; if I be not mistaken, the Indians are living images of them." Language provided one avenue for grasping the essence of these manners. Like an emerging group of Enlightenment writers who grew increasingly enamored of Indian language in the eighteenth century, Colden argued that Indians were uniquely eloquent in their speech. "For, the Indians having but few words, and few complex Ideas, use many Metaphors in their Discourse." This presented a problem to translators, who often failed to capture the vivid complexity of Indian speech, and as a result "may not have done Justice to the Indian Eloquence." But that eloquence was essential, in Colden's view, to an understanding of "the Genius of Indians." While Colden acknowledged that "it will be a difficult Task to show the Wit, and Judgment, and Art, and Simplicity, and Ignorance of the several Parties, managing a Treaty, in other Words than their Own," he provided lengthy accounts of treaty proceedings in which he hoped to illustrate those qualities.[13]

In the spirit of the classical analogy, Colden presented a historical narrative that placed Indian and European actors on an equal footing and included expansive accounts of Indian speeches, sympathetic assessments of Indian interests, and admiring narratives of Indian exploits. Aided by the minutes of the commissioners for Indian affairs, Colden offered a detailed record of Iroquois history during an eventful period of interaction with both French and English colonies. The story was complicated, but its message was simple: the Iroquois were a formidable people, and Britain neglected its alliance with them at its own peril. In Colden's mind the Iroquois held the balance of power in the contest between France and Britain for northeastern North America, and he produced his narrative to drive the point home to colonial officials in both New York and London.[14]

$$\mathcal{H}$$

The message took. Nor was Colden the only messenger; since 1710, correspondence between governors and the Board of Trade had provided many opportunities for London officials to appreciate the virtues of both the Iroquois Confederacy and the Covenant Chain. In their eyes, the Iroquois alliance gave Britain enormous leverage in Indian country. Not only did it stabilize relations with a formidable and strategically situated people; the influence of the Iroquois among their neighbors meant that the Covenant Chain was also a potent mechanism for managing relations with other Indian groups. In the years following the visit of the four Indian kings, some imperial officials were tempted to view the Iroquois Confederacy as something like a proxy state, whose special relationship with the empire made it paramount in its relations with other Indian nations.

The growing enthusiasm for the Covenant Chain in London is illustrated by the attempts to use it as a model for Britain's relations with southern Indians. In 1730, with the example of Hendrick's delegation firmly before him, Sir Alexander Cuming escorted seven Cherokee "kings" to England. Cuming was an adventuresome Scot who had managed to gain influence among the Cherokees and convinced them to declare their loyalty to King George II. Without any kind of official authorization, he arranged for his delegation of seven "kings" to cross the Atlantic. Despite Cuming's marginal status and only the most limited knowledge of the Cherokees in London, George II agreed to receive them. In the end, they visited Windsor Castle four times, met with other leading figures, and toured many of the same sites visited by the four Indian kings in 1710. The Board of Trade, persuaded that the Cherokees were a formidable and strategically pivotal power, proposed a treaty of alliance and trade. The Cherokees accepted, thereby inaugurating a new alliance system with the Crown that was maintained in subsequent years through regular visits to Charles Town.[15]

In recommending to the king a formal treaty with the Cherokees, the Board of Trade invoked the Covenant Chain as a model. "Your Grace is well apprized of what Consequence the good understanding between His Majesty's Subjects of New York and the five Indian Nations in their Neighbourhood, has been to the British Interest in those Parts," they wrote. "It may truly be said that they are our Frontier Guards there, always ready to defend our out Settlements and to make War upon any other Nation whenever we require them to do so." A formal treaty with the Cherokees might bring similar benefits. Since the Cherokees "are a Warlike People and can bring three Thousand fighting Men upon Occasion into the Field," a treaty would give the British a powerful ally in the Carolina backcountry. Moreover, "in such a Treaty, words may easily be inserted acknowledging their Dependence upon the Crown of Great Britain, which agreement remaining upon Record in our Office, would upon future Disputes with any European Nation, greatly Strengthen our Title in those Parts." Their analysis of the Chero-kee alliance sheds light on the board's understanding of the Covenant Chain. They concluded their memorial to the king by noting offhand-edly, "As this Treaty is to be only with Savages, we presume His Majesty's Orders signified to us by your Grace in a Letter, may be a suitable Power for us to act by upon this Occasion."[16]

Four years later, the Cherokee example emboldened General James Oglethorpe, a founding trustee of the colony of Georgia, to organize an embassy of nine representatives of the Creek Confederacy for a similar mission. The Yamacraw headman Tomochichi and the rest of his party spent four months in London and Westminster, where they met with King George II, the Georgia trustees, and other leading gentlemen and once again explored the city's many tourist attractions. Like the Iroquois and the Cherokees, the Creeks came to enjoy a special relationship with their neighboring colony, renewed through regular diplomatic and gift-giving encounters, and were considered by British administrators to hold a preeminent and privileged place among the Indian nations of the Southeast.[17]

The Cherokee and Creek visits, and the alliances they helped to cre-ate, highlight the ways the Covenant Chain was being transformed in the minds of London ministers from a local phenomenon into a cor-nerstone of imperial policy. Imperial officials encouraged the most ex-pansive account possible of Covenant Chain diplomacy, and Iroquois leaders obliged by describing their chain of friendship as a comprehen-sive alliance system that governed Indian relations from Maine to the Mississippi. Though the Covenant Chain was originally an expression of Iroquois influence with the Confederacy's neighbors, British officials began to blend the idea of Iroquois influence with that of imperial au-thority, and to conceive of a single, undifferentiated chain of friendship that united their interests with the most powerful Indian nations of the eastern seaboard.

It served the purposes of Anglophile Iroquois leaders to accept this expansive view, because it enhanced their apparent authority and kept diplomatic presents flowing into Iroquoia. In a conference with Lieutenant Governor George Clarke in August 1740, an Iroquois spokesman noted that only the southern Indians had failed to confirm a league of friendship with the Confederacy; he asked that representatives from the South be invited to Iroquoia by the colony in order to remedy this defect in the Covenant Chain. Clarke, in turn, recommended to the Board of Trade that representatives of the Cherokees and Catawbas, both allies of South Carolina, should be sent to Albany for a conference with the Iroquois. In the same letter, he proposed that all of Britain's American colonies should contribute to a fund that would buy presents for the Iroquois in time of war, since they were the "only barrier" between British America and French Canada.[18]

This idea—that the Iroquois served as a vital line of defense in case of war with France—was not new. But Clarke's coordinated, intercolonial vision was. So, too, was the willingness of Iroquois spokesmen to accept so fully Clarke's expansive account of the Covenant Chain. As George Clinton came into office as New York's new governor in 1743, Iroquois relations were entering a new era. The added weight placed on the Covenant Chain raised the stakes of events in Albany that had previously been governed by local interests and understandings, and required Clinton to adopt new methods for managing the Iroquois interest. With the outbreak of the War of Austrian Succession in Europe, which spilled over into the North American theater beginning in 1744, this new view of the Covenant Chain and the Iroquois Confederacy would face its first great test.

The transformation of Mohawk country

These heightened expectations for the Covenant Chain alliance echoed through a Mohawk landscape transformed by contact with New York. A series of interrelated developments threatened Mohawk interests and challenged the logic of the Covenant Chain. A thriving trade between Albany and Canada belied the central premise of the alliance: that it united Britain and the Iroquois against the French. Merchants in Albany and Montreal profited handsomely from the trade, as did the Mohawks' Kahnawake relatives, but in time of war it called local loyalties into question. At the same time, a growing number of large land transfers threatened the Mohawks' territorial integrity. The rise of European settlements in Mohawk country was matched by accelerating out migration of Indians. By the 1740s, Mohawk country bore little resemblance to the region where Hendrick Tejonihokarawa grew to adulthood.

Canadian scholars refer to the trade between Montreal and Albany as the "contraband trade" because it was outlawed by the French Crown. In New York, however, it was legal except for a few years' prohibition. Despite French efforts to discourage the trade, it was a common practice, since furs were more valuable in British markets and the manufactures available in Albany were generally both less expensive and of better quality than the French goods. British strouds—blankets made of a short-napped, closely woven woolen fabric in red and blue—were especially prized and a principal article of the Indian trade; many Indian customers would not accept French-made substitutes. Generally, the contraband trade was conducted by Indian couriers who carried beaver pelts, deerskins, and muskrat hides from shops in Kahnawake down the Richelieu River to the merchant houses of Albany. In return, they brought a wide variety of goods back to Canada: luxury articles like lace, muslin, calico, gold buttons, silver forks, chocolate, and sugar, along with supplies for the Indian trade, including strouds, wampum, and copper kettles. The traffic between Montreal and Albany was almost impossible to police, especially since the Kahnawake Indians, unlike their French Canadian neighbors, were not forbidden to trade in Albany. Nearly all Montreal merchant houses participated in the trade, often with the collusion of Canadian officials. By the second decade of the eighteenth century, the contraband trade was estimated to account for half to two-thirds of all the beaver production in Canada, and in succeeding decades it continued apace.[19]

The effect of the trade was to blur the boundary between New York and Canada. It was widely accepted because everyone profited: the Kahnawake Indians, the Albany traders, the Montreal merchants—everyone, that is, except the New York Mohawks, who played no role. The trade did affect them in one way. The constant traffic between Kahnawake and Albany helped sustain family ties and kin networks among the Mohawks that might otherwise have grown attenuated. For the Mohawks of Canajoharie and Tiononderoge, regular contacts made the prospect of migrating northward easier to imagine and to undertake, and such movement was common, especially when new pressures were felt in Mohawk country. Colonial officials on both sides of the border worried about the trade's implications. "The greatest fortunes" in Albany, noted Peter Wraxall, "have been got & are at this time getting by the Canada Trade." That trade, in turn, "increases & extends" Canada's "Indian Interest, for which they wisely pay us." But if British officials worried that the contraband trade helped New France, French officials developed the opposite concern. "Almost all the people" at Kahnawake, wrote the governor of Canada, Charles de Beauharnois de la Boische, in 1741, "have English hearts, as the Indians express it. For this I can blame only their Missionaries and the Misses Desauniers," three sisters with a shop in Kahnawake that specialized in the contraband trade, "who make them trade with New-York." Traversing as it did a great fault line of empire, the contraband trade between Montreal and Albany was an uncomfortable fact of life.[20]

The decade that intervened between the death of the first Hendrick and the emergence of the second was an eventful one in Mohawk country.

The events were not the kind that left prominent traces in the historical record: peace prevailed between Britain and France during the 1730s, and there are few accounts of dramatic violence or conflict. But the pressure on Mohawk lands, which had dropped off in the previous two decades, now entered a new phase. Throughout the 1720s, the region beyond Schenectady was still predominantly Mohawk country. The principal settlers west of Tiononderoge were the Palatines who took up lands on the Schoharie, and then farther west at German Flats and Stone Arabia, with the permission of the Mohawks. The Indian trade was centered in Schenectady and Albany, and the paths along the Mohawk River remained Indian paths that carried traders to their destinations.

Change came quickly. In 1727, New York Governor William Burnet built a fort at the western outpost of Oswego to counter the influence of the French post at Niagara. Soon the locus of the colony's Indian trade shifted from Albany, which was a long way from most Iroquois villages, to the southeastern shore of Lake Ontario, which was a more convenient destination for Indian hunters and a strategically important site for Great Britain. The rise of Oswego corresponded with the decline of the Mohawks as intermediaries. Albany merchants sent supplies to Oswego and received furs and skins in return through the efforts of small traders and hired laborers, and the Mohawks were largely cut out of the trade. As the fur trade declined, the Mohawk Valley trade in wheat and flour picked up. The German settlers on the Schoharie and Mohawk rivers pioneered wheat production in the region; Schenectady quickly became a milling center; and Albany had soon established a growing trade in flour and bread with the West Indies.[21]

Then around 1730, Mohawk lands once again became a target for large-scale speculation and settler recruitment. Governor William Cosby initiated the land rush, and his successor George Clarke carried it to new heights. The two men had partnered in the eighty-six-thousand-acre fraud at Tiononderoge that colored the last years of Hendrick Tejonihokarawa's life. In 1734, Cosby obtained a survey of twenty-eight thousand acres at Tiononderoge. In the same year, he acquired by royal grant an enormous tract in the western Mohawk Valley that came to be known as Cosby's Manor, which ran for eleven miles along the Mohawk River and three miles inland from its banks on either side. Unlike the Tiononderoge tract, no Indian purchase had yet cleared title to the Manor. When it did, however, Cosby's claim would take precedence.[22]

Cosby's efforts were little more than a shadowy portent of Clarke's full-scale assault on Mohawk lands. Born in England, Clarke arrived in New York in 1703 to serve as its secretary and deputy-auditor. He was appointed to the council in 1715 and succeeded to the governorship on Cosby's death in 1736. He served for seven years, during which time he pressed forward his interest in developing and settling western lands as energetically as he could. Clarke proposed to set aside one hundred thousand acres of land to be granted "gratis . . . to the first five hundred protestant familys that come from Europe in two hundred acres to a family." He hoped the settlers would be recruited principally from Ireland and Holland. It was not his intention to give settlers land outright; by "gratis," he meant that he was willing to absorb most of the usual patenting fees himself, in exchange for making the newcomers tenants on his own estates. Clarke recommended that the one hundred thousand acres be located somewhere in "the Mohacks Country." In fact, he noted, "we have already some Lands purchased which we design for this use." Though he had a personal interest in the project, he did not expect to profit immediately. "[T]he advantage I propose to myself is at a distance," he emphasized. The real benefit would be to the public, since poor immigrants would gain land on easy terms, the merchants who transported them would profit, the colony's frontier would be populated, and Britain would have "nothing to fear from Canada."[23]

With this vision in mind, Clarke supported nearly every land deal that came before him, and he claimed a personal stake in most of them as well. By the end of his term as governor, Clarke had acquired an interest in twenty-eight tracts amounting to nearly 120,000 acres, the vast majority in Mohawk country. It proved more difficult to populate these lands than it had been to patent them. Clarke worked with several partners to bring tenants to his estates, but with only limited success. But although his reach exceeded his grasp, Clarke's efforts challenged the Mohawks' control of their ancestral lands. Between Schenectady and Schoharie Creek, European titles covered nearly every acre of land. Beyond the Schoharie, the Mohawk Valley corridor was claimed, almost without a break, all the way to Oneida country. It would take many years to act on all of these claims, but the foundation for Mohawk dispossession had been laid.[24]

Mohawk leaders responded to these developments with alarm. Cosby and Clarke had triggered a mania for speculating in frontier lands, and unscrupulous purchasers kept arriving with disconcerting regularity to propose yet another sale. Often they dealt with young men who lacked the authority to sell land but could be flattered, plied with rum, or otherwise tricked into signing a deed. Even before the Butler purchases were complete, the Tiononderoge sachems noted that "most of their Lands on the Mohawks River were already sold to the Christians w[hi]ch grieved them to their hearts." They knew all too well that through "the Enticem[en]t of the Christians (to which their young men are too ready to give Ear) the remaining Small parcels of Their Lands are Likely to be sold in Like manner[,] by which means they would be utterly destroyed and scatter[e]d among the French and others and so Make a breach in the Covenant Chain." To prevent that eventuality, they had asked before, and now asked again, that no further licenses be granted to purchase their lands.[25]

As Tiononderoge leaders witnessed the culmination of this process, the Canajoharie Mohawks contested its earliest manifestations. Eight Canajoharie sachems who visited Albany in the spring of 1732 noted that they had sold Philip Livingston a small tract of land "Lying along the river to the Eastward of David Schuyler's land," but had since learned that Livingston had obtained a patent "that Takes in all our land that Lyes to the North and West along the Mohawk river" for many miles. "[I]f this is true," they lamented, "then Mr. Livingston has Murdered us asleep, for our Land is our Life." They contended that they had not agreed to such a sale and were now "fully resolved never to sell him a foot of Land." The Livingston purchase on Canajoharie Flats would be a source of controversy for many years to come.[26]

Two months later, a group of Canajoharie Mohawks appeared again before the Albany commissioners. They reiterated their complaint against the Livingston patent. They noted that they had lodged a similar complaint with Governor Montgomerie several years earlier about a purchase made by John Schuyler and Harmanus Wendell. They had requested an investigation and gave the governor a large belt. Now the governor was dead, and the belt had not been answered. The group's spokesman noted that there had always been a "good understanding" between the colony and the Mohawks, "and now we have accepted the Christian faith, we are Closer united together." But he worried "that there will soon be a difference between us which will occasion a dispute and a dispersion . . . of the Six nations, some to Canada others to Sughsaghrondie, some East, some West." He hoped for justice, but despaired of its likelihood. "I Grow more angry and my mind is full. . . . [I]f any come to Survey on Land not purchased we shall break the Compass and Chaine, and if any Settlements be made we shall destroy it, and their Cat[t]le."[27]

These were not idle threats. In the previous fall, thirteen European residents living in the vicinity of Canajoharie complained that the Indians had destroyed at least sixty head of livestock. Most of the complainants were descended from the Palatine refugees who had been granted asylum years earlier by the Mohawks, but now the Indians expressed hostility toward them. A Canajoharie spokesman noted that the Palatines were originally granted lands on the Schoharie, far to the east of their current homes. "[T]he People who Live there are People who Live on our Lands," he retorted, "and are but Strangers."[28]

Despite the conflict and misunderstanding, Canajoharie Mohawks continued to sell their land. Twice—in 1735, and again in 1737— Hendrick Peters Theyanoguin was party to a deed. In 1735, Hendrick, Nickus, and William, "Native Indians of the Maquas Nation of the Canajoharies Castel," sold an eighty-four-square-mile tract to John Lindesay and several partners for £100 New York currency. Two years later, Hendrick, Thomas, and Joseph sold another parcel, forty-nine miles square, to Lindesay and two partners, this time for £80. Hendrick had not yet learned the English alphabet; each deed is signed with a bear totem.[29]

In the fall of 1741, the Albany commissioners reported the arrival of two Canajoharie sachems who appeared in their records for the first time. Their names were Hendrick and Nickus. Hendrick announced, "We are Come here in the Name of the Two Castles of the Mohawks." They came in "great fear." The reason for their concern was the steady loss of Mohawk unity. "We are all scatter'd from our Castles and formerly we used to Live together. Brethren, we come to acquaint you That there is no more a Castle but that all the Nations who are your brethren are Scattered[.] A great Number are gone to Canada and Schohare and those that are left we Imagine will soon be gone." Their ancestors—the Mohawks and the New Yorkers—had made a covenant with one another. But colonists had abused the relationship more and more. Now, Hendrick said, "we fear you will make a break in that Covenant." Hendrick and Nickus had come to alert the commissioners that their confidence in the alliance was nearing an end.[30]

The visit was prompted by several incidents of violence between colonists and Mohawks that the colony had done nothing to address. One of them occurred on the property of a recently arrived Irishman named William Johnson, where an Oneida sachem had been beaten "almost to death" for picking corn. Neither Johnson nor any official of the colony had intervened to do justice to the victim. This is an inauspicious way for Hendrick's name and Johnson's to be paired in the surviving documents for the first time, but it would not be the last. The names of William Johnson and Hendrick Peters Theyanoguin would appear together repeatedly in the fourteen years to come as they developed a partnership that enabled both to rise in prominence and authority.

William Johnson and the Mohawk Valley

William Johnson's arrival in the colony resulted directly from Governor William Cosby's stake in the Tiononderoge purchase of 1733. Though Cosby had initiated surveys and patents on the land, he had done nothing to improve it at the time of his death. His widow, who controlled the rights to his estate, left New York in June 1736 to return to England. She sailed to Boston aboard the man-of-war *Squirrel*, commanded by a young captain named Peter Warren. Warren was the youngest son of a moderately well-to-do Irish family and nephew to Matthew Aylmer, admiral of the British navy. He had entered the naval service himself as a fourteen-year-old, risen quickly in rank, and been commissioned a captain at the age of twenty-four. In 1731 he was posted in New York, where he met and soon married Susannah DeLancey, the daughter of one of the city's most prominent merchants. Warren purchased three hundred acres in Greenwich Village and began looking for opportunities in the rapidly growing colony.[31]

Fortune shone on Warren the day Grace Montagu, William Cosby's widow, stepped aboard his ship. No one knows what transpired between them on the trip to Boston, but by its end Warren had bought a thirteen-thousand-acre tract in the Tiononderoge purchase, already patented for Cosby by Charles Williams, for £110 in cash. With the deed to a vast estate along the Schoharie Creek in hand, he returned to County Meath, Ireland, and enlisted his nephew, twenty-two-year-old William Johnson (whom Warren called "Billy"), to manage his new lands. Johnson recruited twelve families to accompany him on his transatlantic voyage. In the spring of 1737 the party arrived on American shores, probably in Boston, where they would have arranged for an overland trip to Albany. From there they followed the course of the Mohawk River to the mouth of the Schoharie, where they began planning a settlement just miles from Fort Hunter and the Tiononderoge lands that Hendrick Tejonihokarawa had worked so hard, for so long, to preserve.[32]

Johnson bore immediate responsibility for settling the new tenants on his uncle's estate, but he had plans for himself as well. Initially capitalized by Captain Warren, Johnson began to explore the prospects for trade in his new neighborhood. He quickly developed an interest in "Indian truck." He discovered that the competition was intense at Fort Oswego, which had become the principal point of contact between the Albany traders and the western Indians, and he initially preferred to send his merchandise to the remote Oneida village of Oquaga. But he also hoped to gain influence closer at hand. In 1739 he purchased a tract of land near his uncle's estate but on the north side of the Mohawk River, which placed him squarely in the path of travelers making their way downriver toward Albany. Here he hoped to catch the attention of his neighbors and capture some of the Mohawk trade that Peter Schuyler and his Albany circle had monopolized for decades. By year's end, he was living at "Mount Johnson" with Catherine Weisenberg, a seventeen-year-old indentured servant who had fled from her master to the German settlements in the Mohawk Valley. Over the next several years, Catherine gave birth to three children: Ann, or Nancy; John; and Mary, or Polly. During the same time, Johnson gradually broke into the lucrative trade supplying Oswego. By 1743 he had made significant inroads into the profits of the Albany traders.[33]

Johnson's independence made everyone unhappy. His uncle had hoped to keep Johnson as his own estate manager and factor, and he objected to the new land purchase and Johnson's growing prominence in the Mohawk Valley. The Albany traders soon had even greater cause to resent Johnson's interference. In July 1743, John de Peyster and Philip Livingston, Jr., summoned Johnson to Albany on behalf of the commissioners of Indian affairs to swear to the "full Quantity of Strowds or other Cloaths [and] Rum or other distilled Liquors" he had "Sent Carried or transported for Sale to the Indians or french" at Oswego in the previous seven months. Such shipments, they contended, were "contrary to the Tenor Intent and meaning" of an act of the General Assembly to support the Oswego garrison and regulate the Indian trade. Johnson had run afoul of the Albany traders by breaking into the Oswego trade.[34]

At the same time that Johnson supplied traders headed to Oswego, he was gaining influence nearer at hand among the Mohawks. His proximity to Fort Hunter gave him contacts in Tiononderoge, but the center of gravity in Mohawk country had shifted upriver to Canajoharie, and it was here that he made his most important connections. Johnson soon displayed an extraordinary talent for winning the confidence of his Mohawk neighbors. He was a shrewd trader, but that was only the beginning. A generous, warm, funny man, he maintained a growing household of family, friends, retainers, servants, slaves, and visitors with exceptional grace and hospitality. When it was appropriate Johnson and his household could be courtly, but more often, liquor flowed and hilarity prevailed. Indians, traders, and travelers mixed in his home, where they enjoyed the opportunity to escape the formalities of settled society.[35]

Johnson's Mohawk visitors were treated with the same generosity as gentlemen from the colonies or European travelers. He welcomed them in his home and demonstrated a strong intuitive grasp of Mohawk culture and values. He understood the importance of personal ties and intimate trust, as well as the dynamics of a kin-based social structure, and he developed key friendships and family alliances that allowed him to gain and extend personal influence in Mohawk country. Among these contacts, none was more important in the mid-1740s than his connection with an influential Canajoharie family, the most prominent member of which was Hendrick Peters Theyanoguin.

Hendrick Peters Theyanoguin

Like the first Hendrick, the second was baptized in Albany by Reverend Godfridius Dellius, but as an infant. The most plausible reconstruction of his life suggests that he was the son of a Bear clan matron named Canastasi Koaroni and a Mahican father named Peter who died while Hendrick was still a child.[36] A persistent tradition has it that Hendrick was adopted. He appears in the baptismal record for 1692 as "Hendrick Wänis," or "Long Bow." His childhood and early adulthood went largely unrecorded, but he married a woman of the Turtle clan named Mary, with whom he probably had four children, two boys and two girls. Along with his brother Abraham Peters Canostens and half-brother Nickus Karaghiagdatie, he rose in the leadership ranks of the Mohawks' upper castle of Canajoharie.

Hendrick was a large, imposing figure with flowing white hair. Some depictions of him include distinctive facial tattooing, although there is no mention of it in the written sources. In public, he was assertive and commanding; he could also be imperious and bombastic. Yet he won the confidence of those he worked with. The Canajoharie Mohawks considered him an effective agent and spokesman; after 1745, he represented them in public again and again. Despite the strident tone of many of his public pronouncements, British officials also respected and admired Hendrick. He became the most influential figure of his generation in Anglo-Iroquois affairs.

One important influence in the life of Hendrick's family and community was the Anglican mission, which had recovered after William Andrews's departure to become a mainstay of Protestant Mohawk culture. The mission at Fort Hunter was revived by the appointment of Henry Barclay in 1735. Barclay knew Dutch and some Mohawk, and he began to travel regularly to Canajoharie to baptize and minister to its residents. In 1740, three Christians in town granted him three hundred acres of land in recognition of their "love and esteem" for him. Two years later he opened schools in both Canajoharie and Tiononderoge, with the Christian sachems Daniel and Cornelius as schoolmasters. By the early 1740s, nearly every resident of the two Mohawk castles was baptized, and Barclay was a popular, trusted figure in both communities. It was only after Barclay's school opened that Hendrick began to sign his name with his distinctive block initials.[37]

While the first Hendrick came to prominence in the colony through his connection with Peter Schuyler, Hendrick Peters Theyanoguin had limited contact with the Albany traders and voiced extreme displeasure with the power they wielded over his community. In the first few years of the 1740s, the second Hendrick forged a tie with William Johnson that gave him an alternate path to influence in the colony and the empire. Johnson was both patron and tutor to Hendrick (as Peter Schuyler had been to Hendrick Tejonihokarawa). Among other things, it is likely that Johnson outfitted Hendrick with the English clothing he wore on public occasions. His signature attire included a laced hat and matchcoat and a ruffled shirt. The most famous image of Hendrick, which appeared a decade later, shows him dressed this way and is largely responsible for the false but persistent notion that he traveled to London in about 1740 and met George II, who was supposed to have presented him with this suit of clothes (Figure 3). No such trip could have occurred without leaving a trace in the records of either colony or Crown. It is much more likely that William Johnson, who understood the importance of genteel comportment and who was known to provide just such suits of clothing to Indian leaders, provided Hendrick with these garments sometime in the early 1740s. They served him well in the years to come.[38]

In 1744, three years after his first appearance before the Albany commissioners and a year before he met Governor Clinton, Hendrick Peters Theyanoguin traveled to Boston in a diplomatic capacity. He made a strong impression on those who saw him. The occasion was another conference in which a group of Iroquois sachems was asked to mediate a conflict between the Wabanaki Indians and the colony. With Britain's declaration of war against France in the spring of 1744, officials from Massachusetts, Connecticut, and New York met with representatives of the Iroquois Confederacy in Albany to plan for their mutual defense. The Massachusetts commissioners also arranged for a group of Iroquois Indians, led by four sachems, to travel back with them to Boston to meet with the Wabanakis. Hendrick was one of the sachems who made the trip in the summer of 1744; the others were two Cayugas, James and Jonathan, and an Onondaga named Joseph.[39]

Is there any reason to think that Hendrick might have been involved in this mission in part because he shared the same name as the Hendrick who had been at the center of a similar effort two decades earlier? Perhaps his stature in Canajoharie is sufficient to explain why he made the trip. Yet he was regarded in Boston as a figure of more than local significance. A Massachusetts diarist noted that one of the sachems visiting Boston "is look'd upon as a Chief of the Whole Six Nations." This is a curious description, whether applied to Hendrick or any of the other three sachems traveling with him. Curious, that is, unless Hendrick Peters were already being confused with Hendrick Tejonihokarawa, who had visited London as emperor of the Six Nations in 1710, reviewed the queen's troops in Boston in 1711, and returned in 1722 on his way to treat with the Wabanakis. For those with long memories, it is possible that the visit of 1744 brought these earlier appearances to mind. Hendrick looked prematurely old, an impression that was aided by his flowing shock of white hair. Conrad Weiser called him "weissen Kap," or White Cap, and in Boston in 1744 Ebenezer Parkman described Hendrick and James as "elderly men and Chiefs." Soon, Chief Hendrick would also be called King Hendrick on occasion. This title was incommensurate with Hendrick's stature and almost without precedent in reference to the Iroquois, who were well known to have been a confederacy without chiefly or kingly leadership. Almost, but not quite: the one precedent for calling an Iroquois leader a king was the London trip of 1710. When Hendrick Peters was called an Indian king, it was very likely with this earlier association in mind. From the beginning of his public career, the second Hendrick may have been confounded with the first.[40]

If so, the confusion of identities likely originated with the sachems' principal host in Boston, Colonel Jacob Wendell. Though he was a wealthy Boston merchant and influential figure in Massachusetts politics by the time he traveled to Albany in the summer of 1744, Wendell was an Albany native, born in 1691. His father was Johannes Wendell, a prominent fur trader and militia captain who was also a deacon and elder in the Dutch Reformed Church. A year after Jacob's birth, his father died; his mother remarried Johannes Schuyler, the younger brother of the man who had organized the embassy of the "four Indian kings" in 1710. In all likelihood, Jacob was baptized by Godfridius Dellius sometime between the christening of Hendrick Tejonihokarawa and Hendrick Peters Theyanoguin. Though Jacob moved to New York and then to Boston to pursue a career in trade, he maintained close ties to the Albany trading community and the Dutch Reformed Church throughout his life. It was almost certainly Wendell who sent ahead word to Boston in the summer of 1744 that he would be returning with the "Chief of the Whole Six Nations."[41]

Wendell's memory was not only long, it spanned the distance between Albany and Boston. He almost surely possessed some recollection of Hendrick Tejonihokarawa's public career. He may even have met the first Hendrick. Perhaps the passage of time dimmed his memory, and he assumed that the white-haired old sachem he met in Albany was the same man who had traveled to London thirty-four years earlier and whom he may have seen in Boston in 1722. Or perhaps Wendell initiated the confusion intentionally, to inflate the prestige of the visiting delegation. It is equally possible that Hendrick himself saw an opportunity to capitalize on Hendrick Tejonihokarawa's reputation and thereby strengthen his own authority. Perhaps Hendrick and Wendell collaborated on the deception. However the confusion originated, for Wendell it was as plausible as it was useful to claim that Hendrick Peters Theyanoguin was the "Chief of the Whole Six Nations."

Though the confusion of identities—if there was such a confusion—was a fluke, it is no accident that the second Hendrick emerged just as the prospect of imperial warfare loomed once again on Iroquoia's horizon. Like his predecessor, Hendrick Peters Theyanoguin came to the fore and gained transatlantic fame in response to the pressures and opportunities generated by the War of Austrian Succession: the first declared war between Britain and France since the Treaty of Utrecht was signed in 1713.

℞

By 1744, Wendell had become one of Boston's leading citizens. A colonel in the Massachusetts militia and a member of the provincial council, he was often placed in positions of public trust like the one that carried him to Albany as a commissioner to treat with the Six Nations. He knew, perhaps better than anyone in the colony, the dangers posed to Massachusetts Bay by the prospect of a renewed war with France. As militia captain, he took a leading role in demanding that the city prepare its defenses against the possibility of a naval attack. Wendell was also a land speculator. He partnered with Philip Livingston (another Albany native) and Colonel John Stoddard to purchase 24,040 acres of land in western Massachusetts, and in 1738 they laid out sixty-three one-hundred-acre lots in present-day Pittsfield. They began to clear land in 1743, but the threat of French-allied Indian raids led them to suspend the work. That experience must have given his efforts with the Iroquois delegation a personal sense of urgency.[42]

Hendrick and the other sachems stayed in Boston for several days in early July 1744, where they were entertained by leading citizens and made a favorable impression on those they met. They attended a Wednesday meeting in Cambridge with Governor Jonathan Belcher and dined afterward in Massachusetts Hall. The next day, Ebenezer Parkman breakfasted with them in Boston at the home of Josiah Quincy and engaged them in conversation. Their translator was Rachel Kellogg, whose husband had been captured as a child in the Deerfield raid and lived in and around Kahnawake for a decade. He served as an interpreter at Fort Dummer and must have taught his wife Mohawk as well. With her aid, Parkman found Hendrick to be "very ready, pleasant and intelligent"; he "especially gave free answers to our Enquiries concerning their Sentiments in matters of Religion." His association with Henry Barclay apparently served Hendrick well among the earnest Christians he met in Boston.[43]

On Saturday, 7 July, Hendrick and the other sachems sailed east with the Massachusetts commissioners, probably to Casco Bay, to meet with representatives of the Wabanakis, just as Hendrick Tejonihokarawa and his party had done twenty-two years before. Like his predecessor, Hendrick Peters was eager to please his hosts. Unlike that of the first Hendrick, the behavior of the second exceeded the commissioners' fondest hopes. The story of his assertive behavior spread through the streets of Boston on his return, and Alexander Hamilton, an Annapolis physician who was visiting the city at the time, recounted the tale in his journal. When the Iroquois delegation arrived at the "place of rendezvous," a number of Wabanaki "common[er]s" were already present, but their sachems had not yet arrived. Hendrick nevertheless launched into his speech. He declared the Mohawks to be fathers to the Wabanakis and announced that if they were "dutifull and obedient," if they "brighten[ed] the chain with the English, our friends," if they took up the hatchet against the French, then the Mohawks would "defend and protect" them. But if they were "disobedient and rebel[led]," Hendrick warned, "you shall dye, every man, woman, and child of you, and that by our hands. We will cut you off from the earth as an ox licketh up the grass."[44]

Still awaiting their sachems, the assembled Wabanakis were unsure how to reply. One of them made a brief statement of acceptance with equal parts fear and obsequiousness. Then, finally, one of the sachems arrived. When he discovered what had happened, he criticized Hendrick for making his speech before the sachems were present. Hendrick, "with a frown, told him that he was not obligd to wait his conveniency and time, ad[d]ing that what was said was said and was not again to be repeated, 'but do you or your people att your peril act contrary to our will.'" The Wabanaki sachem, according to Hamilton's account, "was silent and durst not speak."[45]

This singularly undiplomatic performance must have appalled the Wabanakis, but it stood Hendrick in good stead with the Massachusetts commissioners. They returned to Boston in glory on July 24. Hamilton was browsing the bookstalls in a King Street auction room that day when a clamor outside led him to the window. There he saw a "parade of Indian chiefs marching up the street with Collonell Wendal. The fellows had all laced hats, and some of them laced matchcoats and ruffled shirts, and a multitude of the plebs of their own complexion followed them." Among them was Hendrick, whom Hamilton—presumably with the story of his speech in mind—called "a bold, intrepid fellow."[46] His reputation must have spread quickly in Boston. Anyone who remembered the debacle of the 1722 embassy to Maine would have been gratified indeed to hear this tale of Hendrick in action: bold, intrepid, and militant, he embodied the new possibilities of Covenant Chain diplomacy.

This appearance captures enduring features of Hendrick's public comportment. Unlike Hendrick Tejonihokarawa—and, for that matter, unlike nearly every effective Iroquois spokesman up to that time—

Hendrick Peters showed a striking impatience and disregard for protocol. Though colonists who met him privately often remarked on his genteel comportment and pleasing manner, in public he could be abrupt, confrontational, even rude. The unvarnished threats he issued to the Wabanakis in Boston stand in stark contrast to the more measured way Hendrick Tejonihokarawa and his contemporaries had sought to mediate the conflict between Massachusetts and the Wabanakis without being drawn into the fray. Hendrick Peters Theyanoguin instead plunged in with both feet, and in doing so helped to commit the Iroquois Confederacy to the war that was now brewing in the New England–Canada borderland.

Stretching the chain

At the same time that Hendrick and his delegation were visiting Boston, a much larger Iroquois embassy traveled to Lancaster, Pennsylvania, to participate in an intercolonial conference. Representatives of Virginia and Maryland were there, alongside Governor George Thomas of Pennsylvania. Some 250 Iroquois men, women, and children from all six nations made the trip, led by the prominent Onondaga sachem and spokesman Canassatego. Unlike Hendrick, Canassatego might plausibly have been called "Chief of the Whole Six Nations" in 1744—at least, he might have been called that in Pennsylvania. A little older than Hendrick—he was perhaps sixty—Canassatego was a "tall, well-made man" who was considered especially eloquent by colonists who heard him speak in public councils.[47]

The Iroquois had had intermittent contact with Pennsylvania, Virginia, and Maryland since the days of Edmund Andros and William Penn, but in the 1720s these colonies made a concerted effort to stretch the authority of the Covenant Chain southward, where they hoped it would help them control escalating violence between colonists and Indians in the backcountry. The initial focus of their concern was the warriors' path that ran through the Pennsylvania backcountry to the Carolina piedmont. Iroquois warriors traveled this path to the south, while refugees followed it northward, throughout the first several decades of the eighteenth century. Because the Onondagas, Oneidas, and Cayugas bore particular responsibility for the warriors' path, their sachems generally took the lead in councils with these colonies, especially when they occurred in Pennsylvania.[48]

The colonies to the south soon discovered for themselves how useful the Covenant Chain could be. In 1728 the Iroquois Confederacy placed an Oneida overseer named Shickellamy near the Susquehanna Valley town of Shamokin, where he could monitor and help to control the behavior of warriors, traders, and refugees in western Pennsylvania. In 1737 Shickellamy and Conrad Weiser, the Palatine who had spent eight months living in a Mohawk community on the Schoharie River as a child and now served as a translator and diplomat for Pennsylvania, helped to orchestrate the infamous Walking Purchase, by which the colony defrauded the Delaware Indians of a half million acres of prime land. The Delawares resisted efforts to remove them and protested the purchase. Five years later, Thomas Penn invited Iroquois and Delaware leaders to a council in Philadelphia to settle the matter. A Delaware named Nutimus voiced his people's objections. Canassatego, speaking for the Six Nations and asserting the authority of the Covenant Chain, gave a withering response. "Let this Belt of Wampum serve to Chastize You," he began. "You ought to be taken by the Hair of the Head and shak'd severely till you recover your Senses and become Sober; you don't know what Ground you stand on, nor what you are doing." He validated the purchase and reminded the Delawares that they had no authority to sell land in the first place, since the Iroquois had "made Women" of them many years earlier. He insisted that they move immediately and never deal in land with the colonies again.[49]

When Canassatego arrived in Lancaster two years later, in the summer of 1744, he was a kind of folk hero to Governor Thomas and many of the other Pennsylvanians who assembled. Representatives of Maryland and Virginia were more cautious; they thought Iroquois land claims overstated, and they mistrusted Weiser and the Pennsylvanians who were orchestrating the conference. Its principal purpose was to settle a land dispute centered on the Shenandoah Valley in western Virginia, where the interests and populations of all three colonies converged. Though the proceedings almost collapsed in discord, an agreement was hammered out in the end. Everyone left Lancaster feeling pleased with the outcome. The colonies had settled an important land dispute; the Iroquois left with "very handsome Presents," including £200 in gold from Virginia and another £100 in gold from Maryland. Equally important, they had reaffirmed the importance of the Covenant Chain and the centrality of the Iroquois Confederacy to colonial affairs. In this sense, Canassatego had once again proven his worth, both to the colonies and to his fellow Iroquois.[50]

Yet once again he had betrayed the interests of other Indians to do so. This time it was an unwitting betrayal. The treaty signed by Canassatego and his fellow sachems recognized "the King's Right to all the lands that are *or shall be* by his Majesty's appointment in the Colony of Virginia." Because the western boundary of Virginia was open-ended— the colony had a sea-to-sea charter—and because its northern border ran northwestward, Virginians would soon argue that, with the king's permission, this cession gave them the right to claim a vast parcel of western land, including all of the Ohio Valley. And since the Iroquois claimed authority over the Indians on the upper Ohio, Virginia treated the Iroquois grant as determinative. The Lancaster Treaty of 1744, like the Walking Purchase of 1737, would soon hold a place of infamy in the minds of Indians whom it claimed to dispossess.[51]

At summer's end, however, that controversy still lay in the future. Canassatego, Hendrick, and the other Iroquois sachems faced more immediate concerns.

Calls to war

In mid-January 1745, the residents of Tiononderoge were awakened in the middle of the night by a terrible clamor. Five or six Indians had just returned from Schenectady with the horrifying news that "the white People were Coming with a Considerable force to Cut them All in Pieces." The messengers, and everyone they succeeded in panicking, then fled into the woods to escape their destruction. The missionary Henry Barclay pieced together the details of this report and, over the next few days, tried to convince his neighbors that their fears were groundless. The "Authors of the Sedition Oppos'd us with Violence," he wrote, but most of Tiononderoge's residents calmed down and accepted his reassurances. Canajoharie was a different story. People there were "all in a Flame, Threatening to Murder the Inhabitants set[t]led about them." Its leaders sent urgent warnings to the other Iroquois nations. Barclay himself was suspect. "Notwithstanding my Seeming Affection for Them," his accusers contended that he "was a very Bad Man and in League with the Devil."[52]

In response to Barclay's report, the Albany commissioners traveled to Tiononderoge and, with some difficulty, persuaded the leaders of Canajoharie to come down and talk. Eventually calm was restored, though "the Villains who first occasion'd This Disturbance Endeavour'd for some time to Kindle the Fire Anew." For such an episode to grip Canajoharie, and to center on Barclay, who had been a fixture there for a decade, highlights the deepening mistrust that the Mohawks felt toward both Albany and the empire.

Though Barclay was the focus of the January uproar, the Canajoharie Mohawks were increasingly unhappy with their Albany neighbors more generally. By 1745 they had come to believe that the threat posed by Albany to their community's interests was dire. As for Hendrick, his time in Boston the previous summer also sharpened his sense that the Albany commissioners were refashioning the Covenant Chain, which had been a symbol of partnership and a badge of Iroquois authority, into a leash that tied the Mohawks to their colonial neighbors and threatened to rob them of their autonomy and their livelihoods.

Conrad Weiser visited Canajoharie in July and recorded Hendrick's sentiments in detail. Hendrick differentiated sharply between the governors of New York, Massachusetts, and Pennsylvania on the one hand, who, he said, "intended no hurt" and "always were kind to Us," and the "Albany People" on the other who "did intend to hurt us,—& have in a manner ruined us, and would prevail upon the foresaid Governours, to destroy us if they could." His ire focused on three issues. First, the Albany circle "cheated us out of our Land" and "Bribed our Chiefs to sign Deeds for them." Second, they traded with the enemy. They sold "many Barrells of Gunpowder, last Fall to the French," part of a larger pattern of clandestine trade that diminished Albany's loyalty to the "English Interest." And third, they dominated the Six Nations' relations with other colonies. They "will never Suffer Us to go to Boston, Philadelphia, or any where else" but insisted on hosting diplomatic conferences themselves. When the Massachusetts commissioners came to meet with them in the previous summer, Albany officials "stopt the Bostoniers for 10 Days, would not suffer them to come to Our Towns; and after all They would not suffer the Bostoniers to speak with us, without it be in their presence."[53]

The cumulative weight of these grievances made Hendrick furious. The last must have especially galled him, given his favorable reception in Boston. The Albany commissioners, he complained, "treat us as Slaves." Speaking on behalf of his community, Hendrick asserted, "We could see Albany burnt to the Ground, or every Soul taken away by the Great King, & other people planted there." He asked Weiser to report their sentiments to Governor Clinton and assure him "that the Quarrel with Albany will never be made up." The Indians, Hendrick warned, "would no more look upon the Commiss[ione]rs as their true friends." They would visit Canada "on the Invitation of the ffrench Governour, to show Albany people, that they would no more be advised, or ruled by them."

At Tiononderoge, the local sachems tried to persuade Weiser that the crisis of the previous January had passed "& all was thrown into the Bottomless Pit never to be thought on more." But Aaron and another resident pulled Weiser aside a few days later to report that "the matter with Albany people was not made up, but only by words of Mouth. . . . [T]he old Cause, That we have been cheated out of Our Lands, stil remains unsetled." Weiser's journal passed into the hands of Daniel Horsmanden, a member of Clinton's council. Neither the council nor the governor nor the Albany commissioners liked what it had to say.

H

The fear of a conspiracy against the Six Nations resurfaced in August, when an Iroquois delegation of about 150 people, including sachems from each nation, traveled to Montreal to confer with the governor of Canada. There they joined another 450 Indians from the upper country in a grand council. They learned of two letters that had been captured from an English ship that described a plan to "Attempt the Taking of Canada & afterwards to root out & destroy the 6 Nations." Governor Beauharnois asked the Iroquois to take up the hatchet against the British colonies. Though they would not make a commitment in Montreal, they carried his war belt back to Onondaga to consider what they should do.[54]

The belt still lay, unanswered, in Onondaga when the Albany conference convened in October 1745. It was here that Clinton called on the Iroquois to "vindicate" their "Honour" by taking up the hatchet against the French, and here that Hendrick delivered his impassioned "harangue," more than an hour in length, "which the Interpreter could make little or nothing of." What made his account unintelligible? Perhaps it was disordered and confusing. Hendrick, truth be told, was no orator. When roused to anger he spoke in furious gusts of passion. But however chaotic his speech might have been, it would not have been hard to understand. From both Schenectady and Montreal, the Mohawks were hearing rumors of a British plan to destroy them. One version of the rumor suggested a grand conspiracy orchestrated in Montreal *and* Albany. The Canajoharie Mohawks were caught in the middle, pressured by the governors of both New York and Canada to take up the hatchet. Their western neighbors, especially the Senecas, favored the French interpretation of events. As the Mohawks looked at the encroachments of settlers all around them—as they considered the fate of the Mahicans, who had "become the property of the Albany people, they were their dogs"—they had to acknowledge that fears of a British conspiracy resonated. Hendrick's harangue probably seemed overblown to an audience that refused to credit its panicked sense of alarm. But Hendrick saw that wolves in sheep's clothing surrounded the Canajoharie Mohawks. The rumors of conspiracy were symptoms of a deep crisis of confidence in Mohawk country. Relations between Albany and Canajoharie were near a breaking point.

The strains were apparent in the Iroquois response to Clinton in October 1745. His request to take up the hatchet against the French met with cautious diffidence. Instead, the assembled sachems said they intended to send four delegates to Montreal, where they would "demand satisfaction for the wrongs done our Brethren." Only if they failed to gain reassurances from Canada, or if the French committed further hostilities against the Iroquois or the British colonies, would they go to war. This response stood in stark contrast to Hendrick's unequivocal insistence in the previous summer that the Wabanakis join in the war against the French. Flattered by his invitation to Boston, Hendrick had been willing to act forcefully on behalf of Massachusetts Bay. But Albany was a site of deep ambivalence for him. Moreover, events of the previous year had rattled the Mohawks, and with them the entire Iroquois Confederacy, and Clinton now faced unexpected resistance in his effort to recruit their warriors for his cause.[55]

Clinton himself only made matters worse. According to Conrad Weiser's private account of the proceeding, the governor was a "Monster of a Man" whose explosive temper set the tone for the conference. At one point, his angry criticism of the Mohawks prompted Hendrick to interrupt him in a "very bold and rude" manner. Weiser intervened in this confrontation, took the wampum belt out of the governor's hand, and insisted that Hendrick "hold his tongue." As it became clear that the Iroquois sachems intended to temporize rather than take up the hatchet, Clinton grew more impatient and frustrated. When he failed to get the desired result, he withheld two-thirds of the present he had assembled for the conference. As the debacle drew finally to a close, Clinton tried to beat a hasty retreat from Albany. A group of Indians stopped him as he was leaving to request a barrel of beer. Even as he complied, Clinton "damn'd them" and complained that "he gave them some the other day."[56] The governor, in short, made no friends in Albany. If he were to succeed in managing Indian affairs, he would need the help of a capable mediator.

ᕼᑭ

Clinton knew little about the deep ties between the Albany commissioners and the Mohawks, nor did he understand the estrangement that had poisoned their relationship in recent years, but the 1745 conference made it clear that Britain's relations with the Iroquois were badly frayed. He blamed factions on the council and divisions in Albany for the difficulties he faced in mounting a war effort, and he leaned heavily on Cadwallader Colden, his closest ally on the council, for his understanding of Indian affairs. Colden had already developed a strong antipathy to the Albany circle. In part, he considered their loyalties to be suspect, especially given the long-standing contraband trade between Albany and Montreal in which they were so deeply implicated. And in part, he simply did not like them. He found their Dutch manners rough and their temperaments dour and sullen. Many Britons who visited Albany remarked on the jarring speech and alien habits of its populace. With the advent of war, Clinton and Colden sought to shift the locus of power in Indian relations away from the tight-knit old Albany circle, dominated as it was by second- and third-generation Dutch traders, and toward people whose loyalties and manners were more reliably British.[57]

The Albany commissioners were equally unhappy with Clinton. The war was closing in around them, and neither the governor nor the Assembly was responding quickly enough. In November 1745, a French-supported raiding party of more than six hundred burned the fort and twenty houses at Saratoga, just north of Albany, killed thirty people, and took sixty prisoners (many of them African-American slaves). The commissioners, scrambling to rebuild the fort and patrol the countryside, called on the neighboring Indians for help. The Iroquois dragged their feet. Finally, in January, Hendrick went to Albany along with several other Mohawk sachems and warriors. They announced that they had come to renew the "Silver Chain" that had held fast the covenant between Albany and the Mohawks for many years, but Hendrick would only renew the covenant on equal terms. "We have one Request to ask of the Commissioners," he stressed, "that we may go hand in hand as in former Times, not that the white People look on themselves as entirely our Masters and despise Us." Hendrick's admonition suggests how mistrustful the Mohawks were, and even after the January visit, help came slowly. In February, a messenger traveled to Onondaga on behalf of the governor, imploring the Six Nations to take up the hatchet. They flatly refused. In March, Hendrick revealed that the Iroquois had received a belt from the governor of Canada, along with an invitation to visit him. The belt had been kept "very private," but its message received serious consideration.[58]

Conditions only worsened in the spring of 1746. Hendrick sent word to Albany—he was apparently unwilling to go again himself—that although the Mohawks had supplied manpower for scouting the frontiers, Albany had not lived up to their expectations. John Schuyler had promised to deliver a cask of gunpowder to each town, but had not yet done so; the commissioners had promised to fortify Canajoharie, but nothing had happened. Now the Mohawks intended to plan for their own defense, which would further limit their availability for service to the colony. The atmosphere in Mohawk country had grown too hostile for Henry Barclay, who left in April. He was called as rector of Trinity Church in New York and never returned to his Mohawk missions. Then further attacks north of Albany led the local farmers to abandon their homes and flee to town. The landscape was emptied out "for upwards of 70 Miles along Hudsons River" as a result of the "universal Terror" the raids inspired.[59]

In the midst of this growing crisis, Clinton began to despair of getting results from the Albany commissioners and turned to William Johnson for help. He granted Johnson the contract for supplying troops at Oswego, and at the same time enlisted him to speak with the Mohawks on the colony's behalf. When the Albany commissioners learned that Clinton was bypassing them in negotiations with the Six Nations, they asked Clinton to dismiss them from their post. Though Clinton did not immediately oblige them—their collective resignation was finally accepted toward the end of the year—from the spring of 1746 forward the commissioners became increasingly irrelevant to the conduct of public affairs.[60]

For Clinton, the prospect of making Johnson the new anchor of the Covenant Chain was likely a congenial one. A career naval officer, Clinton would have known Peter Warren, whose victory at Louisbourg in 1745 brought him new fame in the colonies. He probably knew Johnson by reputation almost from the time of his arrival in the colony, and it is no surprise that he began working through him when he saw an opportunity. But Clinton could not have anticipated the Mohawks' enthusiasm for the change. Hendrick was convinced that the Albany circle was strangling the Mohawks, but until now the Mohawks had been able to hold onto the Covenant Chain only through the Albany connection. Johnson offered something unexpected. An outsider who was hostile, like them, to the close-knit circle of powerful men who dominated Albany's affairs, Johnson bypassed them in his connection to Governor Clinton. The Mohawks responded with alacrity to this alternate pathway to imperial power. Johnson's prominence among them became clear at an Albany conference in June 1746. As his most able biographer has noted, the conference "was a failure in every respect but one. It brought to the fore William Johnson as an Indian negotiator and thus marked the beginning of a new era in New York's Indian relations."[61]

Warraghiyagey

Johnson's challenge in the spring and summer of 1746 was to rally the Mohawks to Britain's cause, even if it meant driving a wedge in Confederacy politics. In the days of Hendrick Tejonihokarawa, Anglophile Mohawks had often resisted the advice of neutralists in Onondaga. Now Johnson did everything he could to win the confidence of Hendrick and the other Canajoharie Mohawks. Colden admiringly described him as "indefatigable" in these months. To gain influence among the Mohawks, he "dressed himself after the *Indian* Manner, made frequent Dances, according to their Custom when they excite to War, and used all the Means he could think of, at a considerable Expence, (which his Excellency has promised to repay him) in order to engage them heartily in the War against *Canada*." No Briton had ever gone to such lengths to win over Indian allies, and it seems safe to say that no one else could have pulled it off. Somehow, Johnson managed it in a way that was compelling rather than ridiculous. The Mohawks had previously named Johnson Warraghiyagey, or "He Who Does Great Things." Now they designated him a sachem. And for the first time since the debacle of 1711, Iroquois warriors were persuaded to throw in their lots with Britain in its unending war with France.[62]

Johnson's diplomatic role dovetailed with his growing dominance of the Oswego Indian trade. As Oswego's official supplier, Johnson leveraged his war contracts to become one of the colony's leading Indian traders. This war was especially good for business at the western posts, because British depredations curtailed the flow of French merchandise almost completely. Britain dominated the Atlantic theater and plagued French shipping from the start of the war. Then, in June 1745, the fortress at Louisbourg, which guarded the mouth of the St. Lawrence, fell to Britain. For several years, Canadian merchants were unable to supply their western posts; as Clinton later noted, the fall of Louisbourg precipitated "the almost total destruction of the French Commerce with the numerous Indian Nations to the Westward." British traders stepped into the void, none so successfully as William Johnson.[63]

But despite his commercial influence, Johnson faced an uphill battle in persuading the Iroquois to take up the hatchet against New France, something they had not done in decades. Yet his appeals were not without force. He could ensure for his prospective allies the steady stream of gifts, scalp bounties, and booty that were staples of war. Moreover, for the Mohawks a partnership with Johnson offered opportunities to dramatize their deep unhappiness with the Albany commissioners and the recently departed Henry Barclay. Beyond Mohawk country, however, Johnson's propositions were a harder sell. The Oneidas and Cayugas, in particular, were leaning toward Canada and wanted nothing to do with Johnson, Clinton, or a British alliance.[64]

In August 1746, Clinton called another conference. Some seven hundred Iroquois streamed toward Albany in anticipation of the abundant diplomatic gifts characteristic of such wartime meetings. When the western delegates arrived at Fort Hunter, they were appalled to discover that many Mohawks were already preparing for war. Furious that they would make such a commitment unilaterally, before even participating in the conference, the other Iroquois separated themselves from the Mohawk delegation. The rest of the way to Albany, "the Mohawks marched on one side of the River, while the other Nations went on the other side."[65]

As they approached the town, observers were astonished to see Johnson at the head of the Mohawk delegation, "dressed and painted after the Manner of an Indian War-Captain." Hendrick, too, had laid aside his matchcoat and laced hat. The entire Mohawk delegation was painted for war—a most unusual sight at such a conference. Their arrival set the tone for the meeting.[66]

Clinton and his allies had much to overcome. Two Mohawk sachems opposed taking up the hatchet. One was Aaron, a Tiononderoge headman. He had recently visited Canada, and was so unhappy with the direction of events in Albany that he had removed permanently to one of the St. Lawrence towns. The other, the principal sachem of the Turtle clan, met privately with Colden and was soon persuaded to support a campaign against Canada. Among the other nations resistance to war was more widespread, but Clinton and Colden chipped away at their commitment to neutrality. Shortly after his arrival, Clinton received two Onondaga Indians and an Oneida, who brought him two French scalps, which they claimed to have taken "at Noon-day, in Sight of the *French Fort at Crown Point.*" Clinton gave them each a gift of money and clothing, including a laced coat, hat, and silver breastplate for their leader. The leader wanted more: he asked that Clinton confer on him a new name, "which in the Language of the *Six Nations* signified the *Path-opener.*" Clinton obliged and won three more friends to his cause. Clinton and Colden met with other sachems privately to offer additional inducements to alliance. Several scouting parties arrived carrying ominous intelligence about the French buildup at Crown Point, so that the gathering became increasingly concerned about the possibility of a large-scale attack on Albany and its environs.[67]

Before formal proceedings could begin Clinton came down with a fever, so his address to the Six Nations was presented by Colden— which may have been an aid to goodwill, given the way Clinton had alienated Hendrick and the rest of the delegation at the previous year's meeting. Colden's speech ranged deep into the past to invoke the Iroquois' experience with the French. He recalled the disastrous fighting of the previous century, with all its doleful consequences:

> You must have heard from your Fathers and I doubt not several of your Old men still Remember, what the French did at Onandaga[,] how they Surprized your Countrymen at Cadarackue[,] how they invaded the Senekas[,] and what mischief they did to the Mohawks[.] How many of your Countrymen suffered by the Fire at Montreal, before they entered upon their cruel and Mischievous designs; They sent Priests amongst you to delude you and lull you a Sleep while they were preparing to knock you in the Head. [A]nd I hear they are attempting to do the same now[.]

By recalling the wars of the 1670s and 1690s, Colden crafted a narrative of ancient grievance against the French that he hoped would overshadow the persistent, but less dramatic, concerns about land sales and insufficient support that were a chronic feature of Anglo-Iroquois relations. "I need not put you in mind," he concluded, "what revenge your Fathers took for these Injuries when they put all the Island of Montreal[,] and a great Part of Canada[,] to Fire and Sword."[68]

Colden reminded the Iroquois delegates of their promise the previous fall to take up the hatchet if the French committed any further hostilities, which they now had done. He also informed them that George II had "resolved to subdue the Country of Canada," and to that end was mobilizing "Many ships of war" and "Thousands of Soldiers." He urged battle on the Iroquois warriors by invoking the spirits of their ancestors. "If your Fathers could now raise out of their Graves[,] how would their hearts leap with Joy to see this day when so glorious an Opportunity is put into their hands to revenge all the Injuries their Country has received from the French, and be never more exposed to their Treachery and deceit[!]"[69]

Colden's exhortation had the desired effect. It is impossible to know which of its elements was most convincing, but the combination was undeniably powerful. The immediate context of their promise in the preceding year; the incendiary recitation of events long ago; the tantalizing prospect of overwhelming military support for an invasion of Canada: all these elements worked together to carry along the assembled sachems, despite the reservations they had brought with them to Albany. After affirming the message Colden had delivered, the Onondaga spokesman for the Six Nations—in all likelihood, this was Canassatego—threw down a war belt and agreed to take up the hatchet. Though they had brought "but a handful of fighting men" with them, they promised to "send down a greater Number" as soon as possible.[70]

Finally, the proceedings were solemnized by a sizeable gift. Clinton provided presents from the Crown, which were supplemented by a gift sent from the government of Virginia. When "the Presents from the King" were "exposed on one Part, and those from *Virginia* separately near them, it was agreed by the People of *Albany,* who had seen many publick Presents given to the *Six Nations* on Treaties with them, that this was the most valuable ever given." A group of Massachusetts commissioners, including Colonel Wendell, was also in attendance and provided an additional gift of their own. At the end of the proceedings, a Mohawk sachem, possibly Hendrick, offered his fellow Iroquois a final thought. "You now see how you are treated, really like Brethren," he began; "the Governor of Canada does not treat his Indians so; they are set on like his Dogs, and they run on without Thought or Consideration:

You see what a noble Present is made to you; if the Governor of Canada should seize all the Goods in that Country, it would not be in his Power to make such a Present." These remarks underscored the enduring power of Albany to flood Iroquoia with trade goods. Even a large share of the merchandise in Canada was British, traded to Montreal as contraband. The sachems' decision to take up the hatchet was informed by history, by prior commitment, and by the opportunity to show valor in battle. It was also a decision to defend the principal source of economic well-being known to the Iroquois.[71]

Hatchet in hand

A smallpox outbreak slowed Iroquois participation in the fall of 1746. Two pathogens—smallpox and a "malignant fever"—were sweeping through Albany at the time of the conference. While Clinton caught the fever, more than twenty of the assembled Indians came down with smallpox. By the time the proceedings ended, two or three were already too sick to leave Albany. The rest boarded wagons to Schenectady and, from there, returned to their homes. The result was an epidemic that swept through many of the Six Nations settlements. A "considerable Number of the briskest young Men of the *Mohawks* died." In a letter to Johnson written a month after the conference, Clinton lamented "the great Sickness & frequent Deaths among the Indians, w[hi]ch are inevitable Obstructions in executing Your Designs."[72]

As smallpox burned through Iroquoia, the colonies prepared for a campaign against Fort St. Frédéric, the French outpost at Crown Point near the south end of Lake Champlain. Some two thousand provincial troops from New York, New Jersey, and Philadelphia massed in Albany in anticipation of the campaign. But then they waited—restlessly—for events to be put into motion, gradually growing mutinous over the issue of pay. They would wait, as it turned out, for a long time.[73]

Johnson, reluctant to call together a large body of Indian warriors until he had a definite timetable for the campaign, tried to organize raiding parties to harass the Canadian frontier. But only a few went out in the fall. One group traveled to Soulange, just across the river from Montreal, where they took eight prisoners and four scalps. They did not stop in Canajoharie on their return, but traveled the two hundred additional miles to New York to deliver their prizes directly to Governor Clinton, along with a complaint against Reverend Barclay and Philip Livingston, the colony's secretary for Indian affairs. Barclay, they claimed, had kept the land they had made available to him while he served their mission, despite the fact that he had now accepted a call in New York. And Livingston they accused of fraudulently claiming a much larger tract at Canajoharie Flats than they had agreed to sell him. Thus did the return of imperial warfare to Iroquoia provide the Canajoharie Mohawks with a new means to bring their local grievances before the governor.[74]

Both Clinton and Barclay doubted the loyalties of their Indian allies in the fall of 1746. Clinton observed that Mohawks were traveling back and forth between New York and Canada and worried that the Kahnawakes who visited Canajoharie were spies, though it is more likely that they were conferring with relatives to decide what to do. And when the Mohawk raiding party returning from Soulange arrived in New York to present Clinton with prisoners and scalps, Barclay charged that they had not actually taken their prizes in war. He claimed instead that their French-allied relatives had surreptitiously handed them over. He believed that the collusion of the two Mohawk communities put it "beyond All Doubt, that these Savages are in League with Each Other, to Destroy both English and French, and to Observe a Strict Neutrality between themselves." Neutrality was indeed important to the Iroquois, divided as they were by the New York-Canada border. As an Onondaga spokesman explained, the Iroquois of New York and Canada were "sprung of one blood[.] They have made Alliances & Marriages with each other[.] One hath his father[,] another his Uncle[,] another his Son, another his Brother[,] and all of them some Relation or another living at Cachnawage so that they could not go to War against one an-other."[75] In the battle that was taking shape around them, Iroquois war-riors would try, with mixed success, to fight without compromising their complex loyalties.

In early November, Hendrick and eight other Mohawks traveled north. They visited Kahnawake, where they renewed their ties and con-ferred about the prospect of war. Governor Beauharnois soon learned they were there and invited the delegation to Montreal. If Hendrick's account of the meeting was truthful, he was astonishingly forthright and confrontational with the governor. Beauharnois asked whether it was true that the Six Nations had agreed in Albany to take up the hatchet. "I answer'd," Hendrick later reported, "We have accepted of it, and brought it with us, We hold it up, but have not yet struck with it." Beauharnois advised them to "put it behind our Backs, lay it down un-der Us and Sitt upon it for we had nothing to do with the War, It being only between the French and English." If that was so, Hendrick re-torted, why had Beauharnois sent out Canada's Indian allies against the New York frontier? The governor replied that the Indians had under-taken the raids of the previous year on their own initiative. Then, chang-ing the subject, Beauharnois addressed Hendrick directly. "He told me he thought I was a bold fellow to come to Canada at such a time and wonder'd that I was not afraid." Hendrick told him that he "was afraid of no man living" and gestured dismissively with his finger and thumb. Then, in the presence of the governor, Hendrick turned to the Kah-nawakes and the other Indians who had assembled. He delivered a belt and warned them to stay away from Crown Point, "for it wou'd be taken in a Short time, and it would be best for their people to leave it, or Else they would all be kill'd."[76]

Despite Hendrick's aggressive mien, Beauharnois hosted the delega-tion generously for five days. Since he had not invited them on official business, he did not offer a large present. But he gave each of them a coat, a shirt, a blanket, a pair of stockings, and some powder and lead; Hendrick also received "a good Gun." After spending two more nights in Kahnawake, they set out for home "in a Canoe the Governour of Canada gave us." As they passed Ile à la Mothe, they came upon a group of carpenters cutting timber. They decided that the time had come to raise their hatchet. Lying outside the woodcutters' house through the night, they attacked the first two men who appeared in the morning. They killed and scalped one, took the other prisoner, and inflicted wounds on three more as they shot at their pursuers. Then they returned to Albany. Beauharnois and his officers regarded this as an act of supreme treachery. From that point forward, Hendrick was a marked man.[77]

HP

Hendrick fell ill late in 1746 or early 1747, though it seems unlikely that he contracted smallpox. By spring he was regaining his health. His frame of mind must have been something like that of the first Hendrick in 1711 as he awaited the invasion of Canada, and Johnson's position was similar to Nicholson's. Both Hendrick and Johnson had put their reputations on the line; both hoped for a major victory that would vindicate them. In March 1747 Johnson wrote, "Old Hendrick is in a pritty fair Way of recovering again, w[hic]h will be of great Service to our Cause." Clinton acknowledged the news: "I am very Glad to hear my Friend Hendrick is on the recovery & pray let him know yt I Say so." They must have been happy indeed to see Hendrick on the mend. Neither man had a closer friend in Iroquoia, and neither could afford to lose him.[78]

Johnson outfitted nine bands of raiders in the spring of 1747. Hendrick led one, sixty-five or seventy warriors strong, which Johnson expected to return with an "abundance of prisoners and scalps." But Johnson's expenses, and his impatience, mounted. The storehouse at Mount Johnson was nearly bare; he begged Clinton both for more supplies and for repayment of the costs he was incurring in the government's interest. Clinton, meanwhile, had financial woes of his own. Facing an Assembly that refused to pay for the colony's defense, and a ministry that seemed utterly indifferent to his plight, he was forced to pay the New York levies in Albany with bills of credit and hope they would be honored in London.[79]

Meanwhile, in Montreal, Governor Beauharnois responded to the raids of early spring by calling together a large assembly of Indians. Warriors came from the Great Lakes, the Illinois country, and northern New England, as well as the local mission towns of Kahnawake and Kanesatake. Beauharnois asked them to take up the hatchet against his enemies: not the British, but the Mohawk raiders who were wreaking such havoc on his outlying settlements. His Indian allies agreed. At the same time, Beauharnois dispatched a messenger to Onondaga to explain his actions to the other nations of the Iroquois Confederacy. French and British documents give strikingly different accounts of the messenger's reception. According to a French chronicle, the messenger was assured that all of the nations but the Mohawks maintained a "perfect neutrality," and that the rest of the Six Nations had cut off all contact with the Mohawks since the Albany conference. Johnson reported, on the contrary, that an Onondaga spokesman told the French messenger that the raids were being conducted "by the whole body meaning the Five Nations, & that they were surprised how they could yet be ignorant of their taking up their Brother the Governour's ax, last fall, at Albany."[80]

The inconsistency in these reports is surely due, in part, to the differing motives of their authors. But it also reflects divisions among the Iroquois, whose factions struggled to maintain the appearance of unanimity as they battled fiercely with one another behind the scenes. The principles of neutrality and unanimity were victims of war.

For more than a year, Hendrick was the most sought-after target of French raids. An official report in the spring of 1747 referred to "Toyennoguen, the Mohawk chief who deceived us last year." In August, a party of Menominee and Nipissing warriors was sure they killed him. Forming an ambush along the road near Schenectady,

> they were not yet concealed when a big and tall Mohawk made his appearance, carrying a kettle, a sword and a gun. No sooner did this Mohawk perceive them, than he uttered a loud cry. Lamothe, a Fol Avoine [Menominee], chief of the party, called to his men to take him alive, but the man named Caron had already fired and killed him. According to the scalp they have presented, and the height, the voice and the marks they have described, there is every reason to suppose that they have killed Toyenoguén, the Mohawk chief who deceived us. All the Indians maintain that it is his scalp, which is remarkable in being clean and white.

Soon, French officials learned that it was not Hendrick, but another Mohawk called the Big Fish, who had been killed. Again in May 1748, a Kahnawake war party set out to "carry off, if possible, the Mohawk chief named Theya[n]oguin, who attacked the carpenters on Ile à la Mothe."[81]

Hendrick continued to provide ample provocation. In June 1747, he led another party north that included thirty-seven Iroquois warriors and at least two Englishmen and five Dutchmen. Forty-five miles from Montreal, they stashed their belongings—seven large canoes capable of carrying fifteen or twenty men each, and one small bark one, along with food, powder, shot, deerskins, and trade goods—and split into two parties. The smaller group, made up of four Senecas, an Oneida, and a Dutchman, captured three women at the upper end of Montreal Island. Hendrick—the French report calls him "*Thoianoguen*, White Head, a Mohawk"—led thirty-two Indians and four Dutchmen in the direction of Chateauguay, a small settlement just south of the island of Montreal, where they crossed to Montreal. They reportedly captured and killed between thirty and forty people. In the meantime, four Kahnawake

Indians had discovered their canoes and supplies and alerted their French allies. The first party was caught and taken into custody. When Hendrick's group returned, an ambush had been set for them. At two o'clock in the morning on June 18, they approached in four canoes and were fired on by a party of Canadian militiamen and their Indian allies. One canoe was captured. The men in the other three, alerted to the trap, hastily beached their canoes and fled into the woods.

Though they escaped, Hendrick and his party of twenty-four had nothing: no food; no blankets, clothing, or shoes; and no canoes. The overland route from Montreal to the Mohawk Valley was considered to be nearly impassable: more than two hundred miles through the Adirondack Mountain wilderness, all but trackless because anyone who made the trip did so by water. The group had nothing to hunt with. Two-thirds of them died of starvation along the way. The eight survivors finally straggled into Schenectady, where two Dutchmen spent the next month "sick unto death."[82] Hendrick made it, but it had been a harrowing year.

$$H P$$

Johnson reported that the death of four Senecas in Hendrick's raiding party brought even that westernmost nation "heartily to our interest." By midsummer he claimed to have the support of warriors from all of the Six Nations. Though the campaign against Crown Point had apparently stalled, the warriors who were committed to the British interest only grew more desperate to support a large-scale invasion. Belts were making their way from the Mohawk towns through Iroquoia, and Johnson expected to have a fighting force of a thousand warriors by the end of August.[83]

As Hendrick made his miserable way home from Montreal, Johnson spent the summer of 1747 meeting with warriors and sachems from throughout the region, attracted to Mount Johnson by the prospect of a major military expedition. They came until "my house and all my out-houses [are] continually full of Indians of all the Nations, and more so of late than ever." He met in Indian councils for five or six hours a day. On the basis of those conversations, Johnson developed an ambitious two-pronged strategy—remarkably ambitious, considering that he had the approbation of neither governor nor Crown. He learned that some Detroit-area Indians sought permission from the Six Nations to attack the French fort at Niagara. (According to one report, the Detroit Indians "say a sort of Witches about the said Fort always keep the Path foul and dirty, and for that reason they have resolved to make it clean.") To encourage their efforts, Johnson sent a shipment of arms and ammunition to Oswego.[84]

At the same time, Johnson learned that Fort St. Frédéric, the French outpost at Crown Point, was almost undefended, though a force of five or six hundred men was camped nearby. As the Niagara attack took shape on the western edge of Iroquoia, he quickly tried to organize a mixed force of Indian warriors and New York militiamen to strike against the unsuspecting force to the north. In an audacious move that suggests either impatience or desperation, Johnson proposed to undertake the very campaign that the provincial army encamped at Albany had so far failed to execute. Perhaps he thought a show of initiative would shame the British army into action. In any case, he was convinced that even failure was better than inaction, since the campaign would "terrify the Enemy" and give the Iroquois "a better opinion of us, than they have hitherto had."[85]

In August 1747, as Johnson was making his preparations, Clinton learned that the British ministry had laid aside its Crown Point campaign to concentrate its efforts in Nova Scotia. The troops that had been mobilized in Albany for a year and by July were "reduced by desertion to 40 or 50 discontented men" were finally discharged on the last day of October. Johnson was on his own. At the end of August he reported that he was "just setting off this instant for Lake Sacrament with 400 Christians mostly Volunteers and about as many Indians," with "vast numbers" of warriors still rushing to join him. Yet nothing further was heard of this campaign. Clearly, Johnson hoped the urgency and optimism of his letters would bring the support and resources he needed. Perhaps it was only a paper campaign, and the force was never raised. It certainly never marched—at least, not all the way to Crown Point. Instead, on September 18 Johnson was back in Albany, planning to set out for New York the next day in the company of ten Iroquois sachems, almost certainly including Hendrick, to plead their case directly to the New York Assembly.[86]

Nothing came of this either. The campaign season of 1747 ended, like its predecessor, in futility. When his Indian allies placed the losses they had suffered during two years of raiding in the balance against the utter inactivity of New York and Great Britain, Johnson began to fear that "there will be no living for me, or any one else in this part of the world."[87]

The failure of arms

The harbingers of futility that colored the 1747 campaign season were fully realized in the subsequent, and final, year of the war. Both empires had massed large forces along the Hudson–Lake Champlain corridor, but neither army had marched. Instead, small raiding parties traveled back and forth with impunity along that very route. Clinton, caught between an intransigent Assembly and an inattentive ministry, could do little to push forward any military initiative of consequence. Johnson had promised action for two years while he held together his coalition of warriors and sachems with a combination of small victories and big talk. Now he was left holding the bag: he had run deeply into debt and had put his credibility on the line, not only with his Mohawk neighbors but with Indian sachems and warriors from Tionnonderoge to Detroit. Hendrick, his most prominent Mohawk ally, was equally exposed.

Beginning in the fall of 1747, the momentum of cross-border raiding swung decisively in the direction of the French. By October, raids into northern New England and New York had become "almost continual." For the Mohawks, the most shocking of them came in March, when a scouting party was surprised by a group of Kahnawake warriors. Most of the scouts fled, but two of them, including a Mohawk named Gingego, whom Johnson described as "the Chief Warriour of all the Six Nations," chose to stand their ground. They were both killed in an exchange of fire. Then the Kahnawakes beheaded the men, scalped them, cut off their ears, noses, and lips, and set what was left of their heads on pikes before a fire. The headless bodies were set "on their Shoulders in the Snow, w[i]th their heels up, & mangled . . . in Severall parts." This enraged the Indians, according to Johnson, "to such a degree that I have a hard time of it, telling me it is all my Fault, by bringing them so farr into the Warr, and now can have no help from us, when they are murther'd in our cause." Despite his best efforts, Johnson could not persuade the local militia to respond.[88]

At the same time, the new governor of Canada, Roland-Michel Barrin de la Galissonière (who replaced Beauharnois in 1747), sent belts to all the Six Nations "Earnestly desireing to Speak with them Imediately." He included "a verry kind Invitation to old Hendrick to go & See the governour." Johnson stressed that this "must be put a Stop to as Soon as possible, otherwise all other Endeavours are vain." Accordingly, Clinton instructed Johnson to travel to Onondaga immediately to advise the Iroquois "not to depart from their Respective Castles nor hold any Interview with the French in Canada." He should reassure them that they would continue to enjoy the support and protection of the British Crown. Johnson did as he was instructed, and managed to prevent Hendrick and the other sachems from traveling to Montreal. But although they were persuaded to stay home, they could not be persuaded to keep raiding. From November 1747 onward, the governor of Canada reported that there had been no further attacks on his settlements.[89]

Rumors of an impending peace between Britain and France began to circulate in the spring and summer of 1748. They were finally confirmed in August, when Clinton and Galissonière learned that preliminary articles of agreement had been signed. The calculus of Indian alliance now shifted dramatically as each side began negotiating for the release of prisoners and encouraged their allies to suspend hostilities.[90] In the end, King George's War produced nothing but an inconclusive standoff in the New York–Canada borderlands. The raiding was extensive enough to bring misery to many communities, but neither the provincial army nor Johnson's improvised force ever fired a shot. Nevertheless, Hendrick's standing was dramatically enhanced. In his repeated forays against Montreal, he secured a reputation on both sides of the border as a fearsome warrior and important leader. His name fell easily from the pens of both Governor Clinton and Governor Beauharnois. And his status as a leading spokesman of the Mohawks was permanently secured. King George's War had become Hendrick's war as well.

H℘

The end of war was good news for many; the fighting had torn apart communities and exposed frontier populations to danger. For Hendrick, though, it brought a sense of failure and betrayal. While many Iroquois were probably pleased that the conflict ended in stalemate, Hendrick had committed himself wholeheartedly to Johnson and the British alliance. He did so in the expectation that the empire would commit the resources necessary to vindicate his choice.

Hendrick broke with the neutralists in Onondaga because he saw that the pressures of war heightened the significance of Mohawk interests in the eyes of colonial administrators. Throughout the long peace that followed the Treaty of Utrecht in 1713, Tiononderoge and Canajoharie were all but swallowed in a sea of European speculation and settlement. The leading men in Albany drove the process forward, and there was nothing the Mohawk communities could do about it. With the coming of war, Hendrick discovered that he had leverage. He could demand an audience, he could air grievances, he could make himself heard. He also had status. His laced hat, ruffled shirt, matchcoat, and leather boots were marks of power and authority. During the war, he augmented his status by displaying power of a different kind. His astonishing level of activity in the fall of 1746 and the spring and summer of 1747 testify to the great energy and ruthless determination with which he could pursue his ends. As he approached the age of sixty, apparently too old for such things, Hendrick was paddling a canoe up Lake Champlain, cutting a swath through Montreal, covering the two hundred miles back to Schenectady on foot without food, clothes, or— if the contemporary report is accurate—even shoes to cover his feet. He was a man of vigorous action, and in King George's War he seized the opportunity to gain power and notoriety.

Now, like Hendrick Tejonihokarawa in the wake of the failed invasion of 1711, Hendrick Peters Theyanoguin had to recalibrate his expectations and adjust to the very different demands of life in peacetime.

4   Apotheosis

In early June 1753—five years after the end of King George's War—Hendrick and sixteen other Mohawk sachems traveled to New York to express their unhappiness with the colony. On June 12 they were received in Fort George, at the southern tip of Manhattan, by Governor Clinton, councilors James Alexander and Archibald Kennedy, the city's Mayor Edward Holland, several members of the Assembly, Peter Wraxall acting as secretary, William Printeys as interpreter, and a few others. William Johnson was also in the room, having traveled with the sachems from the Mohawk Valley. Hendrick spoke for the group. The contrast with his Albany harangue eight years earlier, when he had "run on for more than an hour" in a speech his interpreter "could make little or nothing of," could not have been sharper. His remarks were focused and to the point. After giving Clinton a string of wampum and expressing his wish to renew the Covenant Chain, he remarked that the chain "seems now likely to be broken not from our Faults but yours."[1]

Hendrick emphasized that the Mohawks had always been reliable allies and faithful friends to the colony, but were now being treated with "indifference and neglect." The blame did not lie with Clinton; it was the Council and the Assembly who ignored the Mohawks and left the colony's frontier "naked and defenceless." New York was responsible for the danger to which the Mohawks were exposed. "It was at your request that we fought against the French, and they now dayly stand with a knife over our heads." The colony had asked the Mohawks to take up the hatchet, and they had done so; but it had failed to take the hatchet out of their hands or settle matters between the Iroquois and French Canada. New York officials had "always desired us to keep the Roads amongst our Nations open & clear," but their relations now approached a rupture. If the colony failed to address the concerns of this delegation, "the rest of our Brethren the 5 Nations shall know of it and all Paths will be stopped." Hendrick concluded his speech by demanding an immediate answer to their concerns; the sachems would not be put off by vague assurances of future satisfaction. He "then presented the Gov[erno]r with a Belt of Wampum & sat down."[2]

For all its apparent venom, the speech has a strangely understated, even scripted quality. It is odd for Hendrick to begin by predicting that, once the outcome of the meeting was decided, the chain would likely be broken. When he drew a distinction between the governor, on the one hand, and the council and Assembly on the other, Hendrick was making a point of much more significance to Clinton than to the Canajoharie Mohawks. And although he was harshly critical of the colony, his catalog of grievances was so briefly sketched as to seem superficial. The substance of the speech, moreover, is elusive: Hendrick called for stronger defenses along the Mohawk frontier, but at the same time complained that the colony had never formally concluded the hostilities of King George's War by taking the hatchet out of the Confederacy's hands. These remarks seem to point in two different directions. Nor do they fully justify either the peremptory tone of the speech or the uncompromising ultimatum with which it concludes.

The speech and the unconventional meeting that followed possess both text and subtext. Much about this occasion was not as it seemed. One part of Hendrick's performance during that week in June 1753—the part he expressed in this opening address—was a carefully orchestrated collusion with Johnson and Clinton, designed to place pressure on the Albany circle, the New York Assembly, and the anti-Clinton faction on the council. The other part expressed the localized, concrete concerns of the Canajoharie Mohawks. These concerns elicited little sympathy from Clinton, for whom Hendrick was a useful instrument in colonial and imperial affairs but little more. He turned out to be more useful than Clinton could have imagined. The substance of Hendrick's speech was communicated to the Board of Trade, where it intersected with a decades-long transatlantic conversation about the significance of the Covenant Chain in the British Empire. The prospect that the chain might be broken aroused the board, in turn, to an unprecedented level of initiative in American affairs.

Hendrick's appearance in New York in the summer of 1753 was grounded in more than a half century's experience of sustained consultation, collaboration, and conflict between the colony of New York and its Mohawk neighbors. It was a culmination of developments dating back to the beginning of Hendrick Tejonihokarawa's career. It also set in motion a chain of events that would lead to Hendrick Peters Theyanoguin's death in battle two years later.

Politics and prisoners

The most immediate pretext for the Fort George conference was the conflict that had developed during King George's War between George Clinton and William Johnson on one side and the Albany traders, the colonial Assembly, and much of the governor's council on the other. Johnson and Clinton had each made his own enemies, but the two groups substantially overlapped. Clinton had thrown in his lot with Johnson as an alternative to the Albany commissioners during the war, and from that point forward their political fortunes were linked. Both men supported a stronger executive and imperial prerogative in governance, while their opponents sought to preserve the power of the Assembly and a greater degree of provincial autonomy. At the center of the opposition was James DeLancey, chief justice of the colony and archenemy, after 1746, of Clinton and his principal ally on the council, Cadwallader Colden. Clinton was at a disadvantage facing off against DeLancey, the patriarch of an old New York family with strong ties in the city's merchant community. DeLancey's connections were stronger than Clinton's even in London, a fact that helps to explain why Clinton's repeated pleas for support in his struggles against "the faction" fell on deaf ears with the Board of Trade.[3]

After the war, Clinton tried to cultivate an interest to rival De-Lancey's. Though his success was limited, Johnson benefited enormously from the effort. Clinton suspended two of his strongest opponents on the council, Stephen Bayard and Daniel Horsmanden, while he helped engineer council appointments for Johnson, James Alexander, and William Smith, Jr. At the local level, Clinton began packing judgeships and offices like sheriff, recorder, and mayor with individuals who would be more sympathetic to him. In Albany County, one of several focal points for this effort, Clinton relied heavily on Johnson's judgment and influence. It was harder for the governor to challenge his enemies in the Assembly, but he called for new elections in 1750 and again in 1752. Though most of Clinton's supporters lost in these elections, Johnson engineered a monumental coup in Albany County, where his candidates defeated Philip Schuyler and Hans Hansen, both of whom had represented the old Albany trading interest.[4]

In stirring up opposition to the Albany faction, Johnson and Clinton relied on rumors of another impending war with France and the issue of frontier defense. They did not have to invent such rumors, though the threat to the Albany region was indirect. The Treaty of Aix-la-Chapelle, which was signed in October 1748, restored the status quo ante bellum. In North America, this meant the return of Louisbourg to New France, to the outrage of New Yorkers and New Englanders whose blood and treasure had helped to capture it. Farther west, the war's indeterminate outcome encouraged colonial administrators to jockey more aggressively for a favorable position.

Though he was an interim governor-general who served in Canada for only two years, Roland-Michel Barrin de la Galissonière pursued a forceful postwar strategy. He recognized that the war had profoundly damaged French interests among the Indians in western Iroquoia, the Great Lakes, and the Ohio Valley. The fall of Louisbourg in 1745 had cut off Canada's supply of merchandise for the Indian trade, and British traders rushed into the vacuum. Oswego was one important source of western trade goods; in the summer of 1749, more than £21,000 worth of furs and skins were collected there, nearly a third from French traders and Kahnawake Indians. To counter its influence, in June 1749 Galissonière began construction of Fort de la Présentation at Oswegatchie, halfway between Montreal and Lake Ontario, where he hoped trade and missionary activity could draw the Iroquois back to the French interest. In the same month he dispatched Pierre-Joseph, Céloron de Blainville down the Ohio River to proclaim French sovereignty and assess the extent of British influence. Galissonière understood that the Ohio country—a vast, neglected region between Canada and Louisiana—was France's soft underbelly in North America. During the war, it was a mecca for Pennsylvania Indian traders; immediately afterward, it also became a target of Virginia land speculation schemes. Galissonière favored an assertive response. He argued for a string of posts in the valley that would connect Canada and Louisiana and secure the center of the continent against the threat of British expansion.[5]

All of this activity surfaced in the Mohawk Valley first as rumor. In July 1749, Clinton reported to the Duke of Bedford that a thousand men had marched west from Montreal in the spring, their destination unknown. Three months later, Pennsylvania Governor James Hamilton wrote to Clinton to offer intelligence about Céloron's expedition. Early in 1750, the sachems and warriors of Canajoharie and Tiononderoge met at Mount Johnson to share what they knew about the French initiative in the Ohio country. Hendrick spoke for them. He reported that the Ohio Indians had given Céloron a cool reception. At Cuyahoga, a recently settled community that was drawing French-allied Indians from Detroit into the orbit of the Pennsylvania traders, Céloron met a well-armed body of warriors, one of whom grazed him with a bullet. Recognizing that numbers were against him, Céloron took a conciliatory approach. He explained that it was his purpose to drive out the English and invite the Ohio Indians to Canada to speak with the governor. The Ohio Indians, according to Hendrick, all replied that they would not accept the invitation and returned the belt Céloron had given them.[6]

Though Hendrick's account aimed to reassure Johnson, there was much to worry about in the posture of the Ohio Indians. These were nominally British-allied Indians who had been migrating to the upper Ohio since the 1720s. Their numbers had grown quickly in the 1740s. They included Delawares and Shawnees who had left Pennsylvania, western Senecas known as Mingoes, and smaller numbers of refugee groups from New England and the southern piedmont. They shared in common a desire to distance themselves from centers of colonial settlement. Though they had all been subordinate to the Iroquois Confederacy to some degree, the move into the Ohio Valley was also, in part, a declaration of independence from Iroquois oversight. The Ohio Indians were avid commercial partners of the Pennsylvania traders, and beginning in 1747 they met with Pennsylvania officials separately from Iroquois representatives. They also developed independent relations with Canada, though they consistently resisted efforts to be drawn into the French orbit. During King George's War, formerly French-allied Wyandots and Miamis moved into the valley to take advantage of Pennsylvania trading connections. By war's end, the population of the Ohio Indians was burgeoning, and their independence was a source of anxiety for both empires. It was also a source of embarrassment for the Iroquois Confederacy, who claimed authority over the Ohio Indians and assigned "half-kings" to oversee them but could not ignore their growing auton-omy from the Covenant Chain.[7]

The Lancaster Treaty of 1744, in which Canassatego and his fellow sachems unwittingly signed away their claim to the Ohio Valley, further complicated the Confederacy's relationship with the Ohio Indians. A circle of influential gentlemen led by Thomas Lee created the Ohio Company of Virginia in 1747 to capitalize on the Lancaster cession, and in 1748 they received a crown grant of two hundred thousand acres near the headwaters of the Ohio. Though Canassatego had not intended to cede those lands, let alone to sever the Iroquois' relationship with the Ohio Indians, the actions of the Ohio Company challenged the Iroquois' ongoing pretension to manage Indian affairs in the Ohio country.[8]

ℍ

In New York, Clinton and Johnson struggled, with mixed success, to bring King George's War to a satisfactory end. One vexing problem was the prolonged postwar prisoner exchange, an issue of pressing personal interest to Hendrick since his half-brother, Nickus, was a captive in Montreal. When Clinton and Galissonière received orders to cease hos-tilities, they each released the soldiers they held themselves. For Clinton, this meant returning some three to four hundred prisoners to Canada. But while these exchanges were relatively straightforward, those involv-ing civilian and Indian captives were much more difficult to negotiate. Dozens of individuals, both European and Indian, were held on both sides. Many were held in Indian villages, especially Canajoharie and Kahnawake; some were jailed in Montreal. Their status was determined less by European rules of warfare than by Iroquois expectation and practice. Yet both Clinton and Galissonière negotiated as if the release of these prisoners was under their control. Each was actually involved in two sets of negotiations: one with his imperial counterpart, and the other with Indian allies who had their own distinct interests and concerns. Nickus and the rest of the captives, once victims of wartime raids, now fell victim to the complex cross-cultural dynamics of a postwar settlement.

Clinton and Galissonière sparred over the issue for more than a year. Their correspondence reflects both the frustration they felt with each other and the extent to which they were powerless to dictate the terms of the exchange to their Indian allies. In the summer of 1748, forty-one New Yorkers held prisoner by the French-allied Indians near Montreal were returned to their homes, while the Canajoharie Mohawks restored five French Canadians. Yet nineteen French prisoners remained among the Mohawks, while a "much greater number" of New Yorkers—several dozen in all—were "detained like slaves" in Kahnawake and Kanesatake. In the fall, Galissonière sent a delegation to New York to negotiate an exchange, but it got nowhere. Clinton stressed that the effort would have been more successful if the French delegation had brought a Mohawk prisoner with them to return as a gesture of good faith. Galissonière promised to "release the Indian as well as the English prisoners as soon as we shall have our Canadians," while Clinton argued that he had already restored the vast majority of Canadian prisoners and French regulars he had held, but that a further release of prisoners from Canada was necessary before the Mohawks would reciprocate.[9]

This disagreement over whose release of prisoners had to come first ran parallel to another, in which Clinton insisted that the Six Nations were under the protection of the British Crown by the terms of the Treaty of Utrecht. Therefore, he contended, Galissonière could only negotiate for the release of the Mohawk prisoners through him. Galissonière rejected this interpretation of the 1713 treaty and insisted that the Six Nations were an independent power, allies of both the French and the British. As Galissonière's efforts to negotiate with Clinton stalled, he tried to deal directly with the Mohawks. In the fall of 1748 and spring of 1749, the Mohawks received a series of invitations to travel to Montreal. One came in the form of a wampum belt from Nickus and the other Mohawks who were languishing in a Montreal jail; it carried a "very strong" message that the Iroquois should send a delegation "if they had any regard" for the prisoners. Johnson was left in the unenviable position of persuading the Mohawks not to make the trip. Somehow he succeeded. Hendrick, meanwhile, headed a Mohawk delegation that traveled to New York to meet with Clinton. They agreed to deliver the French prisoners under their control. By the end of June, Johnson had ransomed all nineteen of the French prisoners who had been held by the Mohawks; he now faced the task of providing them with food and shelter while he awaited the outcome of events. Yet nothing further happened. In July, Hendrick reported that Galissonière renewed his invitation to the Mohawks to travel to Montreal and negotiate with him directly.[10]

Here matters stood when, in August 1749, Jacques-Pierre de Taffanel de la Jonquière finally arrived in Canada to relieve Galissonière of his post. (Jonquière had himself been a prisoner of war; he was captured at sea by a British squadron commanded by George Anson and Peter Warren while on his way to Canada to take up his duties. Galissonière was appointed to serve in his place; in the end, he acted as governor-general for more than two years while he awaited Jonquière's arrival.) With the change of leadership in Canada, the awkward dance between the governors started all over again. Throughout the fall of 1749, Clinton and Jonquière wrangled while the prisoners on both sides languished. In February 1750, Kings George II and Louis XV interceded to order the immediate release of prisoners on both sides. Even then, delays ensued. The prisoners were set free at the end of June 1750, two years after the first word of peace was received in North America. Nickus finally arrived home in August. A short time later, Conrad Weiser ran into Hendrick, Nickus, and eight other Mohawks in Albany, three of them recently released from captivity. They spent the evening together in a public house. Over several bottles of wine, Weiser listened to the captives complain of their "hard usage by the French."[11]

HP

The return of Nickus and his fellow prisoners must have been a joyful occasion, but they carried dark rumors to Mohawk country. Despite their loyalty to Johnson, Hendrick and the Canajoharie Mohawks had serious doubts about the strength of the Covenant Chain, which were deepened by the reports from Montreal. Immediately upon the prisoners' return, Hendrick and his brothers Abraham and Nickus paid Johnson a visit. They were furious. Johnson wrote that they entered his house "in a great Passion" and "would not even shake hands with me or the Interpreter." Johnson pressed for an explanation and learned that the Mohawks had been persuaded, once again, that the French and British had hatched a plot "to fall upon all the Indians on both sides and destroy them." While Nickus was still a prisoner, the governor of Canada had shown him and the rest of the captives a "very large Belt of Wampum" that, he said, had been sent by Clinton to propose the conspiracy. Galissonière assured them that he would not join in the plot. Then, when a Canadian embassy visited Albany to negotiate the prisoner exchange a short time later, "a York gentleman" told Hendrick that they were not negotiating about prisoners at all, but were "scheming how to destroy all the Indians, in conjunction with your Gov[erno]r." To promote the rumor, the Canadian translator read a letter to the Indians who were traveling with them. It was supposedly from Clinton, and it supposedly proposed a joint plot. "This together with the other story of the large Belt of Wampum . . . made all the Indians imagine it to be actually fact." The rumors gained strength because the Mohawks "plainly saw that there was a Coolness" toward them from Clinton, who "had not spoke to them in so long a time which convinced them you had no love for them."[12]

Johnson wrote that these reports "gave me three days hard work to get the better of." Eventually he persuaded Hendrick and his brothers that the rumors were themselves a French plot "to stir up the Indians against us." But this did not put Johnson's worries to rest. The French in Canada continued to vie for the affections of the Ohio Indians; another party had just been sent out with valuable presents to promote an alliance. If they succeeded—if they "overset our Interest with said Indians"— then the Iroquois "must certainly submit also as them very Indians are the Cheif and trustiest Allies, we or the five Nations have." Here Johnson stood conventional wisdom on its head. In the relationship between the Confederacy and the Ohio Indians, it was the Iroquois, he argued, who were in a position of weakness. The Ohio Indians constituted the essential link of the Covenant Chain in the newly contested territory to the west. If the Six Nations lost their influence on the Ohio, and the Ohio Indians made an alliance with New France, Johnson predicted that the Iroquois themselves would soon have to follow and proclaim an alliance with Canada.[13]

Johnson's dire forecast was self-serving, since it was in his interest to stir up anti-French sentiment. Nevertheless, he believed what he wrote. As he mapped local affairs onto an imperial matrix, he saw troublesome signs everywhere. He had worried for months about the rise of French influence in Indian country. Observing the steady flow of belts from Montreal to Iroquoia, Johnson warned, "The French were never so active among the Indians as at present while we must lay still and only look on[,] not having power to do any thing[,] which give me leave to assure your Excellency must hurt or weaken our Interest prodigiously." In the meantime, Johnson and Clinton seemed to bear the whole weight of their colony's effort to maintain the Covenant Chain. Johnson's personal debt in the public service was reported to be more than £5,000 in 1749. Angling for a royal commission, Johnson noted that the French "never employ a Trader to negotiate any matters with the Indians but a Kings officer, who in whatever Rank or capacity is attended by a Retinue of Soldiers accordingly to denote his consequence."[14]

It was not enough for Johnson to reassure his Mohawk neighbors. Nor was it sufficient for individual governors of individual colonies to make gestures of goodwill—though such gestures were essential. Like Clinton, Johnson was convinced that nothing less than a coordinated, imperial effort would suffice to counter the French initiative. This conviction was one impetus to the Fort George conference of June 1753 that began with Hendrick predicting a rupture in the Covenant Chain.

The decline of Mohawk influence

As long as the conflict between Britain and France in North America pivoted on the Montreal-Albany axis, the Iroquois, and especially the Mohawks, were at the center of the action. But as the focus of imperial competition shifted westward after King George's War, the Mohawk Anglophiles had to contend with the possibility that they would fade into irrelevance. All of Hendrick's efforts in the last several years of his life were aimed at forestalling that possibility.

It was not easy. For one thing, Iroquoia was being drained of people—or, at least, of Indians. Outmigration accelerated during and after the war. In 1749 a group of Onondagas and Oneidas moved north to La Présentation, the new mission and fort at Oswegatchie. With war's end, Mohawks could travel freely once again to Kahnawake and Kanesatake. And the Ohio country served as a new destination for would-be migrants. The Mingoes of the Ohio Valley were principally Senecas, but during the 1740s it is likely that migrants from throughout Iroquoia joined them. In 1750, Pennsylvania's Governor Hamilton wrote to Clinton, "You can't be insensible that many of the six Nations have of late left their old Habitations" for the Ohio and "are become more numerous there than in the Countrys they left."[15]

Those who remained behind were more skeptical than ever of the British alliance. A group of Mohawks told Conrad Weiser that the Onondagas, Cayugas, and Senecas "were turned Frenchmen," and the Oneidas were leaning that way as well. The Onondagas "had accepted of the

French religion." Only among the Mohawks did Anglophiles continue to hold sway, but they were an embattled minority. The rest of the Six Nations "abused the Mohawks and used them ill for being true to the English." Their task had never been more difficult. Since war's end, "Indian Affairs lay neglected and nobody minded them." Clinton "never spoke to the Indians nor offered them anything, and . . . the Mohawks themselves who had fought against the French with much loss of blood, received no thanks for their good service."[16]

At the same time, the problem of Mohawk lands was becoming acute. By midcentury, the combined effect of growing Palatine communities, on the one hand, and large, often contested, grants of land to well-placed colonial officials on the other was impinging on Mohawk communities in new ways. The shrinking settlements at Tiononderoge and Canajoharie were breaking up and spreading out, while all around them grew thriving second-generation communities of European farmers. They were pressing the Mohawk towns toward irrelevance, even extinction. Hendrick and his contemporaries recognized the problem and desperately sought the leverage they needed to check the process, but there was little they could do—especially in peacetime, when their grievances were generally ignored.

William Johnson was a bellwether in the transition to European dominance of the Mohawk Valley. In the heat of King George's War, Johnson began to plan a larger estate to replace Mount Johnson. A mile upriver from his first home, it was begun in 1748. Johnson occupied the new structure in the following year. Sited on thirty acres of cultivable land, the house was built of stone, sixty feet long by thirty-two feet wide. It was two stories high, with a smaller third story tucked under the roof. It could be fortified in wartime; during the Seven Years' War Johnson added wings and barracks, and the result came to be known as Fort Johnson. A visitor during that war noted that Johnson had added a crenellated parapet and four bastions with small guns. Two mills—a sawmill and a flour mill—stood near the site before construction began, along with a miller's cabin. Next to the principal dwelling, Johnson also erected a storehouse and a workhouse. The property was secured with a heavy iron gate.[17]

Johnson's new home signaled his growing wealth and prominence. Despite the debts he and Clinton complained about, the war years had been very good to him. His "fair dealing with the German Settlers &ca up the Mohawks River, who are grown Considerable, & will in a time possibly be ye majority in the County of Albany," was one source of influence. At the same time, he wrote that "my Scituation among the Indians, & integrity to them, made those poor Savages Seek to me, so that I have a Superior Interest with them." His growing wealth allowed Johnson to consider importing lead or slate roofing from England. In May 1749, he asked a New York correspondent to acquire one or two "likely" slaves fourteen to sixteen years of age on his behalf, in addition to a "good Cliver lad of a white man." He also asked for a "good Matross, to lye upon." Even as he planned his new Mohawk Valley estate, Johnson bought a house in Albany—"one of the best" in town—and another in Schenectady. The latter was a two-story structure, forty feet long, with three fireplaces, two cellars, a garret, and a loft. It sat on a large lot on State Street with an adjacent stable. Its owner, Peter Felinck, reported to Johnson that his brother-in-law had offered him £200 for the property, but he was willing to sell it to Johnson for "a little more."[18]

Yet Johnson was hardly alone on the Mohawk frontier. By 1750, European settlements pressed far past his new home. It was about twenty-five miles from Johnson's estate to Canajoharie, and the route took a traveler past more than a dozen farmsteads, two mills, the old German settlement of Stone Arabia (first settled by Palatine families in the 1730s), and the home of George Klock, a second-generation Palatine, among other notable landmarks. Beyond Canajoharie, European farmsteads stretched for another twenty-five or thirty miles, nearly halfway to Oneida country. The largest concentration of farms lay at German Flats, which was settled in the 1720s. In 1750, the westernmost European farmstead belonged to George Cost, more than fifty miles upriver from Johnson.[19]

It would be a mistake to think of these settlements as a single, westward-pushing thrust of British occupation. Most of the farmsteads beyond Johnson's property were still in the hands of second-generation German farmers. The Mohawks had sponsored the Palatines' settlement and generally regarded them as poor and friendly neighbors, the conflicts of the 1730s notwithstanding. By midcentury, their situation was not unlike that of the Mohawks themselves. Most were without powerful friends in the colony, spoke little or no English, and did not read or write in the language used to record land deeds. Their land claims, as much as those of the Mohawks, were at risk.

As usual in such matters, the Mohawks' closest friends pursued their own interests most assiduously. In 1752, for example, Arent Stevens, who had served as New York's official interpreter to the Iroquois for the past five years (though Peter Wraxall complained that he "understands neither Dutch nor English Well"), petitioned for a license to purchase twenty thousand acres of land north of the Mohawk, near Stone Arabia. Permission granted, he and his companions set out for Canajoharie, where six Mohawks—two from each clan—signed a deed to the land. By February 1753 it had been surveyed. Whatever those six sachems believed that they had signed, the Mohawks were shocked by the size of the purchase and charged that Stevens had pressured the surveyors to extend its boundaries.[20]

The leverage that King George's War brought to the Mohawks was quickly eroding. They were losing influence among their fellow Iroquois and quite literally losing ground to their Anglo-American neighbors. Both trends deeply worried Hendrick.

The chain gathers rust

If the difficulties of reaching a postwar settlement and fear of Mohawk decline were preconditions to the meeting in New York in June 1753, its immediate context was shaped by the contest for political ascendancy in the colony. Throughout King George's War, Clinton and the faction that opposed him rehearsed their grievances. The Assembly—where the opposition was concentrated—claimed that Clinton kept them in the dark about the war effort, harassed them with repeated adjournments, spent the astonishing sum of £70,000 on the colony's defense, and made a series of poor choices in executing the war. One of his most serious errors was the decision to mobilize the Six Nations. The Assembly argued that Iroquois neutrality dampened conflict along the Canadian frontier, and the efforts of Clinton and Johnson had heightened the war's violence and jeopardized the colony's interest. Clinton, for his part, continued to lobby the Lords of Trade with tales of a self-interested cabal that frustrated his efforts to lead the colony and starved the war effort of cash. He claimed to have received a total of only about £18,000 from the Assembly during the war, which defrayed only a fraction of his costs.[21]

Clinton had labored to build a coalition that could act as a counterweight to the opposition group he called "the faction," with limited success. In an effort to move the contest to a new field of battle, in 1751 Clinton proposed to convene a united council of representatives from all of Britain's mainland colonies. He had two related issues in mind. One was the problem of collective defense; the other was the contest between royal prerogative and popular authority. Vexed by the power of the Assembly to thwart his efforts, Clinton believed that an intercolonial conference, and perhaps some kind of permanent union, might strengthen the hand of imperial administrators and give them leverage over local representatives in the colonies. The Lords of Trade called this a "very wise" plan, and with their blessing Clinton extended invitations to every province. The conference was to be held in Albany in June 1751.[22]

The result was a stunning disappointment. Only Massachusetts and South Carolina responded favorably—and South Carolina was principally interested in brokering a peace between the Catawbas and the

Iroquois. Clinton blamed recalcitrant assemblies that refused to pay commissioners' costs, but in reality few colonies felt a pressing need for such a conference.[23]

Though the plan for an Albany conference in the summer of 1751 proceeded, the lack of interest from other colonies and the token level of support from the New York Assembly discouraged Clinton and Johnson. Both men planned dramatic gestures to highlight their unhappiness. Clinton had begun to beg for a leave of absence from his post—the New York winters, he said, were ruining his health—and in early June he reported that he would depart for England as soon as the conference ended.[24]

Johnson, meanwhile, sent a belt through Iroquoia to announce that he would no longer act with them in public affairs. Though he had no formal title other than his wartime post of commander of the Six Nations, he had continued to act in the place of the Albany commissioners, who had resigned in 1746. Johnson's departure came as a shock to the Iroquois, and particularly to the Mohawks. As Hendrick said to Clinton when they met in Albany, Johnson had been

> Like a Tree, that grew for our use, which now seems to be falling down, tho it has many roots; his knowledge of our affairs made us think him one of us (an Indian) and we are greatly afraid, as he has declined, your Excellency will appoint some person, a stranger both to us and our Affairs; and we give your Excellency this Belt of Wampum in order to raise up the falling Tree.[25]

Johnson's abrupt withdrawal was one reason the Albany conference in the summer of 1751 was a disappointment, but it was not the only one. Attending along with Clinton were four members of the New York council, three commissioners from Massachusetts, two from Connecticut, and one from South Carolina. Yet despite the high hopes Clinton originally had for the conference, there was little business to transact and, in the end, little to say. Clinton declared his intention "to renew the Covenant Chain, to cleanse away all rust, to Brighten it, and Strengthen it; so that it may forever Indure." He stressed the value of a trading alliance linking the western Indians to Albany through Iroquoia, and asked that the Six Nations prevent the French from building a fort at Niagara. He also asked that the Iroquois maintain peace with all British-allied Indians, particularly the Catawbas, whose representatives were present. And he concluded by reporting his plan "to pass over the Great Water" as soon as the conference ended. With Johnson having already cast off his public role, news of Clinton's imminent departure must have left the assembled delegation, and particularly the strongest Anglophiles among them, feeling abandoned and uncertain.[26]

The Iroquois speaker began by noting pointedly, "It is a Long time Since we have had the pleasure of seeing Your Excellency at this place of Consultation." He affirmed each element of Clinton's speech but had little to add. He asked Clinton to "recommend us to our father the King," to let him know that the French were taking away Iroquois lands, and to ask him to "reinstate Collo. Johnson among us." The perfunctory exchange concluded with gifts. But although Clinton gave Nickus and another former prisoner laced coats, hats, and ruffled shirts, the paucity of the larger present was unmistakable. Twelve shirts, twelve guns, fifty flints, a dozen knives—as Clinton would have complained (and probably did in private), the Iroquois had the miserly Assembly to thank for this poor showing. Even the attempt to broker a peace with the Catawbas ended uncertainly. The Iroquois speaker handed them a white belt of peace, gave them "Short horns" to keep them from fighting, and reported that they must return with all their Iroquois prisoners in a year's time or the tentative agreement they now made would be void. The Catawbas asked in response that the Iroquois send a party with them when they returned home; that group could then bring the prisoners back to Iroquoia. The Six Nations considered that proposal to be un-

precedented and unacceptable. The conference ended with the Catawbas promising to return in a year's time, but doubt hung in the air.[27]

Perhaps Clinton was too exhausted by his frustrations and failures to
care about the unsatisfactory outcome of the conference. He raced
home to board the H. M. S. *Greyhound*, a twenty-gun frigate that was
about to sail. I had "all my baggage and necessaries for my voyage on
board the Ship," he later wrote; "I had sold my household furniture, and
was ready to go on Board." Then word arrived that the Duke of Bedford
had denied his request for a leave. Clinton's misery was not over yet.[28]

Stockbridge

Nor was the misery of Hendrick, Abraham, and Nickus, whose disillu-
sionment with the colony had never run deeper. The failure of the Albany conference in the summer of 1751 prompted them to consider
abandoning the colony altogether. The opportunity to do so was close
at hand. Two summers earlier, the missionary John Sergeant had written
to William Johnson to report that he had opened a new school in the
mission town of Stockbridge, Massachusetts, some forty miles southeast of Albany, and to propose that Johnson help him recruit Mohawk
children to attend. Nothing came immediately of that invitation, but by
1751 the Mohawks had begun to show some interest. At the Albany conference, the Massachusetts commissioners talked privately with Hendrick and Nickus. They asked them to bring "as many of their chiefs as
they could" to Stockbridge, where the commissioners, the minister, and
the schoolmaster would outline the opportunity more fully.[29]

John Sergeant founded the Stockbridge mission among the Mahican
Indians on the Hoosic River in 1734. Sergeant's first converts included
the daughter and grandson of Etowacaum, who had traveled to London
with Hendrick Tejonihokarawa in 1710. Timothy Woodbridge joined
Sergeant as the mission's schoolmaster, and the colony of Massachusetts
soon established a township to support their efforts. The missionaries

oversaw the construction of a meetinghouse and school, and by 1740 120 Indians lived there. Sergeant's next project was a boarding school, which prompted his letter to Johnson in 1749. He did not live to see its fruition; he was already ill when he wrote the letter, and he died less than a month later, at the age of thirty-nine. Jonathan Edwards was called to succeed Sergeant in 1751. Edwards was a controversial choice. The grandson of Solomon Stoddard, Edwards had gained notoriety in the 1730s through the religious revivals he oversaw in Northampton. By the 1740s he had fallen out of favor with his congregation. He was dismissed from his pulpit, and only the Stockbridge call forestalled exile from the colony.[30]

As this transition took place, if not earlier, Hendrick began to visit Stockbridge periodically. The tie between Mohawks and Mahicans was an old one. Hendrick's own father had been a Mahican, and he may have had relatives on the Hoosic. In December 1750 his younger daughter, Margaret, married a Mahican man there. After Margaret's wedding, Hendrick seems to have visited Stockbridge regularly. As the Massachusetts commissioners traveled to Albany in the summer of 1751, they stopped at Stockbridge expecting that they would find Hendrick there.[31]

In response to the invitation extended in Albany, Hendrick, Abraham, and Nickus arrived in Stockbridge on August 13. Their party included seven sachems from Canajoharie, six from Tiononderoge, and a "great train" of followers. In all, ninety-two Mohawks made the trip. They stayed for nine days, during which they had "many friendly meetings." According to Edwards, "good humour, and well pleasedness appeared on all sides." He was especially impressed with Abraham, whom he called "a man of great solidity, prudence, devotion, and strict conversation" who "acts very much as a person endowed with the simplicity, humanity, self-denial and zeal of a true christian." At the end of their meetings, about fifty Mohawks, "old and young," stayed in Stockbridge. Those who returned to their home villages promised to send more children at summer's end. By the end of the year, ninety-five boys from Mohawk, Oneida, and Tuscarora villages were enrolled in the boarding school.[32]

Why did the Stockbridge mission appeal to Hendrick, his family, and the other Iroquois? For one thing, conditions close to home were worrisome. Exposed to enemy raiders during times of war and land-hungry colonists in times of peace, they felt abandoned by the governor and neglected by the colony. Massachusetts, by contrast, appeared to be solicitous and supportive. Hendrick had looked favorably on a connection with the Bay Colony since his trip to Boston in 1744, and the invitation to Stockbridge, which was extended by leading men of the colony as well as the town's grandees, must have been gratifying. Hendrick, his brothers, and many other Iroquois also took the prospect of regular instruction and Christian worship seriously. The Tiononderoge and Canajoharie missions and schools had languished since Barclay's departure in 1745. Though both communities had lay schoolmasters and readers (Abraham had himself been named a reader), their residents wanted deeper and more sustained engagement, especially for their children. The Stockbridge experiment promised edification for a large number of Mohawk children; it also beckoned as a potential escape valve, should conditions in New York grow worse.

The stakes are raised

A month after the Albany conference in 1751, Cadwallader Colden submitted a document to the governor summarizing the current state of Indian affairs. His recommendations accorded well with those Clinton and Johnson had been advocating. Like them, Colden feared the rise of French power. He compared French and British influence among the Indians in terms that reflected unfavorably on British interests. In Canada, he noted, Indian affairs were under the direct control of a single council. Moreover, the Crown spared no expense to support its efforts. In New York, by contrast, the Albany commissioners—a body dominated by Dutchmen—acted in their own interest, in cooperation with the antigovernment faction in the Assembly, rather than in concert with Clinton and the Crown. They were as likely to cheat the Indians, in Colden's estimation, as they were to strengthen the alliance with them. Johnson's appointment had temporarily eased this difficulty, but since the Crown refused to pay for Indian affairs in peacetime, he could not afford to continue in his public role. Colden argued that this structural difficulty could be overcome if the Crown would appoint a single superintendent for Indian affairs, responsible to the Board of Trade and in correspondence with the governors throughout British North America, to coordinate and implement imperial policy.[33]

Beyond that crucial administrative reform, Colden suggested a variety of measures to curb abuses in the Indian trade and secure the loyalty of the Crown's Indian allies. He suggested that a new legal mechanism should be created to grant summary justice to Indians; it should accept evidence given by Indians and strive to redress grievances that derived from the sharp dealing of unscrupulous traders. He also recommended the creation of a "sloop force" that would patrol the waters of Lake Ontario. It could simultaneously police the Indian trade in western Iroquoia and supply goods directly to the western Indians. Finally, Colden suggested that the Crown fortify the water route between Montreal and Albany before the next imperial war again highlighted its vulnerability.

All of this was calculated to persuade the Board of Trade, which was already worried about the eroding alliance with the Six Nations. Now reports of a major French initiative began to multiply. Yet another new governor-general, Ange Duquesne de Menneville, the Marquis Duquesne, arrived in Canada in the summer of 1752 with unequivocal instructions to drive the British traders out of the Ohio Valley and win back New France's western allies. In April 1753, Johnson heard a panicked report of twelve hundred French soldiers gathering near Lake Ontario. A month later, he learned that a force of six thousand regulars and five hundred Indians under the command of Paul Marin de La Malgue had passed by

Oswego on their way to the Ohio country. Marin had orders to drive off any British traders they encountered, "build Forts in such places he shall think most convenient to secure their right," and "if he met with any opposition . . . to make good his claim by force of Arms." That summer, Marin's force built Fort Presque Isle on a bay on the south shore of Lake Erie, near modern-day Erie, Pennsylvania, and, fifteen miles farther south, Fort Le Boeuf on a branch of French Creek. Before winter set in, they had begun work on a third fort, Fort Machault, where French Creek met the Allegheny.[34]

The contest for the Ohio, and with it the heart of North America, had begun.

℞

Duquesne's Ohio initiative could not have been better calculated to confirm the fears that Johnson, Clinton, and Colden had been at pains to dramatize since the end of King George's War. Yet the political winds in New York continued to blow against the unpopular governor and his supporters. If Johnson hoped that his resignation from public affairs would prompt the colony or the Crown to grant him an office and salary, he misread the signs. Instead, the New York Assembly took the opportunity to reinstate the Albany commissioners for Indian affairs in their old public role. The new commission could not have represented a more thorough repudiation of Johnson's leadership. The commissioners were drawn entirely from the ranks of the old Albany trading families—those Dutchmen whom Colden so mistrusted. They included three members of the Schuyler family—Myndert, Philip, and David—along with Jacob Ten Eyck, Johannes Van Rensslaer, Hendrick Bleecker, and six others. Only Myndert Schuyler had served before, but all twelve were drawn from families of old standing and long experience, both in the Indian trade and in the public life of their community.[35]

Johnson learned of the reinstatement from Clinton, who wrote that he opposed the move but could not block it. "I can not help observing," he remarked, "that they are pick'd out of almost all your inveterate Opposers." Clinton thought he might at least insist on the privilege of naming half the members of the new body. In any case, he urgently hoped to confer with Johnson in private. "I shall be at the Fort Tuesday next, where I shall be glad if you would dine with me, and in the interim think what I can do in it."

If the dinner took place, it occurred in early November 1752. Perhaps the groundwork for Hendrick's visit to New York in the following June was laid over that meal. Or perhaps the idea took shape in the following months, as the French threat came into focus. Hendrick and the Canajoharie Mohawks had their own pressing reasons to travel to New York in June 1753, but Johnson traveled with them and had a hand in shaping their concerns and expectations. The imperial crisis gave Clinton and Johnson a golden opportunity in the grinding battle they fought with their opponents in the colony. To take full advantage of it, Hendrick would have an important part to play.

The chain broken

When Hendrick and his entourage arrived at Fort George in June 1753, they set in motion a series of events that was, in all likelihood, partially orchestrated ahead of time. They were met at the fort on the southern tip of Manhattan by Governor Clinton and a small circle of his supporters. From the governor's council, James Alexander, Archibald Kennedy, and Edward Holland were there, but no members of the DeLancey faction. The minutes note that "Several Members of the Assembly & other Gentlemen" were also present. The Assembly was not ordinarily represented in Indian councils, and these men were likely there at the invitation of the governor. These would almost certainly have been friends of Clinton rather than leaders of the opposition.[36]

Hendrick's opening speech expressed so well the concerns and interests of Johnson and Clinton that its content must have been, at least, influenced by conversation with Johnson, if not entirely prearranged. It was here that Hendrick predicted the Covenant Chain was about to be broken, here that he blamed the colony's neglect of the Six Nations on the council and Assembly rather than the governor, and here that he demanded immediate satisfaction for the concerns he expressed. Then the gathering adjourned.

A smaller group met later the same day. Hendrick and three other Mohawk sachems conferred with Clinton, Johnson, and the three members of the council. Hendrick spoke once again, and this time the grievances he aired came straight from Canajoharie. They concerned land. The redress he sought may have been understood by him as a tit for tat: he had helped Clinton, and now he sought the governor's help in shoring up his community's land claims. "When our Brethren the English first came among us we gave and sold them Lands, and have continued to do so ever since," he began, "but it seems now as if we had no Lands left for ourselves."[37]

Hendrick proceeded to offer a detailed complaint against four individuals. He noted, "We have sold several small Parcels of Land to our Brethren and they have taken up a much greater quantity[,] which will appear by the records." Hendrick and the other sachems had not come to renounce any sales—"As to what we have sold we are well satisfied therewith and sensible"—but they named several people who had taken more land than they were due.[38]

The former missionary Henry Barclay had been granted land near Canajoharie during the term of his service but continued to claim it as his own even after leaving the mission. The wife of a man named Pichett had been granted "a little spot of Land and she takes more and more every year"; moreover, she caused trouble among the Mohawks by selling liquor. In her case, they asked for "an order to turn her off the Land." Arent Stevens had made a purchase of Mohawk land, and then, according to Hendrick, pressured the surveyors to expand its boundaries. And a poor man named Conradt Gunterman, to whom the Mohawks gave "a Tract of Land out of Charity," continued to survey and claim additional acreage to which he was not entitled. The Mohawks intended "to take a little Rod and whip him, which may deter others from doing the same," and they sought Clinton's blessing to do so.[39]

Hendrick concluded his speech with a "piece of News" that may have represented a gambit of his own, an effort to ensure that the governor and his councilors took the danger of a broken alliance seriously. Just before they departed for New York, he and Abraham had received a string of wampum from Canada inviting them to a conference at Cataraqui, on the north shore of Lake Ontario. The Mohawks had been absent from such councils since the previous war—"for some time past they had not gone the Road to the French"—but that could always change. Hendrick reassured his audience that they did not intend to accept: the Mohawks "imagined," he joked, that the French "intended to do as they had done formerly, invite them to a Feast and then destroy them." Yet the possibility hung in the air as the council adjourned for the day.[40]

For three days, the Mohawk delegation lodged in the city while they awaited a response. Finally, on the afternoon of June 15, the smaller group reassembled. Clinton had referred the land complaints to his friend and councilor Edward Holland, who was also mayor of New York. Holland had assembled a committee to examine Hendrick's complaints. The committee found that, in the first three cases raised by Hendrick, the grants predated Clinton's administration and were therefore beyond redress. In Gunterman's case, the group concluded that the Mohawk grant entitled him to all the land named in his deed. Hendrick backpedaled. These four cases were only the beginning; there were more instances in which "they have been considerably cheated which were of too great importance to be neglected." Hendrick and another sachem sat down with an interpreter and enumerated the most egregious frauds: Livingston's patent at Canajoharie Flats; the claims of Captain Collins and Cornelius Cuyler; Peter Wagener's land "over against Canajohary Castle"; Johannis Lawyer's patent at Stone Arabia; and an island claimed by Honnes Clock. This was not an exhaustive list, but it comprised the worst instances in which the Mohawks had been defrauded of their lands.[41]

On the following day, the larger group met again: seventeen Mohawks, Clinton and his councilors, and some unidentified gentlemen from the city. This time, a lawyer representing the city also attended. The governor began by offering a string of wampum to renew the Covenant Chain. He noted that the management of Indian affairs would now be once again in the hands of the Albany commissioners. He promised to meet with the Six Nations later in the summer in Albany to take the hatchet out of their hands and brighten the Covenant Chain. He stressed his desire to keep "the Roads between the Nations open and clear" and lamented the "Loss of our Brethren at Ohio." He promised to do what he could to curb French power and protect the Six Nations from attack. All of this followed a familiar formula; like Hendrick's opening speech, it appears in the surviving record to be almost perfunctory. If Hendrick and the Mohawks arrived at the fort thinking that the Covenant Chain was about to be broken, there was nothing here to change their minds.[42]

Then Clinton turned to the issue of land. Again, he could offer no satisfaction. "It would be impossible by examining the Grants of Land registered here," he told the assembled Mohawks, "to find out whether the persons who have purchased them have imposed on you." Their only recourse was to consult with the commissioners of Indian affairs in Albany. "I shall direct to send for the persons interested to appear before them and to examine the matter thoroughly as possible and to make a Report thereupon to me, in order that strict justice may be done you." By passing the buck to the commissioners, Clinton put them in something of a bind. Most of the offenders were prominent Albany citizens, often members of the same circle of families that dominated the commission. Now they would have to adjudicate the land disputes and, if they failed to satisfy the Mohawks' concerns, shoulder the blame for their unhappiness.[43]

Clinton's response may have given him some personal satisfaction, but it did nothing to address the concerns Hendrick had voiced. Hendrick replied by asking that, for the future, the colony never again grant licenses to purchase Indian lands unless the Mohawks had a representative present, and he threatened that if anyone appeared on their land to conduct a survey without their permission, "should any accident happen we hope you Brother will not expect any satisfaction from us." At the same time, though, Hendrick asked that Peter Schuyler and Jerry (or George) Klock be granted licenses to purchase Mohawk land. The governor and his advisors briefly withdrew to consider this last request. Upon their return, Clinton informed Hendrick that he could grant a license to Schuyler, who was one of Albany's most respected residents. Klock was another matter. A Palatine without influence in Albany who was also regarded as an interloper by Johnson, Klock was a controversial figure. Though the Canajoharie Mohawks considered him to be a friend, they were the only friends he had. Clinton announced that Klock's license would have to await approval of the whole council.[44]

Hendrick rose to make his final response. It was not long, but it carried ominous implications. He may have been in a terrible passion as he spoke, or his tone may have been quiet and regretful. "Brother," he began, "All what we have desired to be done for our Good is not granted which makes our hearts ache very much." Though they had come to the city expecting their grievances to be redressed, Clinton had sent them instead to confer with the Albany commissioners. "[B]ut we know them so well, we will not trust to them, for they are no people but Devils, so we rather desire that you'l say, Nothing shall be done for us."[45] For all the similarities between Hendrick Tejonihokarawa and Hendrick Peters Theyanoguin, their views of the Albany circle could not have been farther apart. Hendrick's fortune was intertwined with Johnson's, and the Albany traders had always bedeviled their efforts.

Hendrick concluded with a flourish:

> Brother, By & By you'l expect to see the Nations down which you shall not see, for as soon as we come home we will send up a Belt of Wampum to our Brothers the 5 Nations to acquaint them the Covenant Chain is broken between you and us. So brother you are not to expect to hear of me any more, and Brother we desire to hear no more of you. And we shall no longer acquaint you with any News or affairs as we used to do; and as to Jerry Klock there are people who want to do him some harm but we will not agree to it.[46]

"The Covenant Chain is broken." Was this part of a plan hatched by Johnson and Clinton, or had events gotten away from them? It is impossible to know. Certainly Hendrick's defense of Jerry Klock had not gone according to any script provided by Clinton or Johnson; that issue was pressed on Hendrick's own initiative, and it would plague Johnson for many years to come.[47] But the broken chain may have been prearranged to pressure the Albany commissioners and call down the wrath of empire. Though it entailed a considerable political risk, Clinton and Johnson may have calculated that it would aid their cause in the end. For both men knew that however rusted or strained the links of the chain had grown over the past several years, from the vantage point of London it had never been more important for the chain to shine brightly. In the years since King George's War, it had come to be seen as an indispensable bond of empire.

Covenant Chain and empire

Word of Hendrick's dramatic declaration reached Britain at a time when the Covenant Chain was taking on a new depth of meaning there.

In the 1720s, several colonial governors had placed new pressures on the Iroquois alliance, while Colden's *History of the Five Indian Nations* offered a sympathetic account of the Iroquois to English-speaking readers for the first time. A decade later, the Board of Trade explicitly invoked the Covenant Chain analogy in shaping the Crown's relations with the Cherokees and the Creeks. In the wake of King George's War, a growing circle of officeholders and writers sought to reconceive the constitutional and administrative underpinnings of the empire, and in so doing turned to Indian relations as one critical component of imperial authority. Then, as conflict with France heated up again, a host of pamphleteers turned to a consideration of British rights and power vis-à-vis the French in North America. Many of these writers combined a generous account the Iroquois' capacity to act as partners in empire with an expansive reading of Iroquois territorial claims, and on that basis argued for a vigorous defense against French encroachments in the Ohio Valley and elsewhere.

In this rapidly evolving imperial discourse, the always fraught and imperfect connection between Albany and Iroquoia was extracted from its original context and reified into something transcendent. It became both symbol and substance of the possibilities of empire in British North America. That fact helped to vault Hendrick Peters Theyanoguin to international fame in the last two years of his life.

ᚼᛈ

King George's War educated a generation of administrators in the shortcomings of Britain's imperial constitution. Clinton, Colden, William Shirley, James Abercromby, Henry McCulloh, and Archibald Kennedy, all officeholders in North America who served during the war, worried about what they saw, and wrestled with the problem of imperial reform in the late 1740s and early 1750s. They addressed a wide range of issues affecting the relationship between Britain and its colonies.

Colden was the progenitor of the group. When his *History of the Five Indian Nations* was published in New York in 1727, it exerted a deep influence on the thinking of writers and administrators with long-standing ties to New York and the Iroquois. A second edition appeared in London in 1747, just as a host of administrators and pamphleteers were giving sustained attention to the problems of empire. Colden's central themes—the analogy between the Iroquois Confederacy and ancient republics, the threat posed by New France's superior methods in Indian relations, and the importance of coordinated frontier defenses to British interests—threaded through many of the manuscripts and pamphlets that surfaced in these years. Those with access to Colden's "Present State of Indian Affairs," which he submitted in 1751, were deeply influenced by its recommendations as well. Though Colden was an unpopular figure in New York politics, he was profoundly influential in imperial circles.[48]

All the colonial officeholders who argued for reform in the late 1740s and early 1750s began with the problem that Britain lacked a clearly defined imperial constitution. Some colonies originated as chartered corporations, some as royal colonies, some as proprietary grants, and efforts to centralize and standardize their administration had been halting and incomplete. Though Parliament had focused considerable attention on maritime regulation, the colonies managed internal affairs largely on their own. King George's War highlighted, for the first time in two generations, the problem of directing a military effort among semiautonomous colonies. One element of that problem related to Indian alliances. Each colony maintained its own relations with Indians, yet imperial warfare required coordinated action. The emerging contest over the Ohio country illuminated a related difficulty: since the Treaty of Utrecht in 1713, Britain had neglected its territorial claims and interests in North America. These four issues—the imperial constitution, defense, Indian relations, and territorial claims—cropped up again and again.[49]

One participant in these discussions was Archibald Kennedy, a Scot who came to New York under the patronage of Robert Hunter and served as receiver general and customs collector for the colony. In 726 he was appointed to the governor's council. A longtime observer and participant in the colony's affairs, Kennedy published a series of pamphlets beginning in 1750 that spelled out a coherent plan for more centralized and rationalized colonial governance. His writings encapsulated the views of would-be imperial reformers. The first of his pamphlets held that Parliament should encourage all forms of economic activity in the northern colonies. The second emphasized the importance of "gaining and preserving the Friendship of the Indians to the British Interest," which, Kennedy contended, was "of no small Importance to the Trade of Great-Britain, as well as to the Peace and Prosperity of these Colonies." Like Colden, Kennedy argued that although France's American colonies were inherently weaker than Britain's, "yet, by a proper Management of their Indians, they keep us all, both in Time of Peace and War, in a constant Dread and Terror." He argued for stronger fortifications along the northern frontiers, careful regulation of the Indian trade, and more attention to the costs of effective Indian alliances. To this end, he proposed—again, following Colden—a general council for Indian affairs and an intercolonial union for defense, to be supported by a common fund. In his third pamphlet, Kennedy argued that the principal barrier to such rational planning and governance was the power of the colonial assemblies, in which, Kennedy believed, lay the seeds of tyranny. To offset their power, he promoted a uniform land tax throughout the colonies, the proceeds of which would go to support royal officers in the Americas.[50]

Kennedy's series culminated in a meditation on the emerging conflict with France on the eve of the Seven Years' War. Here, the administrator's concern with a rationalized imperial constitution intersected with the growing fear, common by the early 1750s, that France had implemented a grand design to seize control of North America. The initiative in the Ohio country gave proof to the scope of French ambition. Like Britons everywhere in the mid–eighteenth century, Kennedy took it as an article of faith that French law and the French monarchy were incompatible with liberty. Louis XV he characterized as "an ambitious, all-grasping Monarch, whose Will, often the Caprice of a Miss, or a Favourite, is the Law; For such is our Pleasure, is their whole Corpus Juris." Nothing in French law stood to protect subjects of the Crown from the ambitions of their all-powerful monarch. And his ambitions, in the view of many Britons, were as expansive as his power. He wanted nothing less than universal monarchy. "One great step," Kennedy concluded, "if not the greatest, to this grand Monarch's universal system, is that of being possess'd of this Northern Continent of America, a Territory boundless as is his Ambition, in which he has made not a little Progress." The key to frustrating Louis's aspirations, Kennedy argued, lay in the proper management of Indian alliances. Only the careful supervision of Indian affairs could assure Britain's control of the Ohio country, and with it the heart of the continent. In making this case, Kennedy reiterated his view that the colonists' liberties could only be preserved in the impending war if the individual colonies sacrificed a measure of their autonomy in support of a common defense.[51]

Imperial reformers often repeated this claim that colonists could only preserve their liberties by surrendering some of their autonomy. Its logic depended on the specter of French absolutism, which, according to these commentators, posed a much greater danger to colonial liberties than the authority of Crown and Parliament ever could. As Britain veered toward another war with France, other writers picked up on themes developed by Colden and Kennedy to make the case for a vigorous defense of British claims in North America. An increasingly mythologized view of the Iroquois was central to their arguments.

John Huske, the son of a New Hampshire judge who had moved to London and eventually became a member of Parliament, carefully rehearsed the basis for Britain's claims in North America and, in doing so, offered an extended account of the Iroquois Confederacy. He leaned heavily on Colden. "[A]s to Histories of *Indians*," he noted, "there is not one published in our Language that deserves the Title . . . but that of *Colden*, which is justly called a History of the *Five Nations*, and is a masterly Performance." Huske recounted the Iroquois' "just and necessary War" with the Algonquins, and noted that they "so far recovered their spirits" as a result of their victory that they carried their aggression to other enemies. Their success in a series of wars with the Hurons, the Ottawas, and other nations would not have been possible "had they not strictly followed one Maxim formerly in use among the *Romans, viz.* the encouraging the people of other Nations to incorporate with them." Huske assured his audience that the Iroquois' conquests were not "temporary, or merely nominal, for all the Nations round them have for many Years entirely submitted to them, and pay a yearly Tribute to them in *Wampum,* or *Indian* Money." Huske reasoned from this history of conquest that the Iroquois had a "fair and indubitable Title" to a vast territory—by his own calculation nearly a million square miles, ranging from New England to Lake Michigan and down the Mississippi as far as Georgia. Wherever the Iroquois could claim land by conquest, French territorial claims were illegitimate. "The Five Nations never alienated any Part of their hereditary or conquered Country," according to Huske, "to any but his Majesty and his Subjects." Iroquois land was British land.[52]

Huske was not alone in his assessment. In 1755, an anonymous author penned an extended analysis of the situation in North America. Like Colden and Kennedy before him, he emphasized that though France's colonies had many fewer people than Britain's, their careful attention to Indian alliances and military preparedness made them more formidable. "If we consider the strength of the [British] colonies, in respect to military forces, altho' so full of people, we shall find them almost destitute of fighting men." The problem was heightened by the fact that Britain's colonies had, almost without exception, alienated their potential allies among the Indians. Why? "[A]ll the considerable wars or slaughters made by the *Indians* in the Colonies have been owing to the provocations given them, either by seizing their lands, or maltreating them in trade or otherwise." "'Tis true," the author notes, "The Indians never forgive very grievous injuries till satisfaction be made them. The same principles influenced the ancient Greeks and Romans. It is, indeed, the necessary result of liberty, and so inseparable from it, that wherever it is wanting in any nation, once possessed of it, it is a sure sign that they have degenerated, and are hastening to their downfall."[53]

In short, "every thing which tends" to the security of the British colonies "has been neglected, and every thing which tends to their ruin, or to give the French advantage over them, pursued." The author's solution echoes Colden, Kennedy, and other advocates of a rationalized imperial administration. First, the colonies must join in a "general union" for the purposes of defense and Indian alliances. Second, the Indians must be cultivated as allies. On this point, the writer deferred to Colden's account of the Iroquois. "The six nations," he concludes,

> from a small beginning, have made themselves formidable likewise throughout the *Indians* of all north *America.* . . . In short, these people are considered by judicious *Americans,* both *English* and *French,* as equal, if not superior to either the antient *Greeks* or *Romans.* . . . However, the generality of our vain unthinking countrymen, for want of the *Indian* understanding, look on them as a despicable people, because they are content with poverty, and do not make a figure like other nations, things for which they more justly hold the Europeans in contempt: for they rightly place the happiness and dignity of man, in living according to the simplicity of nature, and cultivating political and social virtues.[54]

This anonymous pamphleteer took his characterization of the Six Nations farther than most. But he illustrates the way that a growing circle of writers and administrators emphasized the significance of Indian relations and inflated, as far as possible, the reputation of the Iroquois Confederacy as they argued for an expansive sphere of imperial dominion.[55] By the mid-1750s, the fortunes of the British Empire in North America appeared to be linked inextricably with those of the Iroquois. And the Covenant Chain was the tie that united them.

The road to the Albany Congress

The Lords of Trade, having been bombarded with arguments about the importance of Indian alliances and the French threat to British interests, received word of Hendrick's speech with deep consternation. It coincided with an imminent change in leadership in New York: Clinton's plea to be relieved of his post had finally borne fruit. In May 1753 the board recommended Sir Danvers Osborne for the post, and in August it drafted his instructions. Osborne was a promising choice. The brother-in-law of the energetic new president of the Board of Trade, George Montagu Dunk, the second Earl of Halifax, Osborne had distinguished himself in service under the Earl of Cumberland during the Jacobite Rebellion of 1745. He entered Parliament as a member from Bedfordshire, and in 1750 he traveled with Halifax to Nova Scotia, where he served on the governor's council. At the time of his appointment to the governorship of New York, Osborne was thirty-eight years old and regarded as a man of ability and consequence. Supported by Halifax's patronage, his future looked bright.[56]

A few days after Osborne sailed to take up his post, the board received word of Hendrick's declaration. It quickly dispatched additional instructions. Given the "great consequence the friendship and alliance of the Six Nations is to all His Majesty's Colonies and Plantations in America," its members wrote, they were "greatly concern'd and surprized" at the colony's inattention to the alliance. Even more surprising was "the dissatisfactory answers given to the Indians and . . . their being suffered to depart . . . without any measures taken to bring them to temper, or to redress their Complaints." The board recommended that Osborne immediately send "some person of character and discretion" among the Indians to announce an imminent meeting. Osborne should arrange a conference as soon as possible—perhaps at Onondaga rather than Albany, given the Mohawks' antipathy to the place—where he would take the hatchet from the Six Nations' hands and renew the Covenant Chain with presents from the Crown. At the same time, the board wrote to the governors of six other colonies, recommending that they attend the meeting, join in the treaty of friendship, and add presents of their own to those offered by the Crown.[57]

Osborne received an ecstatic reception in New York. Local residents, weary of Clinton's aggrieved petulance, met his arrival with the "greatest acclamations of the People and the sincerest demonstrations of Joy that were ever known on any occasion here." Two days later, the joy turned to shock. Early in the morning of October 12, Osborne was discovered in his garden, "strangled in his Handkerchief." James DeLancey attributed the death to suicide. He noted that Osborne had appeared cheerless and melancholy, with "a great indisposition of body & disturbance of mind" in the short time since his arrival. DeLancey himself was the chief beneficiary of Osborne's mysterious and untimely death. Thomas Pownall, Osborne's secretary, described the scene that followed: "As soon as His Excellencys death was known the Council of this Province was convened and I sent for to produce the Commission which I carryed and delivered to the Council in the Council Room. Mr. Chief Justice Delancey produced in Council a Commission appointing him Lieutenant Governor and he qualifying took upon him the administration accordingly." Suddenly elevated to the role of acting governor, DeLancey held the position for two eventful years.[58]

DeLancey's rise, though it did not cancel the legacy of infighting and disagreement over the direction of Indian policy in New York, did place the principal leader of the opposition in a new position of responsibility. The ill will generated during Clinton's term in office between the governor and the Assembly was immediately dissipated. Underlying sources of tension remained, especially the bitterness between Johnson and the Albany commissioners, but the petulance and acrimony of the Clinton years fell by the wayside, replaced by an era of relative harmony in New York politics.[59]

ℍℙ

In Iroquoia, Hendrick's angry speech began to produce results in the summer of 1753. Johnson called together the sachems of the two Mohawk towns in July to report that he had been "raised up" by the colony to act in Indian affairs once again. Speaking for the assembled Mohawks, Hendrick said they were "highly rejoyced" at the news and noted that "had the Governor sent for us by the [Albany] commiss[ione]rs whom we hear are appointed, we would not at this time harken or move a foot." Though the tenor of the meeting was upbeat, Johnson began the proceedings with a stern message. The governor instructed Johnson to upbraid the Mohawks for their "unfriendly and rash behavior"; Hendrick's "loud and foul words" at Fort George "almost shook and Soyled that firm and bright Chain made by our wise forefathers." Now, he reported that a new governor was on his way and asked them to be patient until Clinton's replacement could address their grievances. In the meantime, Johnson had been instructed to travel to Onondaga to convene the Iroquois council in the governor's name. He asked the Mohawks to help him decide what to say.[60]

Hendrick was willing to swallow his pride and accept Johnson's reproof. He promised that the Mohawks would "bury all animosity and dispute in a deep pool . . . and hope there may never be reason for the like again." As if he had never declared the Covenant Chain broken, Hendrick concluded, "small provocations shall never weaken the Chain of friendship so long subsisting between us and our Bretheren." Then Johnson sat down with the Mohawk sachems to plan the visit to Onondaga.[61]

Two weeks later, Hendrick was in Albany on his way to Stockbridge. Reports from the Massachusetts mission had been bad and were getting worse. However pressed the Mohawks may have felt at home, the factionalism, infighting, and greed that divided Stockbridge were every bit as troublesome. Edwards was at odds with powerful members of the community, and the Indians had become pawns in a contest for land claims and local ascendancy. The Stockbridge Mohawks began to leave in 1753, and Hendrick instructed those who remained to return by spring. With Johnson's reinstatement, the Mohawks' prospects in New York were looking up. Hendrick and the other sachems concluded that it was time for the Mohawks to return to their homes.[62]

ᕼᕈ

In September, Johnson and a party of Mohawk sachems traveled to Onondaga. Conrad Weiser had visited Johnson in August, intending to go to Onondaga himself with a message from Pennsylvania. He thought they might make the trip together, but Johnson preferred to be on his own. "He said he left it to me" whether to accompany him, Weiser reported, "but I perceived some Coolness in him as to my going; I thought it was best not to proceed any further at this time, but to return." Though he bore no ill will toward Weiser, Johnson wanted free rein to deliver an unequivocal message.[63]

A mile from town, a group of Onondaga sachems met Johnson and his delegation and guided them to the council house. Ordinarily, Johnson would have relied on a translator to deliver his message. In an unprecedented move, Johnson instead made Hendrick his spokesman throughout the proceedings. He began by offering condolence for the loss of three sachems who had died since Johnson's last visit. Then he delivered a series of messages intended to shore up the Covenant Chain. On Johnson's behalf, Hendrick noted that the road to Onondaga had become choked with weeds and the council fire had nearly gone out. "You know it was a saying among us that when the Fire was out here, you would be no longer a people." He offered a belt to clear the road and renew the fire, and a string to sweep their rooms clean with a "new White Wing." Then he lamented, "the fine shady Tree which was planted by your forefathers for your ease and shelter" was "now leaning, being almost blown down by Northerly winds." He gave another belt to set the tree upright so its roots could spread and it could offer protection from any future storms coming out of Canada. He insisted that the Onondagas quench the council fire at Oswegatchie, the new settlement associated with the La Présentation mission on the St. Lawrence.[64]

Next, Hendrick delivered a series of messages aimed at the constituent nations of the Iroquois. The Onondagas, he said, needed to resume their role as messengers to all the Six Nations. The Senecas had begun to fail in their responsibility as keepers of the western door of the Iroquois longhouse, and he gave them a new door that would never decay. The Oneidas, Tuscaroras, and Cayugas were too scattered and needed to move closer together in order to act more effectively in concert with one another.

In short, Johnson hoped that his trip to Onondaga might not simply renew the Covenant Chain, but begin to remake it. In this effort, Johnson and Hendrick stood shoulder to shoulder. By committing to Johnson as fully as he had, Hendrick had invested his political fortunes entirely in the Anglo-Iroquois alliance. Now, the question was whether the alliance could be saved. Johnson, Hendrick, and the Anglophile Mohawks understood that the Covenant Chain was badly decayed, and the rot was worst at its center, in Onondaga. The messages and exhortations delivered by Hendrick had no precedent in earlier meetings; never before had a colonial representative presumed to reorder relations among the Six Nations in the way Johnson was attempting. "As I proceed to reform every thing relative to the Old Covenant between you and us," he concluded, "I must remind you on your part to hold fast by that strong Chain of friendship made by your forefathers, the memory of whose actions you have always regarded."[65]

The Onondaga sachem Red Head responded on behalf of the confederacy. He expressed gratitude for all of Johnson's efforts, but he remained ambivalent about the alliance. "[W]e dont know what you Christians, English and French together, intend; we are so hemm'd in by both, that we have hardly a hunting place left. In a little while if we find a bear in a tree there will immediately appear an owner of the land to challenge the property, and hinder us from killing it, which is our livelyhood. We are so perplexed between both that we hardly know what to say or think." Yet he accepted the renewal of the Covenant Chain on behalf of the Six Nations. "It was high time, being almost eat thorough with rust for want of proper care and inspection." For all the pressures felt by the Iroquois, the Covenant Chain was their only hope in relations with the British colonies. It continued to promise a means to air grievances and pursue justice. It was left to Johnson—and to Hendrick and his fellow Anglophiles—to ensure that it fulfilled that promise.[66]

Ꚑ

The spring of 1754 brought additional, worrisome news from the Ohio country. The string of forts that rose in the previous summer to secure France's claim to the Ohio Valley had roused Virginia's Governor Robert Dinwiddie to action. A partner in the Ohio Company, Dinwiddie worried that the French initiative jeopardized the company's plans to develop lands near the forks of the Ohio. As winter was setting in, Dinwiddie dispatched a militia unit, commanded by the twenty-one-year-old major George Washington, to reconnoiter and to warn the commanding officer at Fort Le Boeuf that he was trespassing on the property of the king of Great Britain. Washington arrived at the fort in mid-December. He delivered his message; Captain Jacques Legardeur de

Saint-Pierre countered by asserting France's right to the Ohio country. Washington took note of the building supplies and the fleet of canoes at the fort, signs that work would begin on a fourth fort as soon as the season allowed it. He also learned along the way that the Ohio Indians wanted little to do with their ostensible British allies. Washington returned to Williamsburg with nothing good to report.[67]

Alarmed accounts of the French initiative soon circulated through the colonies and across the Atlantic. Dinwiddie hastily arranged to have three traders with Ohio Company ties, led by William Trent, travel to the headwaters of the Ohio in early spring 1754 to throw up a hasty stockade and lay claim to the site. They did so, only to be chased off in mid-April when a French force, five hundred soldiers strong, arrived to begin their much more substantial fortification. A month later, Benjamin Franklin's *Pennsylvania Gazette* ran an alarmed account of this run-in, accompanied by the famous "Join, or Die" cartoon. It featured a segmented snake; each segment was labeled with the name of a colony or region of British America. Franklin hoped to emphasize that the French initiative could only be countered by a unified plan for colonial defense.[68]

Franklin well knew that an Indian conference was about to convene in Albany that would bring together representatives from an unprecedented number of colonies. Though its principal purpose was to renew the Covenant Chain with the Six Nations, Franklin, for one, hoped that the conference would also provide an opportunity to hammer out a plan for colonial union.

Exhortation and acquiescence

As summer weather descended on Albany in June 1754, with sultry heat interrupted by frequent thunderstorms, delegations from New York and six other colonies made their laborious ways toward the isolated trading town. They came at the instruction of the Board of Trade and the invitation of New York's new governor, James DeLancey. From the beginning, there was considerable confusion about what they were supposed to do. In the previous September, upon receiving word of Hendrick's declaration that the Covenant Chain had been broken, the Board of Trade had instructed the governor of New York to convene a conference as soon as possible. Its purpose should be to bury the hatchet, thus bringing King George's War, finally, to a formal end; to address the land grievances Hendrick had raised at Fort George; and to renew the alliance. The board further recommended that neighboring colonies should participate, both to strengthen the declaration of friendship and to augment the gifts the Iroquois would receive. Since Hendrick had made it abundantly clear that Albany was a place "obnoxious to them," the board suggested that the meeting should take place in Onondaga— a radical proposition that, had it been heeded, would have shifted the conference to ground controlled by the Iroquois. At the same time, the Board sent a circular letter to the governors of New Hampshire, Massachusetts, Pennsylvania, New Jersey, Maryland, and Virginia, instructing them to confer with their councils and assemblies and recommend that they appoint commissioners and allocate funds.[69]

Much had happened since the board's letters were sent. DeLancey had succeeded Osborne as New York's governor, and it was he who extended invitations and formalized the agenda for the conference. A native of the colony with close ties to Albany, DeLancey had no interest in meeting at Onondaga. He proposed a gathering that would convene on June 14 in Albany, the "most proper and usual place" for such conferences. He invited commissioners from the six colonies already notified by the Board of Trade, and included Connecticut and Rhode Island as well. In correspondence with the other governors, DeLancey stressed the importance of frontier security and suggested that they consider a plan for union, or at least for sharing the cost of mutual defense, while they were gathered in Albany. The colonies' responses varied. In Virginia, Governor Dinwiddie had already committed to an Indian conference of his own involving several southern nations, so he demurred. New Jersey had never had diplomatic relations with the Six Nations in the past, and its Assembly scoffed at the notion that it should participate now. Pennsylvania and Maryland sent commissioners, but both assemblies instructed them to focus on mending the Covenant Chain and avoid any commitment to a plan of union. The New England colonies all participated, and the assemblies of all but Rhode Island endorsed at least the idea of exploring a defensive union.[70]

The delegations arrived in Albany under a cloud of uncertainty about how to proceed. In all, the six neighboring colonies sent twenty commissioners, while DeLancey and four members of his council constituted the New York delegation. Of these twenty-five participants, about a third had some experience in Indian affairs. Though the conference was supposed to start on June 14, delegates straggled in while those who were already present bided their time by dining together and comparing notes on their instructions. On June 19, they decided that the commissioners should collectively draft the opening remarks that DeLancey would deliver, and on June 21 a committee was appointed for that purpose. The remarks were drafted, edited, and debated for a week. On June 24, still awaiting the arrival of all the Iroquois delegations, the commissioners appointed a committee to draft a plan for the union of the colonies. In the meantime, Indians finally began to appear. While the commissioners crowded into Albany's four inns or accepted hospitality from local merchants, the Iroquois camped in a village of makeshift huts just beyond the town's palisades. By Saturday, June 22, some two hundred Indians had arrived.[71]

But Hendrick was not yet among them. He and the Canajoharie Mohawks were still another week away; they finally turned up on Friday, June 28, a full two weeks after the proceedings had been scheduled to start. There was considerable speculation about their delayed arrival. Thomas Pownall, former secretary of the ill-fated Danvers Osborne and an unofficial observer of events, recorded the rumors he heard. According to his sources, the Mohawks had not wanted to participate in an Albany conference at all until Johnson agreed to assist the governor.

Then their progress toward Albany was slowed because "they held many Councils." They were debating two issues. First, what responses should they accept to their complaints before the Covenant Chain could be considered whole? According to Pownall, they decided to insist that they would have nothing more to do with the Albany commissioners in the future, and that their complaints about land had to be fully and finally settled. The second issue was, then what? Once the Covenant Chain was renewed, the Mohawks feared that DeLancey, instead of burying the hatchet they had been carrying since King George's War, would ask them to strike with it once again. They knew as well as anyone that trouble was brewing in the Ohio country, and they feared that a renewal of imperial war would once again expose them to devastation. Experience taught that the British would exhort them to arms, but then fail to offer protection and support. This prospect must have weighed heavily on the delegation as it made its way downriver.[72]

Hendrick's own explanation for their delay differed from Pownall's. If the Mohawks were slowed by internal disagreements, he did not admit it. His remarks did, however, suggest that there were real tensions among the nations of the Iroquois. "We the Mohawks are in very difficult circumstances," he told DeLancey, "and are blamed for things behind our back which we dont deserve." When Johnson, Hendrick, and the other Mohawk sachems had traveled to Onondaga in the previous September, and Hendrick had spoken for Johnson, the sachems liked what they heard but did not trust it. They concluded that "the Mohawks had made" the speech and that it expressed the Mohawks' wishes rather than those of Johnson and New York. Now, Hendrick contended, they had stayed away to dispel the notion that they might have written DeLancey's speech. This explanation had the double merit of masking tensions among the Mohawks themselves and signaling to De-Lancey at the outset that the Canajoharie Mohawks were on thin ice with their fellow Iroquois; it was incumbent on the governor to prove his goodwill to the assembled Indians.[73]

Already, in fact, the Six Nations had expressed their skepticism toward the Albany conference by staying away in large numbers. Even after the Mohawks' arrival, the Iroquois delegation was ominously small. Only about 150 Iroquois attended, perhaps half of them Mohawks. (In addition to the Iroquois, a smaller number of Indians from Stockbridge, Schaghticoke, and Kahnawake were also present.) The Senecas, Cayugas, and Onondagas—those nations Conrad Weiser had been told in 1750 "were turned Frenchmen"—were scarcely represented at all.[74] Though many of the commissioners in Albany were too inexperienced to recognize what a poor turnout they saw, this was, by Covenant Chain standards, a worrisome sign. Seven hundred had participated in 1746. Only the widespread perception that New York had utterly ignored the Covenant Chain alliance in the intervening years could explain the indifference shown by the Iroquois now.

$$\maltese$$

Before Hendrick and the Canajoharie Mohawks arrived, their Tiononderoge counterparts met privately with DeLancey and his four councilors to complain about an especially objectionable land transaction. "We understand that there are writings for all our lands," their spokesman began, "so that we shall have none left but the very spot we live upon and hardly that." They raised no complaint against "those who have honestly bought the land they possess," but one tract in particular troubled them: the Kayaderosseras Patent. The purchase was half a century old. Dating to October 1704 and encompassing some eight hundred thousand acres, it involved a poorly defined and little understood tract of land north and east of Tiononderoge, a hilly region that the Mohawks used as a hunting ground. Four Mohawks, representing two clans, had signed the original deed. One of the four was Hendrick Tejonihokarawa. The purchase price was £60. The rights to the Kayaderosseras patent had since passed through many hands in the colony, but the Mohawks insisted that the original sale was invalid, both because they contended that the money was never paid and because sachems of only two of the three Mohawk clans had signed the deed.[75]

The governor promised to take up the issue with some of the current claimants to the land and give the Tiononderoge Mohawks an answer. In the end, both DeLancey and Johnson made appeals to the Lords of Trade requesting the nullification of the grant. The Lords of Trade considered the issue for two years, then passed it back to the New York Assembly by asking the legislature to annul "these exorbitant and fraudulent Patents." But it was not that simple. Powerful families in New York and England held portions of the Kayaderosseras grant and were reluctant to abandon their claims. The issue bounced back and forth between Crown and colony for seventeen years after the Albany conference before it was finally resolved, in 1771, to everyone's partial satisfaction.[76]

Ᵽ

Hendrick and the Canajoharie Mohawks arrived in Albany on the same day DeLancey met with the Tiononderoge delegation. They may have expected a private audience of their own with the governor: if Pownall's report was correct, the Canajoharie sachems had agreed to seek full satisfaction on the matter of their land grievances before they would declare the Covenant Chain mended. Instead, DeLancey began the public proceedings immediately. On Saturday, June 29, the day after Hendrick and his delegation came to town, all the conference participants gathered on the parade ground in Fort Frederick, on a high hill overlooking the town. The Indians assembled on ten rows of benches facing the governor's house, while DeLancey, the New York councilors, and the visiting delegates sat in a row of chairs facing them.[77]

DeLancey opened the proceedings with the speech he had written in consultation with the commissioners. He announced that the Six Nations were invited "by the command of the great King our Common

Father, to receive a present from him, and in his name to renew the ancient Treaty between this and all his other Govern[men]ts, and you our Brethren." He condoled the Iroquois' recent deaths; then he offered a large chain belt and explained its design. A line ran the length of the belt that represented the king's arms embracing the colonies and the Six Nations. On one side, a set of figures represented the colonies; on the other, figures represented the Six Nations, with "a space left to draw in the other Indians." In the middle of the belt, another, vertical line "draws us all in under the King our common Father"—and, though DeLancey did not say it, separated the Indian nations from the colonies.[78]

DeLancey then noted that the Iroquois "now live dispersed from each other contrary to the Ancient and prudent custom of your Forefathers," and expressed particular concern about the recent settlement at Oswegatchie. He asked the Iroquois to gather once again in their "National Castles," where they would be more formidable to their enemies. Finally, he remarked that the French were making "continual incroachments" on both British and Iroquois territory in the west, and he asked "whether these things appear to you in the same light as they do to us, or whether the French taking possession of the lands in your Country and building Forts between the Lake Erie, and the River Ohio, be done with your consent and approbation."

DeLancey's speech was both disappointing and dangerous. It made no mention of the grievances Hendrick had raised a year earlier, though the ostensible purpose of the conference was to offer satisfaction for them. Nothing about land; no explanation or apology for the colony's inattention to the alliance in the years since King George's War; no effort to take the hatchet out of the Six Nations' hands. DeLancey offered the chain belt without mentioning the bushes and thorns that had grown up in the path between them in recent years. Then he introduced the subject of the French, and did so in the form of an ultimatum. Were the Six Nations as concerned about French encroachments as Britain was—or had they consented to the fort-building plan in the Ohio country? Though DeLancey had not quite issued a call to war, he challenged the Iroquois to declare their loyalties.

The speech was met with something between dissatisfaction and disbelief. Customarily, each nation would have responded by shouting "Yo-heigh-heigh" in turn. Thus "they express their solemn acceptance of ye Belt deliver'd & approbation of ye proposition made." In this case, there was no such response. Instead, the whole gathering called out at once, indiscriminately. Someone present—perhaps Johnson or the Albany commissioners—reminded them what was expected. Only then did each nation call out separately, one by one. This may have been inadvertent, but it was more likely, as Pownall explained, that "they had a mind to disguise that all ye Nations did not universally give their hearty assent to ye Covenant 'till they saw what redress they were likely to find & upon what terms they were likely to be for ye future."[79]

After three days' deliberation, it was left to Hendrick to offer the Six Nations' response. When everyone had once again assembled within the fort, Abraham rose and asked, "[A]re you ready to hear us?" DeLancey said they were. Hendrick rose and addressed the gathering. "Hearken to me," he began. Holding the chain belt in his hands, he thanked for the opportunity to renew it. "This Chain Belt is of very great importance to our united Nations, and all our Allies, we will therefore take it to Onondaga, where our Council Fire always burns, and keep it so securely that neither Thunder nor Lightning shall break it." He acknowledged that DeLancey was correct when he said the Iroquois were now living in a "dispersed manner." Why? The speech turned sharply as he offered an explanation. "The reason is, your neglecting us for these three years past." Then Hendrick held up a stick and threw it behind him. "You have thus thrown us behind your back, and disregarded us, whereas the French are a subtle and vigilant people, ever using their utmost endeavours to seduce and bring our people over to them." This was a remark perfectly calculated to play on British fears and stereotypes. The themes of British neglect and French subtlety and vigilance had been staples of imperial political discourse for years; these lines might have been penned by any one of a dozen colonial administrators or London pamphleteers.[80]

Hendrick next addressed the question of French encroachments, and once again turned DeLancey's inquiry against him. None of the Six Nations had "either sold or given the French leave to build the forts you mention." Nor, for that matter, had they given permission to either Virginia or Pennsylvania, who had "made paths through our Country to Trade and built houses without acquainting us with it." Now the governors of Virginia and Canada "are both quarrelling about lands which belong to us, and such a quarrel as this may end in our destruction."

Hendrick took up an image from DeLancey's speech, but shifted the context in which it had been employed. "It is very true as you told us that the Clouds hang heavy over us, and 'tis not very pleasant to look up, but we give you this Belt . . . to clear away all Clouds that we may all live in bright sunshine, and keep together in strict union and friendship; then we shall be strong and nothing can hurt us." By offering the belt only after he had detailed the ways the alliance had been neglected by the colonies, Hendrick made it clear that a cloudless sky and a strong union, though achievable, would require sustained attention and effort.

That effort must begin in Albany. "This is the ancient place of Treaty where the Fire of Friendship always used to burn," Hendrick acknowledged. But it was now "three years since we have been called to any publick Treaty here." Moreover, although "Tis true there are Commiss[ione]rs here, . . . they have never invited us to smoak with them." The "Indians of Canada," on the other hand, "come frequently and smoak here, which is for the sake of their Beaver." Hendrick invoked the clandestine trade with Kahnawake to cast aspersions on the Albany commissioners, in contrast with the Mohawks, who were loyal adherents to the Covenant Chain. "[B]ut we hate them (meaning the French Indians) [and] we have not as yet confirmed the peace with them." Here, wrapped in a declaration of loyalty to Great Britain, was a subtle reminder that the colony had failed, for six years, to take the hatchet from its allies' hands.

Up until this point, the transcript of Hendrick's speech suggests that he had been forceful but restrained. His criticisms, if not exactly veiled, were at least balanced by promises that the alliance would endure. But now, with the Albany commissioners squarely in his sights, Hendrick unleashed his fury.

> Tis your fault Brethren that we are not strengthened by conquest, for we would have gone and taken Crown Point, but you hindered us; we had concluded to go and take it, but we were told it was too late, and that the Ice would not bear us; instead of this, you burnt your own Forts at Seraghtoga and run away from it, which was a shame & and a scandal to you. Look about your Country & see, you have no Fortifications about you, no, not even to this City, tis but one Step from Canada hither, and the French may easily come and turn you out of your doors.

After this angry gust, Hendrick gathered himself for a final flourish. "Brethren," he began. "You desire us to speak from the bottom of our hearts, and we shall do it. Look about you and see all these houses full of Beaver, and the money is all gone to Canada, likewise powder, lead and guns, which the French now make use of at the Ohio."[81]

Hendrick's indictment of the Albany traders was more than that: it was an indictment of the empire itself, whose will never matched its pronouncements. He drove the point home in words that would be quoted on two continents. "Brethren. You were desirous that we should open our minds, and our hearts to you; *look at the French, they are Men, they are fortifying everywhere—but, we are ashamed to say it, you are all like women bare and open without any fortifications.*"[82] Behind this simple declaration lay two lifetimes of experience: the disasters of the 1670s and 1690s; the failures of 1709 and 1711; the bluster and indecision of King George's War. Hendrick had seen enough to understand the pattern, and his audience knew enough to recognize the truth of it.

Hendrick sat, and Abraham rose to make one final point. Though they had given Governor Clinton a belt to take across the ocean with him, asking that Johnson be reinstated by the Crown to manage Indian affairs, they feared that it had been "drowned in the sea." He gave De-Lancey a belt renewing their request. The belt, according to Pownall, "was as rich & larg a Belt as that which they gave in answer to ye Covenant Belt." The implication was that Johnson's restoration was as important to them as the alliance itself. Then Abraham turned to the Albany commissioners and declared, "The fire here is burnt out."

Hendrick's speech exposed the cracks in the alliance that DeLancey had hoped to paper over. Now the governor and the commissioners from the various colonies had to decide how to respond. What they said publicly amounted to little. Conrad Weiser, who accompanied the Pennsylvania delegation as interpreter and advisor, defended the actions of Pennsylvania and Virginia in the Ohio country. DeLancey began his remarks by saying, "The Covenant is renewed, the Chain is brightened, the Fire burns clear, and we hope all things will be pleasant on both sides for the future." Yet nothing else he said eased the concerns Hendrick had expressed. He defended the Albany traders—"this is a Trading place, and the Merchants have a right to traffick for Beaver or other skins"—and asked the Iroquois to confer with the commissioners for another year. Then, and only then, if they were still dissatisfied, De-Lancey would take action—presumably by reinstating Johnson.[83]

But even as he was preparing this response, DeLancey, under pressure from the other colonies' delegates, undertook a series of private meetings with Hendrick and the Canajoharie Mohawks. The subject was land. The governor managed to settle one controversy relating to a purchase by Teady Magin. He then learned that William Livingston and William Alexander, two of the heirs to the Livingston Patent who between them controlled a quarter of the purchase, were willing to vacate their claims if the Mohawks wished. Thus, although he made no prior provision for addressing the Mohawks' land issues, DeLancey was able to offer two key concessions at the last minute.[84]

The strength of the Mohawk delegation in comparison with the other Iroquois nations, and Hendrick's growing prominence in Covenant Chain diplomacy, opened other doors at Albany as well. The commissioners from Pennsylvania and Connecticut each hoped to purchase title to frontier lands. Pennsylvania's Governor James Hamilton instructed John Penn and Richard Peters to make a purchase west of the Susquehanna River, in what is today the northwestern quadrant of the state, "and the larger the better." Because the Oneidas, the Cayugas, and, after they became the sixth Iroquois nation, the Tuscaroras had always managed the warriors' path leading down the Susquehanna, these nations traditionally mediated Iroquois relations with Pennsylvania. But at Albany, Penn and Peters discovered that the few Oneidas in attendance "insisted on taking Hendrick and the Mohocks into Council to help them to treat with the Propr[ieto]r of Pennsylvania." In the negotiations that followed, Hendrick spoke for the Iroquois. He drove a hard bargain. He stressed that "Land is grown very dear," and he refused to sell the vast tract the commissioners were seeking. He wanted to retain the Wyoming Valley and Shamokin, which had long been indispensable as a corridor of migration and settlement for refugee Indians. Nor did he want the sale to extend west beyond the Allegheny hills.[85]

Conrad Weiser, who was interpreting for the Pennsylvania commissioners, responded to Hendrick in kind. Knowing that the Mohawks had no traditional ownership of the lands in question, he instructed Hendrick to communicate Pennsylvania's offer directly to the Six Nations' council and to let them know that, if they would not approve the sale,

Pennsylvania "would take no further Notice of them." Hendrick did as Weiser asked. After explaining the situation to his fellow sachems, Hendrick argued that they should approve the larger tract. The council gave its unanimous approval. Though he had done what he could to limit the purchase and assure a good price, in the end Hendrick had no choice but to acquiesce in Pennsylvania's wishes. If he resisted, the colony would eventually get what it wanted in any case, and the new path Hendrick had just managed to open to Pennsylvania would be blocked to him and the Mohawks. On July 6, twenty-four Iroquois sachems agreed to the sale in exchange for £400 New York currency delivered immediately, with the understanding that when the lands were settled, the sachems would receive an additional payment not to exceed £400. The names of Hendrick and Abraham headed the list. Hendrick closed the proceedings by noting that "as Times were likely to become troublesome, if the Governor wanted to know the true Disposition of the Indians or to consult on Affairs, and would at any time send for him, he would be sure to come with a few of the principal Mohocks and confer with him." Thus he hoped to seal his new status as the leading sachem and spokesman of the Iroquois in their relations with Pennsylvania.[86]

A second, and more controversial, land purchase took place in Albany as well. This one was arranged by John Henry Lydius on behalf of a Connecticut partnership called the Susquehannah Company. Lydius was a longtime Albany trader, heavily involved in the contraband trade to Canada and a controversial figure in the New York borderlands. Now he agreed to act as agent in a transaction that the Susquehannah Company tried to conduct as quietly as possible. In contrast with the Pennsylvania commissioners, who ensured that every step they took was publicly witnessed, Lydius and the Connecticut purchasers operated in secrecy. The company's agents knew that the lands they sought—the Wyoming Valley on the upper Susquehanna—overlapped with the purchase just completed by Pennsylvania, but they promised an extravagant price to any Iroquois Indians who would sign them away again. The offer was for £2,000 New York currency, though only 10 percent would be paid initially. Hendrick was present at Lydius's house when he made the offer, and he is named in the text of the Susquehannah Company deed, but he refused to sign. Abraham did sign, however, along with thirteen other Indians; five were among those who had also agreed to the Pennsylvania sale. The Pennsylvanians were furious, the Iroquois came to regard Lydius as a "snake" and a "Devil," and the conflicting deeds would soon bring grief to colonists and Indians alike.[87]

The Albany conference was less than fully satisfactory for Hendrick and the Canajoharie Mohawks. Key concerns went unaddressed. Though Johnson had reported in the previous summer that Clinton had raised him up again in Indian affairs, DeLancey was unwilling to promote Johnson over the Albany commissioners. And nothing had been said about burying the hatchet. As they gathered at Albany, the delegates were still absorbing the most recent news from the Ohio country, where a force of Virginia provincials under the command of George Washington had skirmished with a French reconnaissance party near Fort Duquesne. Thirteen French soldiers were killed, including an ensign named Joseph Coulon de Villiers de Jumonville. Jumonville's death blow had been delivered by Tanaghrisson, an Iroquois "half-king" who had been sent by the Onondaga council to oversee the Ohio Indians and was acting as a scout for Washington's party. (Five weeks later, Washington would surrender to a French force that had been detached from Fort Duquesne to avenge Jumonville's party.) Hendrick had heard the news as well, and he knew what it meant. He remarked, "if it be a Fact that the Half-King be engaged in blood, 'tis of more consequence to ye English than twenty such Treaties." Though there had been no formal declaration of war, this was no time, as it turned out, for burying hatchets.[88]

But although the Mohawks did not get everything they wanted at

Albany, they got enough to reassure them. DeLancey had acknowledged and acted on land complaints at both Tiononderoge and Canajoharie. They had long been New York's strongest allies, and now their pre-eminence in the Covenant Chain had been confirmed. They dominated the proceedings, and Hendrick stood apart as their most eloquent spokesman and their most powerful sachem. He had succeeded, too, in establishing a new relationship with Pennsylvania—a tie that might give him additional leverage in his ongoing struggle with the Albany com-missioners. Alongside the Indian conference, the commissioners were hammering out a plan for colonial union in which frontier defenses and Indian alliances would play a central role. And the Indians who came to Albany also got the most tangible benefit of a seven-colony confer-ence: thirty wagonloads of presents to carry home. Such bounty would strengthen the hand of Iroquois Anglophiles and heighten their bat-tered reputation among the western nations.[89]

Hendrick closed the conference with a far different tone than he had taken at the outset. He reminded the assembly of the former power of the Mohawks. "[I]f any of our Enemies rose against us, we had no oc-casion to lift up our whole hand against them, for our little finger was sufficient." Now he hoped the tree of friendship between the Iroquois and the British colonies would "grow up to a great height, and then we shall be a powerful people." If they were "truly earnest" in the partner-ship they had created, then they might "retrieve the Ancient glory of the Five Nations."[90]

Newspaper accounts of the Albany conference, including reports of Hendrick's words and actions, circulated in New York, Philadelphia, and Boston in the weeks that followed. They took longer to cross the Atlantic, but in June 1755 his speeches ran in the *Gentleman's Magazine*. The "faithful Translations" offered in its pages could not "fail to be agreeable to our Readers," the magazine's editors predicted, "as they contain not only the Sense of the *Indians* on our State of Affairs there, but some Strains of native Eloquence, which might have done Honour to *Tully* or *Demosthenes.*" The account ran to four pages; nearly every word of it was Hendrick's.[91] His most famous speech at Albany—the one in which he cast a stick behind his back and compared the British colonies to women—resonated with English-speaking audiences in a way that no Indian's speech had ever done before. It warned of French persistence and challenged Britain to defend itself. It recounted the failings of the Covenant Chain alliance and wondered whether the British were men at all. The speech grew more persuasive the farther it traveled from Albany. It sounded both eloquent and prophetic in London, where growing numbers believed the time had come to mount a vigorous defense of British interests in North America.

Yet the speech that got so much press was only a small part of Hendrick's activity during the Albany conference, and much of what he said and did seemed to run counter to the tenor of his famous exhortation. At the Albany conference of 1754, all the complexities and contradictions of Covenant Chain diplomacy were personified in the single character on whom it depended above all others. Hendrick could offer stern words, but in the end compliance was his only weapon. In the end, he agreed to everything.

Apotheosis

Hendrick's support for the British alliance can appear to be nothing more than an expedient, forced on him by circumstances. And it was forced on him: by 1754, he had little choice but to pursue its logic to its final end. But he was also pursuing a principle, one that dated to Hendrick Tejonihokarawa's youth and animated generations of Mohawk Anglophiles. As Thomas Pownall put it, they "never loved the French nor their politics & alway considerd Alli[ance] with them as putting themselves under subjection to them." The idea of a French yoke of subjection dated to the 1670s and burned itself into the minds of the Protestant Mohawks who endured the crises of the 1690s. It had remained an article of faith for many ever since. "The Indians, unwilling to undergo ye Yoke of a French alliance yet dreading to defye their power," Pownall reasoned, "have acted hitherto a timid & double Part. But if they could hope for a real & effectual Support in our Measures, . . . The English Party would be strong enough to make all declare in our favour." This was Hendrick's hope and conviction. It remained to be seen whether, after more than half a century of futility, Britain could finally provide "real & effectual Support."[92]

The signs were promising. Washington's clashes in the Ohio country roused the ministry to action, and during the fall of 1754 it formulated a comprehensive plan to push back against French power across the frontiers of North America. In February 1755, Major General Edward Braddock arrived to take command of British forces in North America. Two months later he called a conference with the governors of New York, Pennsylvania, Massachusetts, Virginia, and Maryland to lay out his strategy and enlist their support. He invited William Johnson as well, and informed him that he was now appointed superintendent of the northern Indians. Braddock then proceeded to outline a breathtakingly ambitious, four-pronged plan of attack. He would lead two regiments against Fort Duquesne in the Ohio country, while William Shirley, governor of Massachusetts and, until now, no military man, would lead a second attack against Niagara. A third expedition would sail against Nova Scotia from Boston. The fourth prong of Braddock's 1755 initiative was to be a campaign against Crown Point, led by William Johnson.[93]

The prospect of a renewed effort against Crown Point must have felt like déjà vu to Johnson, who watched such a campaign dissolve before his eyes during King George's War. Hendrick must have been gratified by the news. If Washington's ignominious retreat from the Ohio country dramatized the vulnerability of Britain's colonies, Hendrick's bracing words at Albany had served as a call to arms. Braddock had come to show the world that the British were men, after all.

ᕼᑭ

In the meantime, Hendrick was being flattered by the attentions of colonial governors. In December 1754, William Shirley wrote to Johnson to ask that he "let the Indians know, that I will espouse their Interest in the warmest manner both here, and with the King's Ministers." He hoped that nothing would damage the Iroquois' "ancient alliance" with the colonies. "Be pleased in a particular manner, Sir," he continued,

> to let my Old Friend Hendrick know yt I have read over his Speech to the Commissioners of the Congress at Albany with great attention, and much like the spirit, he hath expressed in it, and that I retain the same good Opinion I at first conceiv'd of him, when I saw him at Boston, and met him at Albany afterwards upon an Interview with the Indians of the Six Nations; and assure him that I will let the King's Ministers know how good a friend I look upon him to be to the English, of how much Importance his friendship is to them, and the great regard and Esteem, I have for him as well as the dependance I have upon him for his future attachm[en]t to the English Interest, w[hi]ch I doubt not he will promote to the utmost of his power not only in his own, but the other Castles of Indians.[94]

In Philadelphia, Robert Hunter Morris had his own reasons to appeal to Hendrick's vanity. Having just succeeded James Hamilton as governor, Morris was trying to unravel the Lydius affair. He had been informed of Hendrick's offer to give his "Sentiments on any Thing that might be proposed for the publick Service" at Albany. "I now earnestly desire that You would Favour Us with a Visit," Morris wrote. He enclosed his letter to Hendrick in another, addressed to Daniel Claus, who was living with Hendrick in Canajoharie.[95]

Born in Württemberg, Claus had arrived in Philadelphia several years earlier, at the age of twenty-two, in the hope of making his fortune. He fell in with Conrad Weiser and was soon introduced to William Johnson and the world of the Mohawks. Under Johnson's patronage, he entered Hendrick's household. Hendrick was "very proud" to have Claus join him and "did everything in the world to make his Situation agreeable to him." Traveling back and forth between Johnson's estate and Canajoharie, Claus quickly mastered two new languages, English and Mohawk, and made a home for himself in the Mohawk Valley. Now, at Morris's request, he escorted Hendrick to Philadelphia.[96]

Claus drafted a narrative of his experience that is remarkable in several respects. One of its surprising features is that he refers to Hendrick as "King Henry" throughout. Though Hendrick Tejonihokarawa had been called a king in London, and though Hendrick Peters Theyanoguin was described as the "chief of the whole Six Nations" in Boston, no one with personal knowledge of Iroquois governance, let alone intimate familiarity with Canajoharie and Hendrick's household, had ever suggested that Hendrick held such a status. But Hendrick achieved an entirely new level of renown and influence in the last year of his life. In the months after the Albany conference, references to "Chief" and "King" Hendrick multiplied rapidly as Hendrick came to be treated more like a paramount leader of all the Six Nations than a sachem of the Mohawks. In Philadelphia in particular Hendrick gained an exalted, almost mythical, status.

On their way to Philadelphia, Claus remarked on the "great . . . Curiosity of the Inhabitants to see King Henry and his Attendants." As they approached the city, several members of the governor's council met them and asked that Hendrick and his party pause to allow the city time to prepare for their arrival.

Accordingly entering Second Street coming from Germantown the Town Militia was drawn up on both sides & a numerous populace assembled & following with Acclamations of Huzza for King Henry until he entered the State House where the Governor & Council rec[eive]d and compliment[e]d him and every imaginable respect to Friendship was shown him by every one that had an opportunity of having his Company.

Much to Governor Morris's relief, Hendrick disavowed the Lydius purchase. He blamed it—dishonestly—on "a few drunken Oneida Ind[ia]ns" who, he claimed, agreed to the purchase "without the Knowledge & Consent of the Six Nations in Council."[97]

For the ten days of his visit, Hendrick was the talk of Philadelphia. He and his entourage were entertained at the State House and attended a dancing assembly, where, according to a Trenton newspaper, "they danced the Scalping Dance with all its Horrors, and almost terrified the Company out of their Wits. I must tell you they brought with them a beautiful young Lady, who in publick made the Indian Compliment, a Tender of her Person to the Governor; as gallant a Man as he is, he was quite confounded at that Time. I know not if he accepted her." The Fishing Company of Fort St. David's, a local association of which Governor Morris was himself a member, embraced Hendrick as a hero and adopted him as a symbol. During his visit, the company commissioned William Williams to paint his portrait. Born in Wales, Williams arrived in Philadelphia in 1747 and was well established as a painter by 1755. Upon its completion, the portrait was prominently displayed on a wall of the company's clubhouse.[98]

The same newspaper account that related the tale of the dancing assembly is also noteworthy for another reason: it explicitly conflated the two Hendricks in print for the first time. "The antient King of the Mohawks, (the same who was in England in Queen Anne's Time)," it reported, "came down with some of his Warriors this Winter to Philadelphia." This must have been the word on the street. There is no evidence to suggest that it was a common notion prior to the Albany conference, but Hendrick's dominating presence there seems to have encouraged the association with Hendrick Tejonihokarawa's London visit. The idea had a certain symmetry: as the Crown prepared for yet another military offensive in North America, the distant events of 1710 and 1711 seemed more relevant than they had for many years.

$$\maltese$$

But if Hendrick's star was on the rise, the alliance appeared to be dissolving around him. In October, an Iroquois sachem on the Ohio sent a "very large Belt of Black Wampum" urging the other members of the Confederacy to join with the French at Fort Duquesne. Claus reported from Canajoharie that a hundred members of the Six Nations had recently left for Canada in defiance of the Albany commissioners, to whom they declared they would no longer listen. The Albany council fire, he said, was now "burning at Colonel Johnson's." The Mohawks were openly mocked by members of the other nations for hanging onto the Covenant Chain.[99]

These issues weighed on Hendrick's mind during his visit to Philadelphia. Given the opportunity to talk about something besides the Lydius purchase, he unburdened himself to the governor and council. "I am glad of this Opportunity to open my Heart," he began. "It has been heavily oppressed these Seven or Eight Years, and I have wanted to disclose it." In an apparent attempt to reroute his connection to British authority through Philadelphia, Hendrick complained at length about the Mohawks' mistreatment by New York. The people of Albany had cheated them out of their lands, and neither Governor Clinton nor Governor DeLancey had so far delivered the redress they promised. "Several People of New York" even told the Mohawks that they "should move away to Ohio among the Rest of our Brethren, that they had Patents for all our Lands."[100]

Hendrick complained that the Mohawks were caught in a power play between Johnson, to whom they were willing to listen, and the Albany commissioners, who continued to care more about their ties to the French Indians than their allegiance to Great Britain. The Mohawks fought valiantly and suffered many losses during King George's War, but Clinton "never took any Notice of it. We have the Hatchet still in our Hands. He never took it out. Our Blood is still on the Ground. He never made Us any Satisfaction." Now the governor of New France was entreating them to move north. Hendrick reported that "Many of the Mohocks straggle into Canada," where they were kindly received and showered with presents. "Now and then they intermarry with the Caghnawaga Indians, and when this is the Case no Stone is left unturned to draw them from the English." Abandoned by New York and lured by Canada, the Mohawks were at a loss. "We absolutely despair of Redress from New York. If You do not help Us We know they will not. We will give all up."

Of course, the governor did not help them. He expressed his sorrow at hearing their predicament "and wish it was in our Power to give You the Redress You so earnestly sollicit for," but noted that the colonies were independent of one another. All he could do was "in a friendly Way to lay before the Government of New York what you alledge against it." Hendrick and his party "thanked the Governor, and said that this is all they could expect." They set off on their return to Canajoharie, wondering, it seems fair to assume, what the spring and summer would bring.[101]

ℍℙ

They would have soon learned, upon Johnson's return from his meeting with Braddock, of the sweeping campaigns planned for the summer.

Johnson plunged immediately into planning the Crown Point campaign for which he was responsible. Much depended on his efforts: he was expected not only to organize and command an army as it marched toward Canada but also to ensure that the Six Nations were "heartily engaged in & attached to the British Interest." These duties had him moving in two directions at once: toward Canajoharie and Onondaga, where he would have to take the temperature of the Iroquois; and toward Albany, where he was responsible for organizing and outfitting a force of some thirty-five hundred provincial soldiers from New England and New York. The problem of supplying his army was vastly complicated by the fact that he would be competing—for arms, supplies, wagons and boats, and Indian allies—with Shirley's Niagara campaign. For months, Johnson wrote to his New York factors demanding the supplies he would need. "My great concern," he wrote in early June, "is, that Everry thing seems so backward."[102]

As slowly as things moved in Albany, they were even slower in Iroquoia. The Mohawks had met with Johnson in February to insist that forts be erected at Tiononderoge and Canajoharie, and this became an essential precondition to their involvement in the summer campaigns. In May, DeLancey appropriated £500 for the project and ordered Johnson to proceed. In early June, Johnson completed his survey of the proposed sites and returned to Fort Johnson. There, beginning on June 21, Johnson hosted the largest conference of Indians on record in the colony of New York. More than eleven hundred people gathered at his home. Several nations were represented in addition to the Iroquois, including some Delawares. Johnson announced that he was "appointed to the sole management and superintendency of all affairs relating to you and your Allies which may be transacted in these parts." The old Albany fire was now rekindled at his home, and he urged the Assembly to be zealous in their attachment to the alliance, unified in their response to enemies, and attentive to the "ancient forms" of the Confederacy.[103]

The conference lasted two weeks and served as a testament to the patience of everyone involved. Johnson stressed the long history of the Covenant Chain and the betrayals and deceptions of the French. He gradually worked up to a declaration of hostilities. "My war kettle is on the Fire, my Canoe is ready to put in the water, my Gun is loaded, my sword by my side, and my Ax is sharpened," he concluded. "I desire and expect you will now take up the hatchet and join us." The Indians' response came slowly. They offered many professions of goodwill, but they were unprepared to declare for war. The Onondaga sachem Red Head replied that their warriors had business to attend to at home before they could join the fight. Johnson had assurances that the Iroquois would join him for the march on Crown Point, but at the end of the conference he still had no idea how much support to expect.[104]

In Indian country, the spring and summer of 1755 brought as much communication and debate about the thorny problem of imperial alliances as had ever been seen there. Belts and messengers passed from the Ohio country, to Detroit, to Onondaga, to Kahnawake and Kanesatake. Not since the campaigns of the 1670s had the French mounted such a sustained and determined effort to shape events. The British were resolved to launch a response, but they were sluggish and disorganized as usual. With the fort-building project connecting Lake Erie to the Ohio completed, with thousands of French regulars arriving in North America to join seasoned Canadian militiamen, with apparent advantages at every strategic point in the northern colonies, the French appeared to be in control. One of the greatest concerns of the New York Iroquois was to avoid fighting against their Kahnawake and Kanesatake relatives. They sent repeated messages to Montreal, asking their families and friends to remain neutral. The replies were not encouraging. Indians were streaming toward Montreal from throughout the Great Lakes to join in the French campaigns, and the St. Lawrence Indians intended to fight alongside them. Any Iroquois warriors who joined Johnson's campaign ran the risk of encountering their relatives on the battlefield.

By early August, the new fort at Canajoharie was completed, and the men and supplies for the Crown Point campaign were slowly, laboriously moving forward. Disastrous news had recently arrived from the Ohio country: Braddock's army had been routed. It would be hard to overstate the effect of this news, both on Johnson and Shirley and on their prospective Indian allies. Braddock was the one seasoned commanding officer to take the field in the summer of 1755. He had regarded his campaign to be the essential prelude to the Niagara and Crown Point ventures. His loss was a stunning blow to Shirley, whose inexperience and caution were already causing him to drag his feet. He and Johnson had been wrangling for months over arms, supplies, men, and Indian allies. Summer would soon turn to fall, and neither the Niagara nor the Crown Point campaign was yet under way. Shirley's progress slowed to a crawl: he made sure that he could get no farther than Oswego before winter set in, then delayed the march on Niagara until spring.[105]

Johnson, however, pressed slowly on. To the British officers who planned the campaign from a distance, it might have appeared easy to move an army north out of Albany toward Crown Point, since a chain of rivers and lakes created an almost continuous waterway. The Hudson River ran most of the way to Lac St. Sacrement; at the northern end of that lake, it was only a short distance overland to Lake Champlain; Crown Point was just beyond the next portage, guarding the southern entrance to Champlain. But that impression was deceptive. Crown Point was nearly a hundred miles from Albany, and there were chokepoints all along the way. Most daunting were the two major portages. It required hundreds of boats to carry the thirty-five hundred troops and their supplies north from Albany, past Saratoga, and to the upper reaches of the Hudson. There, at the Great Carrying Place, Johnson and his men had to regroup for the sixteen-mile portage that stood between them and the shore of Lac St. Sacrement. They built a fort alongside the river—

Fort Edward, named to honor the Duke of York—and then set to work cutting a road toward the lake.[106]

Good news arrived in Johnson's camp at the Great Carrying Place on August 23, when one of Hendrick's brothers—either Abraham or Nickus—arrived with twelve other Indians and reported that more were on the way. Hendrick came two days later with another two hundred warriors. All things considered—with Braddock's stunning defeat on the Monongahela and indications from Canada that Kahnawake and Kanesatake warriors would be fighting alongside the French—this was a good turnout. Only the combined efforts and strong reputations of Hendrick and Johnson could have gotten this many Iroquois warriors to take the field at a time when British fortunes in North America had never looked bleaker.[107]

By September 3, Fort Edward was substantially completed, and Johnson had pushed his camp forward to the shores of the lake, which he renamed Lake George to honor Britain's king. There he had begun clearing ground for another fort, which would be the staging ground for a final push to Crown Point. From their position on Lake George it was fifty miles to the portage onto Lake Champlain, and another fifteen miles to Crown Point. Johnson thought he could be there in three weeks.[108]

The campaign's prospects changed dramatically a few days later. Johnson's efforts had attracted the attention of Canada's supreme commander, Baron Jean-Armand de Dieskau, who hurried to Crown Point in August with a mixed force of regulars, Canadian militiamen, and Indian warriors, numbering about three thousand in all. While half his force shored up the decrepit Fort St. Frédéric at Crown Point, Dieskau struck out with two hundred regulars, six hundred Canadians, and seven hundred Abenaki and Kahnawake warriors. He hoped to strike quickly, before Johnson could reinforce his positions at the Great Carrying Place. His detachment paddled to a bay at the south end of Lake

George, not far from Johnson's camp, and struck out southward through the woods.[109]

Dieskau's intended target was Fort Edward. But when his force was within a few miles of the fort, the Indian warriors told him they would not join in an attack on a fortified site. Rather than argue, Dieskau changed his plans and turned north on the portage road recently cut by Johnson's men, heading for the camp—still undefended except for a hastily improvised breastwork—on the shore of Lake George (Figure 12). Johnson, meanwhile, had been informed that a large French force was on the road to Fort Edward. Summoning a council of war, he proposed to split the forces at his disposal. Five hundred would march south to reinforce Fort Edward, while another five hundred would follow the lakeshore until they found Dieskau's canoes, then set off along their path through the woods. They would thus have him "between two Fires," and could march on him from both directions. Hendrick conferred with some of his warriors, and then informed Johnson that they would not participate in such a maneuver. It was a mistake, he argued, to divide their small forces. Johnson should send them south at full strength toward Fort Edward. Johnson agreed.[110]

Thus, on the morning of September 8, 1755, two hundred Iroquois warriors led by Hendrick set out from the camp, followed by a thousand provincial soldiers under Colonel Ephraim Williams. Williams was one of the leading landholders in Stockbridge, Massachusetts, and would surely have known Hendrick well. Assuming that Dieskau's objective was Fort Edwards, Hendrick and Williams hoped to surprise him as he invested the fort. But it was they who would be surprised. Dieskau's force had advanced the night before to a position only four miles from Johnson's camp. In the morning, Dieskau learned of the British advance and planned accordingly. His Indian warriors and Canadian militia flanked the road where it passed through a ravine and waited in ambush.[111]

About ten in the morning, Hendrick, Williams, and their men approached the spot. Hendrick was out front on horseback (Figure 13). Daniel Claus, who was with Hendrick, reported that "they had not marched 4 Miles before the Indians were challenged in ye Iroquois Tongue who they were." Hendrick replied, "We are the six confederate Ind[ia]n Nations the Heads & Superiors of all Ind[ia]n nations of the Continent of America." The Kahnawake Indian, who had already spoiled the ambush, replied, "We are the 7 confederate Ind[ia]n Nations of Canada & we come in conjunction with our Father the King of France's Troops to fight his Enemies the English without the least Intention to quarrel or trespass against any Ind[ia]n Nation." He asked that Hendrick's warriors get out of the way, "lest we transgress & involve ourselves in a War among ourselves." Hendrick replied that the Six Nations were there to help their British allies resist French encroachments, and the Kahnawakes should either "join them, or at least follow their advice & keep out of Harm's way &c."[112]

The conversation was finally interrupted by gunfire. One of Hendrick's warriors fired a shot in the direction of the Kahnawake who had been talking, and with that the spell was broken. A "hot running fight" ensued. Some thirty Iroquois and fifty provincials were killed in the initial exchange. The Massachusetts soldiers and Iroquois warriors briefly tried to defend their position, then initiated a steady retreat toward Johnson's camp. Williams lay dead in the ravine. Hendrick survived the initial volley, but his age betrayed him as he tried to join the retreat. Now some sixty-five years old, the years since his exploits in King George's War had taken their toll. Tumbling from his horse, the "heavy old Man" was "soon left in the rear." As he tried to make his way back to camp, he "fell in" with the French baggage guard, which consisted of "young Lads & women." Though they were unarmed, someone got the best of him. Stabbed in the back by a spear or bayonet, he was scalped and left to die. "[S]ome pretend to say," according to Claus, "it was committed by a Squaw, the Lads being too young to attempt it, & by the Manner of his being scalped it is probable a woman did it, as the scalp being taken off [was] not larger than an English Crown."[113]

The battle lasted through the day. Once the retreating provincials and Mohawks regained their camp and regrouped behind improvised defenses, they held off the French attackers. Casualties were high on both sides. Though the British suffered the heaviest losses at first, the

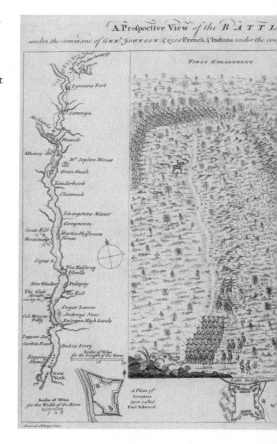

Figure 12. Samuel Blodget, *A Prospective-Plan of the Battle fought near Lake George . . .* (London, 1756). This composite image shows the first engagement of the battle, the ambush in which Hendrick and Ephraim Williams fell (left). Center: French, Canadian, and Indian soldiers attack the camp alongside the lake. Right: the camp and its defenses. Far left: map of the route up the Hudson River. Blodget engraved an earlier, similar, but not identical, image that was printed in Boston in 1755. Courtesy of the John Carter Brown Library at Brown University.

French regulars were devastated as they tried to charge the camp's breastworks. Late in the day, after Dieskau's forces were finally drawing back, reinforcements from Fort Edward arrived to inflict one last slaughter that more or less evened the number of dead and wounded on both sides. Dieskau, first shot in the knee and then blasted with grapeshot in his "Loins," surrendered on the battlefield in terrible pain. Johnson, too, bore a new scar following the battle: he had taken a mus-

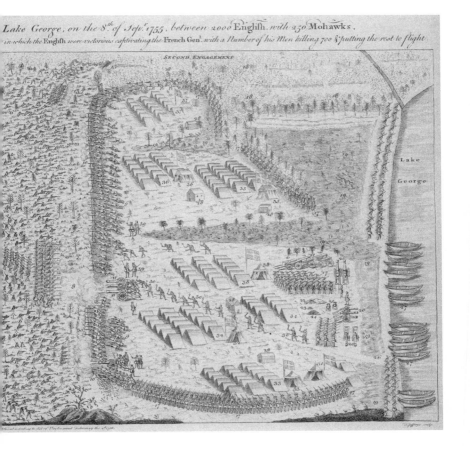

263

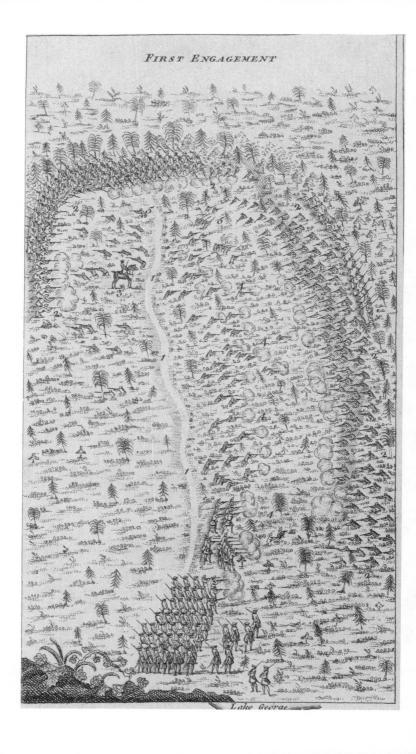

FIRST ENGAGEMENT

Lake George

ket ball in the buttock. At day's end Johnson could claim a victory, as costly as it was. His men had held Fort Edward and defended their campsite by the lake. Dieskau was a prisoner and his force was scattered. Crown Point still beckoned in the distance.[114]

H̸

Dieskau, inconsolable after the battle, blamed the fiasco on the Kahnawake warriors who had disobeyed his orders in the first, critical engagement. Claus recorded Dieskau's analysis of the day's events. Though the French force had Hendrick, Williams, and their men "entirely surrounded," the sight of two hundred Mohawk warriors led by the familiar figure of Hendrick gave the Indians pause. "[T]hey seemingly were pannic struck & instead of attacking & demanding our people to surrender (as it would have been Madness in them to refuse) they began to parley with Henery." His reply to their challenge seemed to "damp their & the Canadians' ardor & courage." Hendrick's men, not Dieskau's, initiated the attack, "which turned out in a scattered Skirmish" and allowed the provincials and Mohawks to retreat. The result was a "confused drawn affair, whereas had his orders been obeyed, he must inevitably have taken the whole party prisoners." Then his men would have "surprised us in our open Camp [and] with very little difficulty completed the Victory."[115]

On Johnson's side, the loss of Hendrick and the other Mohawks who fell was a stunning blow to the Iroquois warriors. To Johnson's surprise and dismay, they announced that they were leaving. "You hung your War Kettle," the Oneida spokesman said to him, "and now brother it seems that you had such a great Fire under it that it made the Water

---

Figure 13. Blodget, *Prospective-Plan*, detail. Hendrick is visible as the only figure on horseback on the upper left. Courtesy of the John Carter Brown Library at Brown University.

boil over." The battle had been a success; now "all of us are determined to return to our several Homes and Families for the present and so we bid you farewell." Johnson offered two strouds to cover the dead, then insisted that the campaign was not yet half over. He passed a belt, saying, "I expect and desire by this Belt that you fulfil your engagements." But the warriors could not be dissuaded. They had many corpses to cover and much to think about. Never again would they join with British arms in such numbers.[116]

Three days after the battle, word reached Canajoharie. According to an account from Albany, Hendrick's son Paulus wailed in grief at the news of his father's death. Then, "suddenly putting his hand on his left breast, [he] swore that his father was still alive in that place, and stood there in his son." Paulus succeeded his father as a Canajoharie sachem. The Reverend John Ogilvie, who had replaced Henry Barclay as the town's Anglican missionary in 1750 and served as Hendrick's minister for the last five years of his life, recorded news of the battle in his diary. "We remained in Suspence till Thursday the Eleventh about one oth'Clock we received the joyful Tydings that we had got the Victory with a very little loss on our Part," he wrote. Dieskau, now a prisoner, he called "a Man of Quality." He noted Johnson's wound and lamented the loss of Williams and five other officers. He never mentioned Hendrick's name, either in that entry or in any other thereafter.[117]

The loss of his Indian warriors, and reports that the French had begun work on a new fort, Fort Carillon, to guard the southern end of Lake Champlain and protect Crown Point, forced Johnson to reevaluate his plans. It appeared increasingly unrealistic to press forward. Instead, he focused on securing his position at the south end of Lake George. By the end of September, work had begun on a substantial new fort, which Johnson named Fort William Henry to honor the dukes of Cumberland and Gloucester. Even though Johnson had not attained Crown Point, the Battle of Lake George was accounted a great victory, from the streets of New York to the offices of Whitehall. Upon his return to

New York, he was "received with Acclamations of Joy & Congratulation thro every Street he passt; the Shipping firing their Guns & the greater part of the Town was illuminated." In November, Johnson was granted a baronetcy "as a distinguishing mark of His Royal favor and approbation of your conduct." His reputation was secure.[118]

Light and shadow

Hendrick's reputation, too, soared after the Battle of Lake George. He was prominently featured in the many accounts of the battle that circulated in the colonial and transatlantic press. The *New-York Mercury* and the *Pennsylvania Gazette* published their first accounts based on flying reports they received within days of the battle. For more than a month, they continued to print supplemental narratives as they came to hand. Their information came from "stragglers" and French prisoners, from William Johnson and Peter Wraxall, from a correspondent in Halifax and the skipper of an Albany sloop. Once printed in the colonies, they made their way across the Atlantic, where they appeared in newspapers throughout Britain and eventually found their way into the pages of the *Gentleman's Magazine*, which published a succinct account of the battle in October, only four months after it carried the story of Hendrick's speeches at the Albany congress. The November issue included a longer account. "Our Indians were prodigiously exasperated," it noted, ". . . by the death of the famous *Hendrick*, a renowned *Indian* warrior among the *Mohawks*, and one of their sachems, or kings." The same issue advertised a "print of old *Hendrick*, the great sachem of the *Mohawk Indians*," which could be purchased for a shilling.[119]

Hendrick's name lived on in other contexts as well. The fort at Canajoharie that Johnson had built in the summer of 1755 was called, by the summer of 1756, Fort Hendrick. At about the same time, a public house named the Indian King Hendrick opened on Third Street in Philadelphia. A few years later, Musgrove Evans opened another Philadelphia establishment with a similar name—the King Hendrick—on Arch Street opposite the Church Street Burying Ground. Ships named for Hendrick soon plied the waters of coastal North America and the Caribbean. In June 1757, the sloop *Hendrick* was captured on its way from Barbados to Virginia and taken as a prize to Martinique. Without a "Chief" or "King" as part of its name, this vessel may or may not have been named for the fallen hero of the Battle of Lake George. The same uncertainty does not hover over the privateer brigantine *King Hendrick*, which sailed from Rhode Island under the command of a Captain Tomkins and captured three French vessels in August 1757. It was presumably the same brig *King Hendrick*, now under the command of Captain Frederick Hamilton, which helped to bring eight enemy ships to port in a six-month period in the following year. At the same time, a sloop named *King Hendrick*, also from Rhode Island, was enjoying similar success as a privateer. While under the command of Captain Christopher Waterman, it captured a small schooner "laden with Sugar" off the coast of Hispaniola in February 1758 and a Dutch vessel headed for St. Eustatia in May. A month later, the same ship under the command of James Eborn arrived in Providence with a large French schooner in tow. In the coastal battles of the Seven Years' War, Hendrick's Atlantic fame became a literal fact.[120]

In October 1756, Richard Footman and Company of Philadelphia offered a new shipment of English goods for sale. Among the merchandise were "pictures of old Hendrick." This was most likely the famous print entitled *The brave old Hendrick, the great Sachem or Chief of the Mohawk Indians* (Figure 3). One of three likenesses to appear after the Battle of Lake George, historians have ever after taken it as an accurate depiction of Hendrick. Yet its source has always been a mystery. Though it is not a mezzotint of the very highest quality, it is the kind of skilled engraving that owners would have hung on their walls. Some surviving copies, like the one reproduced on the cover, were carefully and painstakingly hand-tinted. An engraving of such depth and detail was almost certainly based on a painted portrait, but if so the original has been lost. We know that William Williams painted a portrait of Hendrick in early 1755 that hung for a time on the clubhouse wall of the Fishing Company of Fort St. David's but has long since disappeared. This portrait may well have been the source for the engraving. If so, the image's transmission remains mysterious. All known versions of the print originated in London. How would a London printer have gotten the engraving? Was the engraving struck in Philadelphia, then transported to London? Who executed the engraving, and why was it not first used to print copies in Philadelphia—where Hendrick was, after all, a culture hero? And since the portrait on which the *brave old Hendrick* print was based no longer survives, how confident should we be that the print's likeness is accurate?

When we compare the figure in the print to written descriptions of Hendrick, several key features correspond with what we know. Hendrick is dressed in the kind of laced coat and hat and ruffled shirt he commonly wore to conferences. He also has flowing white hair—the one physical feature that is remarked on repeatedly in the documentary record—and a swelling belly. This sounds like our man. On the other hand, the striking facial tattoos that stand out in this image have no documentary confirmation. The print shows various markings, including two horizontal slashes beneath the left eye, a crescent scar on the left cheek, and, most notably, a sunburst tattoo at the left temple. It seems surprising that if he had such marks, no one would ever have described them in print. On the other hand, tattoos were common among many Indian nations, including those of the Iroquois Confederacy, during the seventeenth and eighteenth centuries, yet European observers almost never remarked on them.

Six months after this image was advertised for sale in the pages of the *Gentleman's Magazine,* a second print (Figure 14) of Hendrick appeared in London that is as striking for its differences with this first image as

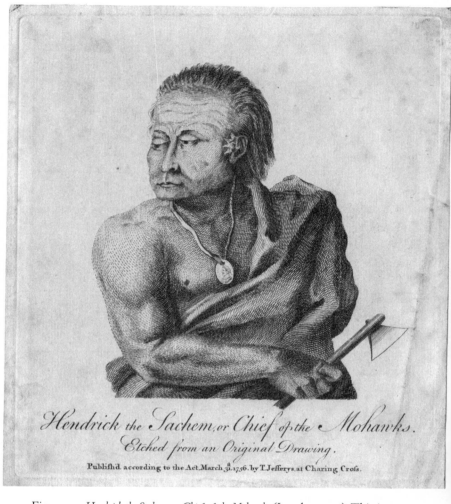

Hendrick the Sachem, or Chief of the Mohawks.
Etched from an Original Drawing.

Publiſh'd. according to the Act, March 31.1756. by T. Jefferys, at Charing Croſs.

Figure 14. *Hendrick the Sachem or Chief of the Mohawks* (London, 1756). This image replicates the sunburst tattoo of *The Brave Old Hendrick* (Figure 3) but otherwise bears little resemblance to it. The painting or sketch it is based on has been lost. Negative no. 7722, collection of The New-York Historical Society.

for its similarities. Like the first image, this one includes a prominent sunburst tattoo next to Hendrick's left ear. In both prints, Hendrick holds a tomahawk.[121] Little else in the second image, however, corresponds with the first. The second picture shows no obvious facial scarring beyond the sunburst tattoo. This Hendrick would be better described as stocky than corpulent. In place of the fine clothing in the first print, this Hendrick, dressed (or undressed) for war, is naked from the waist up except for a blanket tossed over his shoulder. He wears a medal around his neck. His unusual seated posture, which ran against contemporary traditions of portraiture, would have appeared especially unflattering to an eighteenth-century eye. And in place of the flowing white hair in the first print, this Hendrick sports a short, dark, shaggy cut. Viewing these two images side by side, it is tempting to conclude that the first is an accurate depiction of Hendrick and the second a hasty copy that got several key details wrong.

But there is a third image of Hendrick, which also seems to date from the time shortly after the Battle of Lake George, that casts doubt on both prints. It is an anonymous watercolor now owned by Williams College in Williamstown, Massachusetts (Figure 15). The college is named for Ephraim Williams, who died on the battlefield with Hendrick at Lake George. In all likelihood, the painter knew both Hendrick and Williams. Perhaps it was someone who met Hendrick in Stockbridge. The script on the painting identifies Hendrick as "a Mohawk Indian kill'd with Sr. W. Jonson" and asserts that it was "drawn from the life." The comparison between this painting and the famous Hendrick print is surprising and puzzling. There is no facial tattooing, but Hendrick wears two large, beaded hoop earrings and a nose ring (or something like it). He also wears a cross around his neck. His clothing is European, though it is not the kind of lace-and-ruffle finery we see in the first print. He is bald on top, with a short patch of stringy black hair. Oddly, he wears a polka-dot ribbon in it. He looks old and not at all fierce. Yet for all the discrepancies with the *brave old Hendrick* print, a close comparison reveals striking similarities as well. The two men appear to have the same prominent, aquiline nose, jutting upper lip, and receding chin. Their cheeks are lined around the mouth in precisely the same way. For all their cosmetic differences, these two visages appear to

Figure 15. *Effig of King Hendric a Mohawk Indian . . .* , anonymous watercolor. Though it purports to be "drawn from the life," this painting differs in significant ways from other images of Hendrick. Courtesy of the Williams College Archives and Special Collections, Williamstown, Mass., USA.

be nearly identical (though perhaps the watercolor Hendrick appears a few years older).

The surviving images of Hendrick present us with a final enigma. How do we make sense of these partially congruent, partially discordant pictures? Like so much in Hendrick's life, we are left, at the end, with a suggestive but irreducible mystery. Famous on two continents, he remains nevertheless in history's shadow.

Conclusion:
Memory and Meaning

Rufus Grider was a painter, art teacher, and local historian from the Mohawk Valley town of Canajoharie, New York—a thriving little village near the site of the old Mohawk castle. In the spring of 1887 he traveled to Caldwell, near Lake George, to visit a man named George Brown. Brown claimed to own the thighbones of King Hendrick, which he said he had scavenged from his gravesite. Grider carefully sketched the bones, annotated the picture, and placed it in one of his bulging scrapbooks (Figure 16).[1]

According to Grider's note, Hendrick was buried alongside Colonel Ephraim Williams after the Battle of Lake George, near the place where they both fell. A "fine monument" marked Williams's grave; Hendrick's was also marked, though less impressively. Then in 1862 "the ground was needed for Cultivation & the Indian's grave was not respected." Enter George Brown, who "Collected the remains and retains them in his collection." The thighbones were improbably large—nineteen and a half inches, compared to the average human length of about fourteen inches, according to Grider—supporting the theory that Hendrick was a giant of a man: by Grider's estimate, he stood seven feet tall and weighed three hundred pounds.

It is true that Hendrick cut an imposing figure, but this is too much.

Several other elements of Brown's account of the thighbones strain credulity as well. Yet Grider's willingness to believe the improbable reflects a sensibility common to his era. Grider belonged to a generation of men with a strong interest in the local past and a romantic attachment to its legends. The thighbones of King Hendrick had the power of a relic. A giant Hendrick added another element of interest to the little-known, larger-than-life character he was investigating. The world had all

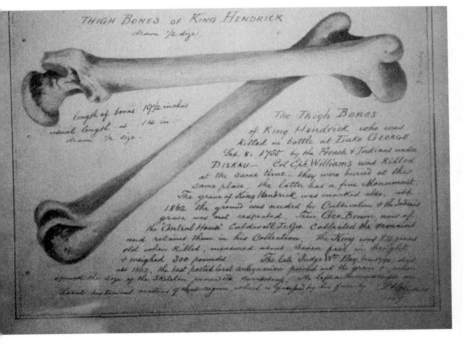

Figure 16. Rufus Grider, *Thigh bones of King Hendrick, drawn half size*, 1887. The accompanying note remarks on the extraordinary—and improbable—size of these relics. Rufus Grider Collection. Courtesy of the New York State Library, Manuscripts and Special Collections. Ann Aronson Photography; reproduced by permission.

but forgotten Hendrick. If Grider had his way, he would be remembered again: all seven feet of him.

In retrospect, the Battle of Lake George, bloody and inconclusive as it was, marked an important victory for Great Britain in the early years of the Seven Years' War. There were not many. Yet against all odds and expectations, British fortunes experienced a dramatic revival in 1759. By 1761, all of Canada had been conquered. In the Treaty of Paris of 1763, France ceded all its territory in North America east of the Mississippi River to Great Britain.[2]

This astonishing outcome carried the seeds of its own reversal: the effort to administer the vast new empire precipitated a crisis that culminated in a war for independence. In the American Revolution, the Iroquois Confederacy was forced, once again, to choose sides in a fight that was not its own. Many people migrated north or west to avoid the worst of the conflict. Some communities sought neutrality. The Mohawks who stayed in their homeland remained attached to the British interest. The Oneidas, under the influence of the missionary Samuel Kirkland, supported the rebels. It scarcely mattered. The war devastated large swaths of Iroquoia, and in its aftermath each of the Six Nations, regardless of its wartime loyalties, was dispossessed of nearly all its territory. Joseph Brant led a migration to Canada; small numbers remained behind on reservation lands. Within a matter of a few years, the Iroquois ceased to be a people of note or consequence in the United States borderlands.[3]

In 1796, as the dispossession of the Iroquois was becoming an established fact, Jeremy Belknap, a Boston clergyman and historian, traveled up the Mohawk River into Oneida country. His journal records the region's transformation since the days of Hendrick Peters Theyanoguin, but it also indicates that Hendrick, William Johnson, and their contemporaries remained alive in memory. After dinner at a house opposite the mouth of Schoharie Creek, Belknap and his companions climbed a hill to view the landscape across the river. Noting the site of Fort Hunter, he wrote, "Here was an Episcopal mission established in the reign of Queen Ann, and kept up till the beginning of the late revolution; a set of books and service of plate [was kept] in the church." As he traveled upriver from the old site of Tiononderoge, the landscape grew rocky and steep, then leveled out again in rich farmland. "The lands through which we passed this day," he remarked, "are all highly cultivated, and loaded with a luxuriant growth of wheat, rye, oats, and peas."[4]

On Saturday, June 18, Belknap ate breakfast at Hudson's, "a good tavern, seated on the same ground where Hendrick lived, the Mohawk sachem who was killed in Johnson's battle, 1755, near Lake George." The site was "a beautiful eminence, commanding a pleasant prospect, and here are many apple trees of at least fifty years old, called Hendrick's orchard. We had some of the cider, and it was excellent."

> Here was a fort, built by British troops in 1756, called "Fort Hendrick," the rampart, ditch, and glacis of which are visible; and here was found, about four years ago, a golden medal, which it is supposed was the property of some Indian chief. It was worth about seven dollars; had an Indian on one side and emblematic figure on the other. It was sold at Albany to a Mr. Lansing.[5]

Belknap noted in passing, "The story of Hendrick's dream and Sir William's counter dream is generally believed to be true." Though he did not elaborate, the story to which he referred has been repeated often. In the late nineteenth century, the journal's editor expanded on Belknap's remark in a footnote:

> The Indian chief dreamed that Johnson would present him with a scarlet uniform similar to the one the agent had just received

from England. This Johnson did. But in due time he summoned the chief, and told him that he too had dreamed a dream, in which the Indian gave him a tract of land. Hendrick is reported to have made the gift, with the remark that the white man "dreamed too hard for the Indian."[6]

This story of reciprocal dreaming—in which Johnson fulfills Hendrick's wish for a fine suit of clothes, but dreams in turn of a large tract of land that Hendrick is obliged to deliver to him—is almost certainly apocryphal: a nearly identical story has been told, for example, about Conrad Weiser and the Oneida headman Shickellamy.[7] Nevertheless, the story about Hendrick and Johnson has had remarkable staying power; many writers and readers apparently see some elemental truth in it. By invoking the Iroquois veneration of dreams, it seems to be informed by ethnographic knowledge and evokes a romantic sense of strangeness. Yet its real point is to emphasize that Europeans like Johnson play the game of life for higher stakes than Indians like Hendrick. There is an element of dishonor and shame in Johnson's unequal bargain, but there is also humor and a quality of soaring ambition that men of the 1790s would have admired. It was a trait that many of Belknap's contemporaries would have agreed was lacking in the Mohawks and their Iroquois brethren. Yes, Johnson cheated Hendrick: nevertheless, he got what he wanted. And, a Mohawk Valley farmer might have added, we are the heirs and beneficiaries of Johnson's cleverly asymmetrical exchange. In the dreaming story, the messy, complex, and deeply corrupted reality of Mohawk land transfers—the Tiononderoge purchase, the Kayaderosseras Patent, Cosby Manor, the Livingston tract, and all the others—is reduced to the form of an amusing and easily digested parable.

As time passed, local and personal recollections of Hendrick and the Mohawks grew hazier. Some stories—especially the story of Johnson and Hendrick dreaming together—endured. Some elements in the characterization of Hendrick—his eloquence, his bravery, and his suit of fancy clothes—were often repeated. But as the era of Hendrick Peters's life faded in memory, the details floated free of context.

In 1808, a former resident of Albany named Anne MacVickar Grant published her recollections of life in the colonies. The daughter of an army officer, she was born in Glasgow in 1755, accompanied her family to the colony of New York three years later, and returned to Scotland for good in 1768, when she was thirteen years old. Forty years later, she wrote a memoir of her experiences in and around Albany. Though it contains many errors of fact, it has been a popular source of anecdotes and local color for generations. More than any other text of the era, Grant's memoir captures a world lost in the violent displacements of the Revolution.[8]

In two passages, Grant recorded specific memories of Hendrick. The first refers to two Hendricks, a father and a son. "It was the fortune of the writer of these memoirs," Grant noted,

> More than thirty years after, to see that great warrior and faithful ally of the British crown the redoubted King Hendrick, then sovereign of the Five Nations, splendidly arrayed in a suit of light blue, made in an antique mode, and trimmed with broad silver lace; which was probably an heirloom in the family, presented to his father by his good ally and sister, the female king of England.

Here Grant evokes a two-generation royal dynasty. She thought that a man named Hendrick had received a fine suit of clothes from Queen Anne, which his son, also named Hendrick and "then sovereign of the Five Nations," wore on the occasion when she saw him. The timing is unclear, but it is certain that Anne Grant could not have met Hendrick Peters Theyanoguin, since he died three years before she arrived in Albany. It is possible, however, that she met Hendrick's son Paulus, who was closely identified with his father and was himself a sachem of Canajoharie, and that she understood that *his* father—Hendrick Peters Theyanoguin—had received a suit of clothes from "the female king of England."[9]

The second passage expands on the first. Grant describes the trip up the Mohawk River that brought her to Fort Hendrick and the adjacent Indian castle of Canajoharie, home of "the principal Sachem, or king of the Mohawks. The castle of this primitive monarch," she wrote, stood "on a rising ground, surrounded by palisades. He resided, at the time, in a house which the public workmen, who had lately built this fort, had been ordered to erect for him in the vicinity."

> We did not fail to wait upon his majesty: who, not choosing to depart too much from the customs of his ancestors, had not permitted divisions of apartments, or modern furniture to profane his new dwelling. It had the appearance of a good barn, and was divided across by a mat hung in the middle. King Hendrick, who had indeed a very princely figure, and a countenance that would have not dishonoured royalty, was sitting on the floor beside a large heap of wheat, surrounded with baskets of dried berries of different kinds; beside him, his son, a very pretty boy, somewhat older than myself, was caressing a foal, which was unceremoniously introduced into the royal residence. A laced hat, a fine saddle and pistols, gifts of his good brother the great king, were hung round on the cross beams. He was splendidly arrayed in a coat of pale blue, trimmed with silver; all the rest of his dress was the fashion of his own nation, and highly embellished with beads and other ornaments. All this suited my taste exceedingly, and was level to my comprehension. I was prepared to admire

King Hendrick by hearing him described as a generous warrior, terrible to his enemies, and kind to his friends. . . . Add to all this, that the monarch smiled, clapped my head, and ordered me a little basket, very pretty, and filled by the officious kindness of his son, with dried berries. Never did princely gifts, or the smiles of royalty, produce more ardent admiration and profound gratitude.[10]

To the two generations of Mohawk royalty mentioned in the first passage, a third is added here: the "pretty boy . . . caressing a foal." The easiest conjecture is that Anne Grant, as a child of four or five, met Hendrick's son Paulus and grandson John, and mistook Paulus for Hendrick. But John was born in 1744, eleven years before Grant, and so he would have been fifteen or sixteen years old at the time of their encounter, whereas her memoir makes him sound younger. Perhaps Grant's childhood memory, recorded nearly half a century after the event, confused the scene. The fine clothing made a strong impression—but in recalling the clothes she saw, it is possible that she was influenced by a memory of the "brave old Hendrick" print, which would have been hanging in Albany homes during the time of her stay.

Despite the pitfalls in Grant's recollection, some descriptive elements of her account are compelling and may be accurate. The friendly pat on the head and the gift of a basket ring true. And her account of Hendrick's dwelling is also persuasive, even if it was not Hendrick whom she met there. It is plausible that Johnson would have instructed the men who built the Canajoharie fort in the spring of 1755 to build a house for the now-famous King Hendrick as well. Grant remembered it as a barn-like structure. Most residents of the Mohawk castles had long since given up their communal longhouses for smaller, single-family dwellings.[11] Among such structures, a new home the size of a barn would have been a substantial mark of distinction. Though Hendrick would not have lived there long—he died only three months after the completion of the fort—his son might have inherited the house, and with it a measure of the status accorded to his famous father.

As midcentury approached, a dawning ethnographic interest in Indians animated the beginnings of scholarly investigation. This took many forms: the excavation and analysis of archaeological sites, inquiries into language and culture, research in archival documents. Henry Rowe Schoolcraft was an early pioneer in this work. Born in Albany County—his grandfather had come from England and served as a surveyor there in the eighteenth century—Schoolcraft was appointed United States Indian agent for the Great Lakes Indians and moved to Mackinaw, in Michigan territory. In 1823 he married Jane Johnston, the granddaughter of an Ojibwa sachem who had been educated in Europe. Schoolcraft served in the Michigan territorial legislature and, in 1836, negotiated a sixteen-million-acre land cession from the Great Lakes Indians to the federal government. He served as acting superintendent for Indian affairs, then as the chief disbursing officer for its northern department.[12]

In 1845, the New York legislature commissioned Schoolcraft to conduct a census and gather information among the members of the Six Nations who remained in the state. He completed his task the same year. But he was not content simply to report his findings to the state senate. The next year he published a landmark book that enfolded his census data in a larger inquiry. Entitled *Notes on the Iroquois: or, Contributions to the Statistics, Aboriginal History, Antiquities and General Ethnology of Western New York*, it was an incomplete work, as much a prospectus for future research as a finished investigation, as he himself acknowledged.[13]

Schoolcraft evinced a rare appreciation for the depth, antiquity, and significance of Iroquois history and culture. "The aboriginal nation, whose statistics and history, past and present, are brought into discussion in the following report," he announced at the outset, "stand out prominently in the foreground of our own history."

> They have sustained themselves, for more than three centuries and a half, against the intruding and progressive races of Europe. During the period of the planting of the colonies, their military exploits gave them a name and a reputation which are coeval with Europe. These events are intermingled, more or less, with the history of each of the colonies, and impart to them much of their interest. But while we have made an extraordinary progress in population and resources, and gone far to build up a nationality, and commenced a national literature, very little, if any, progress has been made in clearing up and narrowing the boundaries of historical mystery, which shroud the INDIAN PERIOD prior to 1492. This forms, indeed, the true period of American Ethnology.

By declaring the Iroquois a fit subject of serious inquiry, Schoolcraft initiated a research agenda that was far ahead of its time. It would gather steam slowly, but reach full flower in the twentieth century, when Native American history, linguistics, archaeology, and ethnography would mature as academic fields. Iroquois scholarship has risen to the apex of these investigations, and Schoolcraft was its first pioneer.

A year later, Schoolcraft published an expanded second edition. More lavishly printed, with a series of beautiful plates, it quickly eclipsed the first. It is the definitive account of Schoolcraft's investigation of the Iroquois. Though the first edition contained no mention of Hendrick, the second added a chapter entitled "Miscellaneous Traits, Etc.," which included a long biographical sketch of him. Schoolcraft relied for his account on correspondence with Giles F. Yates, a local historian of the Mohawk Valley. "There was a time, in our settlements," Schoolcraft wrote, "when there was a moral force in the name of *King Hendrick* and *his Mohawks,* which had an electric effect; and at the time he died, his loss was widely and deeply felt, even in Great Britain."[14]

Yates got a few things right, but his account of Hendrick contained many errors of fact, nearly all of which have long persisted in other historical accounts. Yates erroneously gave Hendrick the Mohawk name Soi-en-ga-rah-ta. He posits a single Hendrick who visited London twice, once in the reign of Queen Anne and a second time about 1740, when "his majesty presented him with a rich suit of clothes—a green coat, set off with brussels and gold lace, and a cocked hat, such as was worn by the court gentry of that period." Then, according to Yates, Hendrick sat for a portrait by a London artist. "From this portrait, which has no date, engravings were made, of a large 'cabinet size,' and colored in conformity with the original."[15] This was Yates' attempt to explain the "brave old Hendrick" print, a copy of which was "preserved in the family of the late Jeremiah Lansing, Esq., of Albany." (The Lansing print must have been tinted differently from the one reproduced on the cover, with a green coat rather than a red one.) Yates repeated the story of Hendrick and Johnson dreaming together. He explained that the Iroquois had an "implicit faith in dreams, which, they said, were sent by the Great Spirit for wise purposes, and that if a dream is not fulfilled, at whatever hazard or sacrifice, some evil may fall upon the dreamer." And he identified the land given to Johnson as "the Royal Grant." Hendrick was "esteemed the bravest of the brave, among the Iroquois," according to Yates, and "his people were ever the fast friends and uncompromising allies of the British" on the New York frontier.

Schoolcraft's second edition includes an engraving of *Soi-en-ga-rah-ta, or King Hendrick* (Figure 17). This image creatively combines elements from several earlier portrayals while it imagines a younger Hendrick, dressed as a warrior. His head is shaved except for a small lock at the back of his crown. The effect is similar to that in the *King Hendric a Mohawk* watercolor (Figure 15), except that feathers have replaced the polka-dot bow. His long loop earrings recall the same portrait. The facial markings are

SOI-EN-GA-RAH-TA, OR KING HENDRICK.

Figure 17. *Soi-en-ga-rah-ta, or King Hendrick,* from Henry Schoolcraft, *Notes on the Iroquois* (New York, 1847). This image combines elements of several eighteenth-century depictions of Hendrick and imagines him as a younger man. Courtesy of the New York State Library, Manuscripts and Special Collections. Ann Aronson Photography; reproduced by permission.

based on the *brave old Hendrick* print (Figure 3): a sunburst tattoo around the left ear, two horizontal slashes beneath the left eye, and a crescent scar on the left cheek. The engraver has added a lightly incised diamond pattern that crisscrosses his face and amplifies the other markings. Like the *Hendrick the Sachem* print (Figure 14), this Hendrick is naked above the waist except for a blanket. In place of the medal that adorns his neck in that print, Schoolcraft's Hendrick wears a beaded necklace. He holds a tomahawk in his hand.

Schoolcraft's *Notes* marked a transition from Belknap's sketchy journal entries and the idiosyncratic memories of Anne Grant to an era of sustained critical research. But Yates's recollections, compounded of personal observation and local lore, made a weak foundation for memories of Hendrick to rest on. By lending to Yates's antiquarian efforts an imprimatur of scholarly rigor that they did not deserve, Schoolcraft simultaneously enhanced the fame of the mythic Hendrick and helped to bury still deeper the reality of the two Hendricks' lives.

At the same time that Schoolcraft was assembling his Iroquois notes, Lewis Henry Morgan, a young lawyer from Aurora, New York, began to seek literary inspiration, fraternal association, and the roots of an ancient American past in the lore of the Iroquois Confederacy. In the early 1840s he founded a secret society alternately called the New Confederacy, or the Grand Order, of the Iroquois. Its members adopted Indian names and costumes, met around campfires in the woods, and cultivated a romantic genre of speech and writing in which they adopted characters and attitudes that they considered to be authentically Indian in spirit. Morgan invented a grand historical timeline to explain their activities. In his imaginary epic, the Six Nations of the Iroquois were founded by Gordius, the mythic king of ancient Phrygia. When Phrygia fell, Gordius led a migration of Phrygian people to the Americas. The Iroquoian empire they established rose, prospered, fell, and finally vanished, so that genuine Iroquois culture had passed from the scene without a trace by Morgan's time. Now, in a third epoch, Morgan and the New Confederacy were reviving the true spirit of the Six Nations. They hoped to use it as the basis for a new, indigenous American literature.[16]

From this starting point in fraternal association and imaginative literary production, Morgan and his associates gravitated toward ethnography. The catalyst for this shift was a young Seneca, Ely S. Parker, whom Morgan met in 1844. Morgan had no prior experience with real Indians, and in Parker he discovered a bright, well-educated man who could serve as an informant and collaborator in his researches. With his help, Morgan pieced together a systematic ethnography of Iroquois governance, society, and culture. Published in 1851, *The League of the Ho-de-no-sau-nee* is a landmark book in both Iroquois studies and the field of ethnography. Though it mentions Hendrick only in passing—Morgan notes his death at the Battle of Lake George—it influenced all subsequent Iroquois scholarship. Shaped by Parker's contributions, *The League* initiated a long tradition in ethnographic research of using native informants to explain alien cultures. In recognition of this achievement, Morgan has often been called the father of American anthropology.[17]

Yet in his own local context—in the midcentury world of upstate New York—Morgan represented more than the search for scientific knowledge. He was one of a generation of men seeking a deeper connection with an indigenous past. They hoped to put the romantic spirit of Six Nations lore to use in their own world, to weave antiquity into the fabric of American culture. Just as Cadwallader Colden developed the classical analogy to make the Iroquois worthy partners in empire, Morgan's ethnography emerged from his search for a useful, epic American past. This sensibility shaped many historical and ethnographic investigations in the later nineteenth century.

While Morgan was assembling the materials for *League of the Ho-de-no-sau-nee*, Edmund Bailey O'Callaghan, an Irish doctor, was settling in to his new job as archivist for the state of New York. By the time of his death in 1880, he had done more than any single individual in the state's history to bring the documentary evidence of its past to light.

Born in Mallow, County Cork, O'Callaghan studied medicine in Dublin and Paris before emigrating to Quebec, where he established a practice. In 1833 he moved to Montreal and became involved in radical politics. Within a few years his role in a riot led officials to place a price on his head; he fled across the border and eventually settled in Albany. He continued to practice medicine but grew increasingly interested in history, and in 1848 he was appointed the state's archivist and plunged into a series of publishing and editorial projects. Between 1849 and 1851, his four-volume *Documentary History of the State of New-York* was published in Albany. Yet that undertaking only scratched the surface of the materials available to illuminate the seventeenth and eighteenth centuries, and in 1853 the first volume of his most significant and enduring editorial project appeared in print. Drawn from archives in London, Paris, and Albany, the fifteen-volume *Documents Relative to the Colonial History of the State of New-York* transformed the context in which scholars would approach the history of the state's colonial era. A wealth of archival materials was now placed within the reach of every writer who had access to a decent library, and they were organized in a way that made it easy to follow historical developments and controversies. While there were precedents for this kind of publishing activity—Peter Force's *American Archives,* Jared Sparks's volumes of Revolutionary-era correspondence, and Hezekiah Niles's *Principles and Acts of the Revolution* come to mind— nothing so comprehensive and far-reaching as O'Callaghan's effort had yet been attempted.[18] Henceforth, writers would have a much greater density of materials to work with as they tried to situate the two Hendricks in the story of colonial New York.

In 1865, the Saratoga Springs lawyer and journalist William Leete Stone published a two-volume biography of William Johnson that also offered the first sustained historical account of Hendrick Peters

Theyanoguin. Son of a writer by the same name who penned biographies of Red Jacket and Joseph Brant, the younger Stone developed a strong attachment to local history and lore. He authored a local guidebook, a collection of reminiscences, and several historical narratives. He was also a founding member of the Saratoga Monument Association. In all these activities, Stone affirmed his connection with the local past.[19]

Though Stone did not cite the primary sources he drew on, he certainly had the O'Callaghan volumes that had already appeared close at hand, and his acknowledgments suggest that O'Callaghan offered him guidance through sources that had not yet appeared in print. The archivist's influence is clear: Stone's knowledge of the eighteenth century is more detailed and coherent than that of any writer since the days of Cadwallader Colden and William Smith. And, necessarily, Stone's biography of Johnson recounts many episodes involving Hendrick Peters Theyanoguin. Yet although Stone unearthed many details of Hendrick's activities, he did little to illuminate his life. An appendix that presents a brief biography of Hendrick is drawn primarily from the Giles Yates material that had been published earlier by Schoolcraft. A few elements are new. Stone contends that Hendrick was a Mohegan (by which he meant Mahican). Extrapolating from Hendrick's statement that his father had been born in Westfield, Massachusetts, Stone writes, "Although this great sachem has been called a *Mohawk,* yet his family was *Mohegan,* and he himself only a *Mohawk by adoption.*" (This is a mistaken inference, since Hendrick's affiliation would have derived from his mother, not his father.) And Stone dissents from both Yates and Belknap when he writes, "The famous story of Sir William Johnson's dreaming with King Hendrick for the royal grant, or indeed for any other piece of land, is a pure fiction." His research into Johnson's life apparently gave Stone confidence that no such conveyance had occurred.[20]

Having debunked the dreaming story, Stone substituted one useful fiction for another, this one drawn from William Campbell's *Annals of Tryon County.* Though it has not had the prominence or staying power of

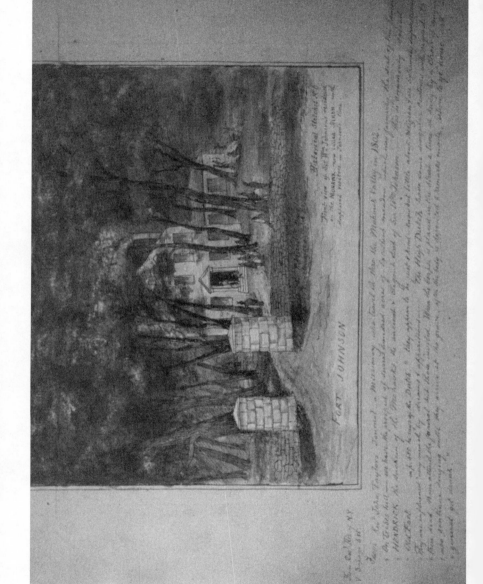

FORT JOHNSON

the dreaming episode or the 1740 trip to England, Stone's anecdote illustrates the persistent desire to make Hendrick a vivid, larger-than-life character. In this case, the story illustrates "the friendship that the Great Mohawk was capable of inspiring in the hearts of the whites towards himself." Stone relates that Hendrick's "likeness was taken" when he was in Philadelphia, "and a wax figure afterward made which was a very good imitation." After Hendrick's death, "an old friend, a white man, visited Philadelphia, and among other things was shown this wax figure. It occupied a niche, and was not observed by him until he came within a few feet. The friendship of former days came fresh over his memory, and forgetting for the moment Hendrik's death, he rushed forward and clasped in his arms the frail icy image of the chieftain."

This story makes Hendrick's effigy an envoy from a lost world. Suddenly surprised by the sight of Hendrick, the "white man" sees in the "frail icy image" the echo of a nearly forgotten past, in which a "Great Mohawk" and a white gentleman could meet as equals and become dear friends. The embrace of the wax figure—a cold, lifeless memento of a once vibrant man—inspires a romantic pang of sympathy for the men whose friendship, like so much else, is lost to the ages.[21]

In Stone's biography of Johnson, as in Schoolcraft's *Notes*, Hendrick figured principally as a shadowy, mythologized figure who added color to the story. In both books, Hendrick was treated in an appendix: a clear indication that neither author knew how to integrate him into the larger story he was telling.

Figure 18. Rufus Grider, *Fort Johnson*, 1886. Rufus Grider Collection. Courtesy of the New York State Library, Manuscripts and Special Collections. Ann Aronson Photography; reproduced by permission.

Ring taken
from the
Grave of Sir
William Johnson
The date is
on the inside
of the Ring
June 26 1739

These histories share in common a half-formed sensibility about the importance of Iroquois culture for those who later occupied the Six Nations' homeland. Rufus Grider, the Canajoharie painter and teacher who sketched Hendrick's thighbones, brought this sensibility to full flower. In nine massive volumes, Grider compiled an enormous collection of watercolors, engravings, tracings, photographs—more than a thousand pieces in all—documenting the historic sites of the Mohawk, Schoharie, and Cherry valleys. Most pages are extensively annotated to explain their subjects' significance. It is an intensely personal act of recovery and reproduction, enormous in scope and rich in local sites, contexts, and stories.

Grider was a transplant to the region. Born in Lititz, Pennsylvania, in 1817, he was a Moravian who studied painting under the Dresden-trained landscape artist Gustavus Grünewald. He spent most of his adult life in Bethlehem and Philadelphia before relocating to Canajoharie at the age of sixty-six. Only then did he begin work on his massive New York sketchbooks.[22]

William Johnson fascinated Grider; the index to his volumes contains nearly two dozen references to him. In August 1886 he sketched three sets of images associated with Johnson. One was a full-page sketch of Fort Johnson, the imposing home he built in 1749 (Figure 18, page 290). Grider mistakenly reported that the site was "formerly the seat of the famous HENDRICK, the sachem of the Mohawks." To give the picture an air of eighteenth-century authenticity, Grider placed groups of Indians throughout the grounds, strolling, chatting, and resting. The second page devoted to Johnson (Figure 19) has two images side by side: a ring

---

Figure 19. Rufus Grider, drawing of William Johnson's ring and prayer book, 1886. Rufus Grider Collection. Courtesy of the New York State Library, Manuscripts and Special Collections. Ann Aronson Photography; reproduced by permission.

Figure 20. Rufus Grider, *View of the Grave of Sir Wm. Johnson*, 1886. Rufus Grider Collection. Courtesy of the New York State Library, Manuscripts and Special Collections. Ann Aronson Photography; reproduced by permission.

taken from Johnson's grave dated June 26, 1739—supposed to be the date of his marriage to Catherine Weisenberg—and a worn Book of Common Prayer that Johnson left in his church pew. The third page is a view of Johnson's grave in Johnstown. It shows a small, overgrown marker surrounded by trees (Figure 20). Beneath the image, Grider wrote simply, "The neglected grave of a great man, when will his worth & services be appreciated?"[23]

In the following spring, Grider traveled to Caldwell, New York, and sketched the thighbones. A year later he devoted another page to Hendrick that wrapped a brief narrative around two small watercolors (Figure 21). One painting was a copy of Schoolcraft's *Soi-en-ga-rah-ta* print (Figure 17); the other reprised *brave old Hendrick*. To the *brave old Hendrick* picture he added a diamond pattern on the face, the kind that was introduced in the Schoolcraft print, to make the images more fully consonant.[24]

Grider's notes highlight the cloud of obscurity that had settled over the lives of the two Hendricks by the 1880s. Like the writers before him, he assumed that there was a single Hendrick, born between 1680 and 1690. He mistook the provenance of both the portraits his sketches were based on, and he repeated the story of a 1740 trip to England. He was confused about which Mohawk village Hendrick came from, and even about how many there were. The errors of fact and inference in these pages testify to the way local knowledge grew hazy as events receded into the past. But accuracy was less important to Grider's project than the act of commemoration itself. Grider's plea about Johnson—When will this great and neglected man be appreciated?—could be a fitting epigram for the entire compendium of paintings and sketches, which sought to recover the lost world of the eighteenth century in the changed landscape of the nineteenth.

SOI-EN-GA-RAH-TA.
OR
KING HENDRICK of the Mohawks.

"A Mohawk he, by Oiondaga stood.
And felt the mighty monarch of the wood."

Was born about 1680 or 90. was slain in
battle at Lake George 1755. when fighting
the French & Canadian Indians, under
Baron Diskau. This portrait was
taken in Indian Costume, he visited
England twice. King George the Second
had a green & flowered suit made for
him such as was then fashionable
in England. the familiar picture of
him was taken by a London artist
when he wore that suit & older in

* See Schoolcraft's note on the Iroquois.

years than the last picture shows.

During the early part of his
life he lived at the Upper Castle
now known as Indian Castle 35 W Sour: R.R.
in 1748 we learn from David Zeisberger's
Journal in Both the Archives & copies in this
Collection, he lived in a large & good house
of his own at the Middle Castle then known
as Canajoharie — now known as Prospect
Hill Fort Plain.

He was a gifted speaker. his oration
before the "Col Gov" of N.Y. in 1754
was masterly & was republished both
here and in England. at the time it
was spoken of: —

" it Contains Strains of Eloquence
" which might have done honor
" to Tully or Demosthenes "
and
" For Capacity, bravery, vigor of mind
and immovable integrity united,
he excelled all the aboriginal inhabitants of whom we have any knowledge."

He was succeeded in office by his Son
and the son by the noted Chieftain
Joseph Brant.

H B Snider
Ap. 27. 1888.

KING HENDRICK Portrait taken when in
England, the Suit given him
by King Geo. the Second

By the end of the nineteenth century, memories of Hendrick depended almost entirely on local folklore. O'Callaghan's heroic editorial efforts made the source materials necessary for a fuller account widely available, but it would take time for scholars to plumb their depths. In the meantime, faulty recollections, false inferences, and apocryphal anecdotes were wrapped around the few known facts of Hendrick's life. Accounts of the Albany congress speech and the Battle of Lake George were consistently reliable, but little else was. The idea that the two Hendricks were a single individual may have originated as early as Hendrick Peters Theyanoguin's mission to Boston and Maine in 1744; a decade later, a Trenton newspaper asserted their common identity in print. If the mistake was already being made in Hendrick Peters's lifetime, it is not surprising that it was so easily perpetuated after his death.

Nor was the conflation of the two Hendricks especially significant. So little was known of either life, and their stories were so encrusted in mythmaking, that the confusion of identities was the least of it. In the last several decades, the rich and complicated world of the two Hendricks has begun, stubbornly, to part with some of its secrets. The work of many scholars has illuminated the contours of the Iroquois confederacy, the Mohawk nation, and the Anglo-Iroquois alliance. This book shines a light on two men whose lives can be portrayed with unusual clarity. Both Hendricks were smart, resourceful, brave, and occasionally impudent; both took bold gambles, which sometimes worked; both also made significant miscalculations. Each sometimes learned from his mistakes. It was entirely appropriate for New Yorkers of the nineteenth century to remember a single, undifferentiated Hendrick as a heroic, romantic, larger-than-life figure. Equally, it is appropriate now that we dis-

Figure 21. Rufus Grider, *Soi-en-ga-rah-ta, or King Hendrick of the Mohawks*, 1888. Rufus Grider Collection. Courtesy of the New York State Library, Manuscripts and Special Collections. Ann Aronson Photography; reproduced by permission.

entangle the skein of stories that have been woven around this name to consider the extraordinary lives that gave rise to them.

When we do so, we discover a narrative of great significance. In most accounts of American history, Indians are depicted as a people who stand apart: they are separated from Euroamerican populations; they are either outside the stream of historical events or standing in futile opposition to them. As individuals, they are fleeting and out of focus; we talk more comfortably about Indians as groups than as living, breathing people. The two Hendricks are important in part because we can see them as individuals. We can sympathize with their dilemmas; we can understand some of their choices and agonize over others. They are important, too, for the relationships they formed with the people around them. What was the British Empire in the early American borderlands, after all, but a tenuous bond between people like Hendrick Tejonihokarawa and Peter Schuyler, or Hendrick Peters Theyanoguin and William Johnson? The two Hendricks played central roles in the construction of imperial power in the borderlands. In the prolonged, dramatic contest between Britain and France to win control of eastern North America, Indians decisively shaped the outcome of events. The choices made by the two Hendricks are with us still today, inscribed on the map of North America and echoed in the images and texts that keep them alive in memory.

Abbreviations

A0272   Applications for Land Grants, 1642–1803, 63 vols., New York State Archives, Albany.

C11A   Série C11A, Correspondance générale, 122 vols., original in Archives Coloniales, Paris; microfilm copy in Library and Archives of Canada, available at www.collectionscanada.gc.ca/index-e.html.

CASHP   Stefan Bielinski, project director, *Colonial Albany Social History Project* (Albany, 1981–), a community history project of the New York State Museum, www.nysm.nysed.gov/albany/.

CO5   Colonial Office Papers, National Archives of the United Kingdom, Kew, England.

CSP   W. Noel Sainsbury et al., eds., *Calendar of State Papers, Colonial Series, America and West Indies,* 39 vols. (London, 1860–1969).

DCBO   John English, gen. ed., *Dictionary of Canadian Biography Online,* www.biographi.ca/index-e.html.

DHNY   E. B. O'Callaghan, ed., *Documentary History of the State of New-York,* 4 vols. (Albany, 1849–1851).

DRCNY   E. B. O'Callaghan and Berthold Fernow, eds., *Documents Relative to the Colonial History of the State of New York,* 15 vols. (Albany, 1853–1887).

ERSNY   Edwin T. Corwin, ed., *Ecclesiastical Records of the State of New York,* 7 vols. (Albany, 1901–1916).

IIDH   Iroquois Indians: A Documentary History of the Diplomacy of the Six Nations and Their League (microfilm) (Woodbridge, CT, 1985).

JR   Reuben Gold Thwaites, ed., *The Jesuit Relations and Allied Documents: Travels and Explorations of the Jesuit Missionaries in New France, 1610–1791*, 73 vols. (Cleveland: Burrows Bros., 1896–1901).

LIR   Lawrence H. Leder, ed., *The Livingston Indian Records 1666–1723* (Gettysburg: Pennsylvania Historical Association, 1956).

MA   Massachusetts Archives, Columbia Point, Dorchester.

MACIA   Minutes of the Albany Commissioners of Indian Affairs, R. G.10, vol. 1819, microfilm reel C-1220, National Archives of Canada, Ottawa (microfilm, Ottawa, 1957).

MHSC1   *Collections of the Massachusetts Historical Society*, 1st Ser., 10 vols. (Boston: Massachusetts Historical Society, 1792–1809).

MPCP   *Minutes of the Provincial Council of Pennsylvania, from the Organization to the Termination of the Proprietary Government*, 16 vols. (Harrisburg, PA, 1838–1853).

NAUK   National Archives of the United Kingdom, Kew, England.

NYSA   New York State Archives, Albany.

NYSL   New York State Library, Albany.

PSWJ   James Sullivan et al., eds., *The Papers of Sir William Johnson*, 14 vols. (Albany, 1921–1965).

RSPGJ   Records of the Society for the Propagation of the Gospel: The Journals, 1701–1850, 50 vols. (microfilm) (East Ardsley, Yorkshire: Micro Methods, 1964).

WAIA   Peter Wraxall, *An Abridgement of the Indian Affairs, Contained in Four Folio Volumes, Transacted in the Colony of New York, From the Year 1678 to the Year 1751*, ed. Charles H. McIlwain (Cambridge: Harvard University Press, 1915).

WMQ   *The William and Mary Quarterly*, 3rd ser.

Notes

Introduction

1. Samuel Blodget, *A Prospective-Plan of the Battle near Lake George* (Boston, 1755), 1; Daniel Claus, *Daniel Claus' Narrative of His Relations with Sir William Johnson and Experiences in the Lake George Fight* (n.p.: Society of the Colonial Wars in the State of New York, 1904), 14.

2. I began work on this project in 1995 under the assumption that there was one Hendrick. Timothy J. Shannon first alerted me to the possibility that there were two, based on a 1997 presentation by Dean Snow, to which Shannon alludes in a footnote in *Indians and Colonists at the Crossroads of Empire: The Albany Congress of 1754* (Ithaca: Cornell University Press, 2000), 30 n. 40. Snow was responding to the work of Barbara J. Sivertsen, whose *Turtles, Wolves, and Bears: A Mohawk Family History* (Bowie, MD: Heritage Books, 1996), first clearly differentiated the two Hendricks. An expanded version of Professor Snow's presentation has now been published as "Searching for Hendrick: Correction of a Historical Conflation," *New York History* 88 (Summer 2007), 229–53. I first learned of Barbara Sivertsen's work through Alden T. Vaughan, whose recent book and essay identify the two Hendricks as distinct individuals and debunk the often-repeated claim that Hendrick visited London in 1740: *Transatlantic Encounters: American Indians in Britain, 1500–1776* (New York: Cambridge University Press, 2006), and "American Indians Abroad: The Mythical Travels of Mrs. Penobscot and King Hendrick," *New England Quarterly*, 80 (June 2007), 299–316. I owe a debt to all these scholars and rely especially on Sivertsen's genealogical work to disentangle some aspects of the two Hendricks' family histories.

3. Those who are interested in pursuing this subject in more depth might be-

gin with "Forum: The 'Iroquois Thesis'—Con and Pro," *WMQ* 53 (1996), 587–636, and Shannon, *Crossroads of Empire*, 6–8 and following.

4. Among contemporary scholars, the idea of an Iroquois myth was first clearly articulated in Francis Jennings, *The Ambiguous Iroquois Empire: The Covenant Chain Confederation of Indian Tribes with English Colonies from its Beginnings to the Lancaster Treaty of 1744* (New York: W. W. Norton, 1984). Jennings argued that the Iroquois' reputation as a fearsome military power was overstated, and that the confederacy maintained its reputation with European empires through skillful diplomacy. His penetrating insights have profoundly influenced the scholarship of the most recent generation; see especially Francis Jennings et al., eds., *The History and Culture of Iroquois Diplomacy: An Interdisciplinary Guide to the Treaties of the Six Nations and their League* (Syracuse: Syracuse University Press, 1985); Daniel K. Richter and James H. Merrell, eds., *Beyond the Covenant Chain: The Iroquois and their Neighbors in Indian North America, 1600–1800* (Syracuse: Syracuse University Press, 1987); Daniel K. Richter, *The Ordeal of the Longhouse: The Peoples of the Iroquois League in the Era of European Colonization* (Chapel Hill: University of North Carolina Press, 1992); and Timothy J. Shannon, *Iroquois Diplomacy on the Early American Frontier*, Penguin Library of American Indian History (New York: Penguin, 2008).

5. L. P. Hartley, *The Go-Between* (New York: Knopf, 1954), 3.

1. New Birth

1. For a discussion of the name, see William N. Fenton, *The Great Law and the Longhouse: A Political History of the Iroquois Confederacy* (Norman: University of Oklahoma Press, 1998), 194, 369–72. Tejonihokarawa became a hereditary chieftainship for the Senecas, who guarded the western door of the longhouse, but there is no such chiefly title among the Mohawks. Nevertheless, it is reasonable to assume that the name implied a ceremonial duty in this case, as it did among the Senecas. I want to stress at the outset, however, that this point is conjectural. For descriptions of Hendrick, see, e.g., *The Present State of Europe: or, the Historical and Political Monthly Mercury*, vol. 21 (1710), 160; for visual images, see figs. 1 and 5.

2. Daniel K. Richter, "War and Culture: The Iroquois Experience," *WMQ*, 40 (1983): 528–59. For an introduction to epidemics and population loss, see Russell Thornton, *American Indian Holocaust and Survival: A Population History Since 1492* (Norman, OK: University of Oklahoma Press, 1987), and David P. Henige, *Numbers From Nowhere: The American Indian Contact Population Debate* (Norman, OK: University of Oklahoma Press, 1998). The connection between epidemics and large-scale raids is demonstrated in José António Brandão, *"Your Fyre Shall Burn No*

More": Iroquois Policy toward New France and Its Native Allies to 1701 (Lincoln: University of Nebraska Press, 1997).

3. Daniel K. Richter, *The Ordeal of the Longhouse: The Peoples of the Iroquois League in the Era of European Colonization* (Chapel Hill: University of North Carolina Press, 1992), 50–74.

4. "Observations of Wentworth Greenhalgh in a Journey from Albany to the Indians Westward," *DRCNY* 3:252.

5. For accounts of torturing prisoners, see, e.g., ibid.; *JR* 47:86–93. For a discussion of torture practices see Brandão, *"Your Fyre Shall Burn No More,"* 39–41.

6. For Hendrick Tejonihokarawa's genealogy, see Barbara J. Sivertsen, *Turtles, Wolves, and Bears: A Mohawk Family History* (Bowie, MD: Heritage Books, 1996), 22–23 and following. If it is true that the name Tejonihokarawa, like Hendrick, was conferred in early adulthood, then Hendrick Tejonihokarawa's birth name is lost to us. This chapter will use his surviving Mohawk name for the period predating his baptism, and Hendrick thereafter. For clan identity and household and community structure, see Richter, *Ordeal of the Longhouse*, 18–21.

7. For the origin and evolution of clans, see Fenton, *Great Law and the Longhouse*, 24–29; clans and moieties for each of the Five Nations are usefully summarized in table form in Dean R. Snow, *The Iroquois* (Cambridge, MA: Blackwell, 1994), 55. For Tekarihoken, see Fenton, *Great Law and the Longhouse*, 61–62, 74, 193, and Sivertsen, *Turtles, Wolves, and Bears*, 22. The structure of the Iroquois League council is outlined in Snow, *Iroquois*, 60–65; the problem of squaring its ideal composition with the historical record is taken up in Fenton, *Great Law and the Longhouse*, 203–14 and following.

8. For village names and sites, see Dean R. Snow, Charles T. Gehring, and William A. Starna, eds., *In Mohawk Country: Early Narratives about a Native People* (Syracuse, NY: Syracuse University Press, 1996), Introduction, xviii–xxiii; for the 1677 account, see "Observations of Wentworth Greenhalgh," *DRCNY* 3:250–52.

9. For the disordered character of late-seventeenth-century community life, see especially Richter, *Ordeal of the Longhouse*, 32–33, 72–74.

10. Ibid., 102–4; Fenton, *Great Law and the Longhouse*, 253.

11. *JR* 51:179–87; quote: 185.

12. *JR* 51:201–09; quotes: 201, 205.

13. *JR* 51:207–9.

14. *JR* 51:187, 211, 191–201.

15. The tradition that Hendrick's father was Mahican derives primarily from evidence relating to the second Hendrick. But there is one document that makes

the same claim about Tejonihokarawa: a letter written by Governor Robert Hunter in 1712. The central purpose of that letter, however, was to minimize Hendrick Tejonihokarawa's reputation and legitimacy as a Mohawk leader. It is possible that Hunter was correct, but there is also good reason to doubt the letter's veracity; see pp. 114–15.

16. *JR* 53: 137–59; *JR* 52:117–21, 127, 141; quotes: 52:119, 117.

17. For an example of the conflict between Iroquois and Christian practices, see *JR* 53:213–39; quotes: *JR* 52:133.

18. *JR* 53:213–39, 137–55; quotes: 281, 155. The Mohegans came from coastal New England and should not be confused with the Mohawks' near neighbors, the Mahicans.

19. *JR* 60:177 (first quote); *JR* 58:171–77; quotes: 173–75.

20. Richter, *Ordeal of the Longhouse*, 130–32.

21. For general accounts of the origins and growth of La Prairie and Kahnawake, see especially John Demos, *The Unredeemed Captive: A Family Story from Early America* (New York: Knopf, 1994), 120–39 and throughout; Gerald F. Reid, *Kahnawà:ke: Factionalism, Traditionalism, and Nationalism in a Mohawk Community* (Lincoln: University of Nebraska Press, 2004), 1–15 and following.

22. "Kahnawake" is a modern, alternate spelling of "Caughnawaga." Scholars generally designated the St. Lawrence Valley town by the latter spelling until recently, but Mohawk speakers have argued for the former spelling as a more accurate rendering of the Mohawk word. The modern reserve community uses the former spelling, and I follow their example. I have designated the seventeenth-century Mohawk Valley town "Caughnawaga" and the St. Lawrence Valley mission community "Kahnawake" to differentiate them clearly.

23. Richter, *Ordeal of the Longhouse*, 114–20. The most famous convert of the mid-1670s was Catherine (or Kateri) Tekakwitha, who was beatified by the Catholic Church in 1980 and remains a candidate for canonization. See especially Allan Greer, *Mohawk Saint: Catherine Tekakwitha and the Jesuits* (New York: Oxford University Press, 2005), and Nancy Shoemaker, "Kateri Tekakwitha's Tortuous Path to Sainthood," in Shoemaker, ed., *Negotiators of Change: Historical Perspectives on Native American Women* (New York: Routledge, 1995), 49–71.

24. For Andros's life and career, see Mary Lou Lustig, *The Imperial Executive in America: Sir Edmund Andros, 1637–1714* (Madison, NJ: Fairleigh Dickinson University Press, 2002). As the imperious governor of the Dominion of New England, Andros earned the hatred of many colonists later in his career. For the Mohawks, though, he was a strong ally and partner during his years in New York.

25. Sir John Werden, Secretary to the Duke of York, to Governor Andros, 15 Sept. 1675, and Werden to Andros, 31 Aug. 1676, *DRCNY* 3:232–34, 238–40; quote: 238.

26. See especially Richter, *Ordeal of the Longhouse*, 133–44. Richard L. Haan has argued that although events of the 1670s laid important groundwork, the Covenant Chain proper was not forged until the 1680s; see Haan, "Covenant and Consensus: Iroquois and English, 1676–1760," in Daniel K. Richter and James H. Merrell, eds., *Beyond the Covenant Chain: The Iroquois and Their Neighbors in Indian North America, 1600–1800* (University Park, PA: Penn State University Press, 2003), 41–57.

27. Richter, *Ordeal of the Longhouse*, 135–36. For the war more generally, see especially Jenny Hale Pulsipher, *Subjects unto the Same King: Indians, English, and the Contest for Authority in Colonial New England* (Philadelphia: University of Pennsylvania Press, 2005), 101–237; Jill Lepore, *The Name of War: King Philip's War and the Origins of American Identity* (New York: Knopf, 1998); and James D. Drake, *King Philip's War: Civil War in New England, 1675–1676* (Amherst: University of Massachusetts Press, 2000).

28. Richter, *Ordeal of the Longhouse*, 135–36.

29. Ibid., 136.

30. *LIR* 42–52; Richter, *Ordeal of the Longhouse*, 137–38.

31. Letter of Father Jean de Lamberville, 25 Aug. 1682, Assembly held at Québec . . . 10 Oct. 1682, and Letter of Claude Chaucetiere, 14 Oct. 1682, *JR* 60:71, 159–61, 185.

32. *DRCNY* 3:559.

33. Sivertsen, *Turtles, Wolves, and Bears*, 22–23; Fenton, *Great Law and the Longhouse*, 194, 369–72.

34. *DRCNY* 3:557–61.

35. For Andros, the Iroquois alliance, and the significance of the name "Father Corlaer," see Francis Jennings, *The Ambiguous Iroquois Empire: The Covenant Chain Confederation of Indian Tribes with English Colonies from Its Beginnings to the Lancaster Treaty of 1744* (New York: Norton, 1984), 193–94; quotes: *DRCNY* 3:558–59.

36. For context, see David S. Lovejoy, *The Glorious Revolution in America* (New York: Harper and Row, 1972).

37. *LIR* 147; Richter, *Ordeal of the Longhouse*, 159–66.

38. Sivertsen, *Turtles, Wolves, and Bears*, 22–26. Sivertsen places these baptisms in North Albany, or Schaghticoke, but that congregation was not established until 1714. See the entry for Schaghticoke, *CASHP*, accessed 6 July 2006.

39. Richter, *Ordeal of the Longhouse,* 165; Sivertsen, *Turtles, Wolves, and Bears,* 7–8; quotes: Jaspar Dankers and Peter Sluyter, *Journal of a Voyage to New York and a Tour in Several of the American Colonies in 1679–80,* in *Memoirs of the Long Island Historical Society,* vol. 1 (Brooklyn, 1867), 301, 315.

40. Dankers, *Journal of a Voyage,* 301–4; Sivertsen, *Turtles, Wolves, and Bears,* 7–9.

41. Dankers, *Journal of a Voyage,* 306–10; quote: 302.

42. Ibid., 312–313.

43. Richter, *Ordeal of the Longhouse,* 178.

44. Diana S. Waite, ed., *Albany Architecture* (Albany: Mount Ida Press, 1993), 27–28. See also the Tantillo diagram, drawn in 1985 to represent the town in 1686, and accompanying materials, *CASHP,* accessed 30 Aug. 2006.

45. On the traditional distinction between sachems, or peace chiefs, and war chiefs, see, e.g., Fenton, *Great Law and the Longhouse,* 7 and following. For Hendrick as raider, see *DRCNY* 4:346.

46. Richter, *Ordeal of the Longhouse,* 166.

47. "Propositions of Christian Mohawks to Gov. Sloughter," 26 May 1691, *DRCNY* 3:771–72.

48. *DRCNY* 4:14–24; Richter, *Ordeal of the Longhouse,* 172–74.

49. Sivertsen, *Turtles, Wolves, and Bears,* 42, 32.

50. Ibid., 37–42.

51. Fletcher's Commission and Instructions, 10 Aug. 1696, *DRCNY* 4:177–78.

52. For intelligence see, e.g., "Report brought from Oneyda by Joseph, a Mohawk Indian," 2 Dec. 1693, and Dellius to Fletcher, 24 May 1695, *DRCNY* 4:77–78, 125; for the trip by Hendrick and Tjerk to Canada, *DRCNY* 4:279–82, 9:665–66.

53. "Report of the Board of Trade on New York's Affairs," 19 Oct. 1698, *DRCNY* 4:391–93.

54. Gary B. Nash, "The Quest for the Susquehanna Valley: New York, Pennsylvania, and the Seventeenth-century Fur Trade," *New York History* 48 (1967): 3–27.

55. Gov. Fletcher's speech to the Five Nations, 18 Sept. 1795, *WAIA* 27.

56. *DRCNY* 4:332–45; 2:73–74; 3:636–48. For context, see Patricia U. Bonomi, *A Factious People: Politics and Society in Colonial New York* (New York: Columbia University Press, 1971), 45–56, 5–77; Michael Kammen, *Colonial New York: A History* (New York: Oxford University Press, 1975), 118–27; and Richter, *Ordeal of the Longhouse,* 164–66.

57. Bellomont's charges were presented in a series of documents. His most detailed accusation against Dellius has been lost, but for the surviving texts see the complaint against Fletcher dated 28 Nov. 1698 in *DRCNY* 4:433–34 and his characterizations of Dellius in *DRCNY* 4:362–66, 488–90, 533–34. For Fletcher's response to Bellomont's charges, dated 24 Dec. 1698, see *DRCNY* 4: 443–51; and for a reply, *DRCNY* 4:462–63. Dellius's defense, dated 31 Oct. 1700, is printed in *ERSNY* 2:1394–1422; see esp. 1402–3.

58. *DRCNY* 4:345–47.

59. Fletcher's response, 24 Dec. 1698, *DRCNY* 4: 443–51; Dellius's defense, 31 Oct. 1700, *ERSNY* 2:1394–1422; quote: 1403.

60. The testimonials are printed in *ERSNY* 2:1305–26; the recantation appears in *ERSNY* 2:1318 and *DRCNY* 4:539.

61. *DRCNY* 4:539–41. This quotation and the following one have been modernized to make their sense clear to the reader.

62. *DRCNY* 4:541. Dellius's opening question—"Do you love me?"—echoes the question Christ asked Simon Peter (John 21:15–17) and highlights the emphasis on Christian love that was characteristic of the Christian Mohawk community at Tiononderoge.

63. *DRCNY* 4:182–83, 337–38, 648, 730–31; Sivertsen, *Turtles, Wolves, and Bears*, 49.

64. *DRCNY* 4:727–46.

65. *DRCNY* 4:730–31.

66. *DRCNY* 4:742–43.

67. *DRCNY* 4:743. Hendrick was correct that Bellomont had written to ask that the grants be vacated by the Crown; Bellomont also persuaded the New York Assembly to invalidate the grants. Fletcher and the grantees had powerful allies at court, however, and the Board of Trade dodged the subject in their communications with the governor and stalled on making any recommendation to the king. Among other things, they complained that they had never received exact copies of the titles in question. How, they wondered, could they recommend that the king vacate titles they had never seen? The issue remained unresolved at Bellomont's death and, despite the Assembly's action, Fletcher's grants were never vacated by the Crown. For Bellomont's pleas to the Board of Trade see, e.g., his letter dated 28 Nov. 1700, *DRCNY* 4:781–97. For the Board of Trade's response, see their letter to Bellomont, 29 Apr. 1701, *DRCNY* 4:852–57, esp. 853.

68. See Bellomont's instructions to Romer, 3 Sept. 1700, *DRCNY* 4:750–51; Romer's account of the visit, 5 Oct. 1700, *DRCNY* 4:798–801; the journal of

Hansen and Van Brugh, [n.d.], *DRCNY* 4:802–07; and Bellomont to the Lords of Trade, *DRCNY* 4:781–97, quote: 783.

69. For the timber trade generally, see Robert Albion, *Forests and Sea Power: The Timber Problem of the Royal Navy, 1652–1862* (Cambridge, MA: Harvard University Press, 1926), and Michael Williams, *Americans and Their Forests: An Historical Geography* (New York: Cambridge University Press, 1989). For Bellomont's plan see Bellomont to the Lords of the Treasury, 23 Nov. 1700, *DRCNY* 4:775–78, esp. 776.

70. For Dellius's charge, see *ERSNY* 2:1416–17; Bellomont to the Lords of the Admiralty, 23 Nov. 1700, *DRCNY* 4:779–81; quote: 779–80. Bellomont's sensitivity to lawyers was due to the fact that the grants to Dellius, Schuyler, and their associates had not yet been vacated by the Crown, which would allow them to argue that any timber cut on those lands belonged to them.

71. Bellomont to the Lords of Trade, 16 Jan. 1701, *DRCNY* 4:833–34; deed enclosed in *CSP* 1701, item no. 38:33–37, IIDH reel 6, 16 Jan. 1701.

72. Bellomont to Lords of Trade, 17 Oct. 1700 and Memorial of Henry and Cornelius, 7 Oct. 1700, *DRCNY* 4:715, 758–59.

73. Bellomont to the Lords of Trade, 16 Jan. 1701, *DRCNY* 4:834.

74. Richter, *Ordeal of the Longhouse*, 195; Brandão, *"Your fyre shall burne no more,"* 120–21.

75. Cadwallader Colden, *The History of the Five Indian Nations Depending on the Province of New-York in America* (London, 1747; reprint, Ithaca: Cornell University Press, 1958), 140.

76. *DRCNY* 4:693–95, 9:715–20; Richter, *Ordeal of the Longhouse*, 190–207.

77. For Bellomont's death see *DRCNY* 4:848–51. For the vacuum of leadership, see, e.g., "Four of the Council of New-York to the Lords of Trade," 10 Mar. 1701, *DRCNY* 4:850–51, "Three of the Council" to same, 30 Apr. and 5 May 1701, *DRCNY* 4:857–63, 867–69, and Robert Livingston to the Lords of Trade, 13 May 1701, *DRCNY* 4:870–79. Bellomont's twenty-four masts were eventually shipped to England, at a cost of nearly £600 plus transportation; see Cornbury to the Lords of Trade, 29 Sept. 1702, *DRCNY* 4: 975–76.

78. Journal of Bleeker and Schuyler, 2 June 1701, *DRCNY* 4:889–95.

79. *DRCNY* 4:893. The second quotation has been modernized to make its sense clear to the reader.

80. Anthony F. C. Wallace, "Origins of Iroquois Neutrality: The Grand Settlement of 1701," *Pennsylvania History* 24 (1957); 223–35. The Montreal conference, known as the "Great Peace," was one of the great public events of the colonial

era. It is ably analyzed in Gilles Havard, *The Great Peace of Montreal in 1701: French-Native Diplomacy in the Seventeenth Century*, trans. Phyllis Aronoff and Howard Scott (Montreal: McGill-Queen's University Press, 2001).

81. Proceedings: *DRCNY* 4:896–908; quotes: 901.

82. Proceedings: *DRCNY,* 4:896–908; deed: *DRCNY* 4:908–11. The original of the deed (a detail of which appears as Figure 2) is in CO5/1046-758; for its rediscovery in 2002 and variations from the printed text, see José António Brandão and William A. Starna, "'Some things may slip out of your memory and be forgott': The 1701 Deed and Map of Iroquois Hunting Territory Revisited," *New York History* 86 (Fall 2005): 417–33.

83. Richter, *Ordeal of the Longhouse*, 208; quote: *DRCNY* 4:908.

2. Odyssey

1. *Dawks's News Letter*, 29 Apr. 1710, quoted in Richmond P. Bond, *Queen Anne's American Kings* (Oxford: Clarendon Press, 1952), 7; for Moorfields and Bishopsgate, see, e.g., Tim Harris, *London Crowds in the Reign of Charles II* (Cambridge: Cambridge University Press, 1987), 82, 148, 191–94, 203–4.

2. The kings' names and titles were printed with many small variations; I have followed the inscriptions on the mezzotints produced by John Faber, Sr. The trip to England is discussed in detail below. For the interpretation of Brant's name, see William Fenton, *The Great Law and the Longhouse: A Political History of the Iroquois Confederacy* (Norman: University of Oklahoma Press, 1998), 372, and Barbara J. Sivertsen, *Turtles, Wolves, and Bears: A Mohawk Family History* (Bowie, MD: Heritage Books, 1996), 64.

3. The crowns of England and Scotland were formally united by the Act of Union in 1707, which created the nation of Great Britain; thereafter, it makes sense to think of the empire as British rather than English, particularly since so many of its administrators in the colonies were themselves of Scottish origins. I have used the term "English" to refer to the period before 1707 and the term "British" thereafter.

4. *DRCNY* 4:928, 977, 920.

5. Daniel K. Richter, "'Some of them . . . would always have a minister with them': Mohawk Protestantism, 1683–1719," *American Indian Quarterly* 16 (1992): 471–84; quote: 475.

6. Thomas Elliot Norton, *The Fur Trade in Colonial New York, 1686–1776* (Madison: University of Wisconsin Press, 1974), 27–59.

7. Conference of Lord Cornbury with the Indians, 9 July–19 August, 1702, *DRCNY* 4:978–999; quotes: 987.

8. Cornbury did not return to Albany until September 1706; thereafter, he preferred fall visits to summer, limited his stay to two weeks or less, and more than once instructed the Indians to deal with the Albany commissioners because he had pressing business elsewhere. See *WAIA* 48, 50, 55–63.

9. G. M. Waller, *Samuel Vetch, Colonial Enterpriser* (Chapel Hill, NC: University of North Carolina Press, 1960), 94–120; Vetch and Nicholson to Sunderland, 28 June 1709, *CSP* 24:399–406. The proclamation by Nicholson and Vetch calling for volunteers was issued from Boston on 9 May 1709; a copy can be found at the John Carter Brown Library at Brown University, Providence. The Indian warriors included 150 Mohawks, 105 Oneidas, 100 Cayugas, 88 Onondagas, and 60 Mahicans; see *WAIA* 69.

10. On the decision to divert the fleet see Godolphin to Marlborough, 31 May 1709 and 20 Apr. 1710 and accompanying notes, in Henry L. Snyder, ed., *The Marlborough-Godolphin Correspondence*, 3 vols. (Oxford: Oxford University Press, 1975), 3:1269, 1467–68; for colonial expenses, CO5/9, 120; for the Congress of Governors, which met in Oct. 1709, see CO5/9, 115–16; Bond, *Queen Anne's American Kings*, 40–42.

11. For a brief sketch, see "Pieter Schuyler," *CASHP*, accessed 7 July 2007; "Colden's Letters on Smith's History," 1759, in *New York Historical Society Collections* (1868), 1:199, cited in Patricia U. Bonomi, *A Factious People: Politics and Society in Colonial New York* (New York: Columbia University Press, 1971), 50 n. 49; Anne Grant, *Memoirs of an American Lady: With Sketches of Manners and Scenery in America, As They Existed Previous to the Revolution* (New York: George Dearborn, 1836; reprint, Bedford, MA: Applewood Books, n.d.), 75; Daniel K. Richter, *The Ordeal of the Longhouse: The Peoples of the Iroquois League in the Era of European Colonization* (Chapel Hill: University of North Carolina Press, 1992), 164.

12. Sivertsen, *Turtles, Wolves, and Bears*, 62–66; *DRCNY* 3:800–85.

13. For the differences between Whigs and Tories in war aims see especially Geoffrey Holmes, *British Politics in the Age of Anne* (New York: Macmillan 1967), 71–75; for blue-water foreign policy in a broader perspective see Daniel A. Baugh, "Great Britain's 'Blue-Water' Policy, 1689–1815," *International History Review* 10 (1988): 33–58; for Anne's turn toward the Tories see W. A. Speck, *The Birth of Britain: A New Nation, 1700–1710* (Oxford: Blackwell, 1994), 176–92.

14. This version of their titles follows the Bernard Lens engraving. Quote: Richard Steele, *The Tatler*, no. 171, quoted in Bond, *Queen Anne's American Kings*, 79.

For Covent Garden, see Peter Thorold, *The London Rich: The Creation of a Great City, from 1666 to the Present* (New York: St. Martin's Press, 1999), 23–24, 102.

15. "Thomas Augustine Arne," in Leslie Stephen, ed., *Dictionary of National Biography* (London: Smith, Elder & Co., 1885), 2:104–7, quote: 105; Alden T. Vaughan, *Transatlantic Encounters: American Indians in Britain, 1500–1776* (New York: Cambridge University Press, 2006), 142.

16. William Smith, Jr., *The History of the Province of New-York* (1757), ed. Michael Kammen, 2 vols. (Cambridge, MA: Harvard University Press, 1972), 1:136. Although Smith's account was not contemporaneous, he had a wide array of printed and manuscript sources at his disposal. This passage, like much of Smith's text, appears verbatim in *The History of the British Dominions in North America* (London: W. Strahan, and T. Becket and Co., 1773), 37.

17. On the tendency to associate outsiders with the Middle East and the Orient in this period, see Troy Bickham, *Savages within the Empire: Representations of American Indians in Eighteenth-century Britain* (Oxford: Clarendon Press, 2005), 22–28; and, more generally, Linda Colley, *Captives* (New York: Pantheon Books, 2002), 23–134, and Brian Cowan, *Social Life of Coffee: The Emergence of the British Coffeehouse* (New Haven: Yale University Press, 2005), 115–32.

18. [Abel Boyer], *The History of the Reign of Queen Anne. Digested into Annals. Year the Ninth* (London, 1711), 9:189. For Cotterell, see Stephen, ed., *Dictionary of National Biography*, 12:291; for Shrewsbury, 55:301–7.

19. Smith, *History of the Province of New-York*, 1:136; Zacharias Conrad von Uffenbach, *London in 1710: From the Travels of Z. C. von Uffenbach*, trans. and ed. W. H. Quarrell and Margaret Mare (London: Faber and Faber, 1934), 104.

20. [Boyer], *Annals*, 9:189–92.

21. Ibid., 9:191; Bond, *Queen Anne's American Kings* (quoting Dickson's *Dublin Intelligence*, 29 Apr. 1710), 12–13; Narcissus Luttrell, *A Brief Historical Relation of State Affairs from September 1678 to April 1714*, 6 vols. (Oxford, 1857), 6:571 (this work is based on a manuscript chronicle written at the time of the visit); [Anon.], *The Four Kings of Canada* (London, 1710), 6.

22. The best discussion of these portraits is Bruce Robertson, "The Portraits: An Iconographical Study," in John G. Garratt, *The Four Indian Kings / Les Quatre Rois Indiens* (Ottawa: Public Archives of Canada, 1985), 139–77. For Kensington Palace, see von Uffenbach, *London in 1710*, 156–58.

23. Luttrell, *Brief Historical Relation*, 6:572; von Uffenbach, *London in 1710*, 20–22; [Boyer], *Annals*, 9:191.

24. *The Present State of Europe: Or, the Historical and Political Monthly Mercury* 21 (1710): 157–60; Luttrell, *Brief Historical Relation*, 574. (According to [Boyer], *Annals*, the speech attributed to the kings in Hyde Park was *"Spurious"*; see 9:191.) On Ormonde and Marlborough see Holmes, *British Politics*, 28, and J. R. Jones, *Marlborough* (Cambridge: Cambridge University Press, 1993). Bond, *Queen Anne's American Kings*, 9, and on Montague House (which was opened to the public in 1759 as the British Museum and stood on the site of the present museum) see entry for John Montague, Second Duke of Montague, in Stephen, ed., *Dictonary of National Biography*.

25. SPG meeting minutes, 28 Apr. 1710, RSPGJ 1:478–82; *Dublin Intelligence*, 6 May 1710, cited in Bond, *Queen Anne's American Kings*, 102.

26. [Addison], *Spectator*, no. 50, 27 Apr. 1711, in Donald F. Bond, ed., *The Spectator*, 5 vols. (Oxford: Clarendon Press, 1965), 1:211; *Daily Courant*, 24, 25, 29 Apr. and 2 May 1710; handbill for Punch's Theatre reproduced in Bond, *Queen Anne's American Kings*, facing p. 4.

27. Two travelers' accounts that provide a useful point of comparison for the kings' visit are von Uffenbach, *London in 1710*; quote: 48, and César de Saussure, *Letters from London, 1725–1730*, trans. Paul Scott (n.p.: Adnax, 2006); quote: 167. Each of them visited the theater frequently and attended both a cockfight and a contest at Hockley-in-the-Hole. (Neither, however, mentions Powell's puppet shows.) The visit of the three kings to the theater on 24 April is noted in H. Isham Longden, "The Diaries (Home and Foreign) of Sir Justinian Isham, 1704–1736," *Transactions of the Royal Society*, 3rd ser., 1 (1907): 199. The anecdote about the kings on stage comes from Arthur Murray, *The Gray's-Inn Journal*, no. 95, 10 Aug. 1754, later collected and published in two volumes (London, 1756); quote: 2:272. It was first recorded more than forty years after the fact, and certain details are inaccurate, but Murphy was well connected in the London theater crowd, where versions of this anecdote may have circulated for many years.

28. De Saussure, *Letters from London*, 60.

29. For the kings's visit to the workhouse, see *Dawks's News Letter*, 29 Apr. 1710, quoted in Bond, *Queen Anne's American Kings*, 7; for Moorfields, see von Uffenbach, *London in 1710*, 52; for the workhouse, see Maureen Waller, *1700: Scenes from London Life* (New York: Four Walls Eight Windows, 2000), 257–60; quote: London, II, Civic and Municipal Institutions, Governors for the Poor, *An Account of the Corporation for the Poor of London; Shewing the Nature, Usefulness, and Management of the Work-House in Bishopsgate Street* (London, 1713), quoted in Waller, *1700*, 260.

30. [Anon.], *Four Kings of Canada*, 6–7. The best discussion of the Verelst portraits is Bruce Robertson, "The Portraits: An Iconographical Study," in Garratt,

The Four Indian Kings, 139–77; this book also includes excellent reproductions of the portraits.

31. [Anon.], *History of the British Dominions*, 37. For an extended analysis of the visit's cultural significance in Britain, see Eric Hinderaker, "The 'Four Indian Kings' and the Imaginative Construction of the First British Empire," *WMQ* 53 (1996): 487–526.

32. *Present State of Europe*, 21:160; [Anon.], *Four Kings of Canada*, 7.

33. Bond, *Queen Anne's American Kings*, 12–15.

34. *DRCNY* 5:217.

35. The principal source for the campaign is Walker's journal, which exists in a manuscript version in CO5 and a published version first printed in 1720. Though they agree in their basic chronology and facts, the entries in each are quite different. See Hovenden Walker, "Journal of the Proceedings of Sir Hovenden Walker," CO 5/9, 17–26, and Sir Hovenden Walker, *A Journal: Or Full Account of the late Expedition to Canada* (London, 1720), 76.

36. Walker, "Journal," entries for 18 and 22 July; Walker, *Journal*, quote: 104–5; Matthew Bishop, *The Life and Adventures of Matthew Bishop* (London, n.d. [1744?], 243–44).

37. Walker, *Journal*, 104–5, 109–10.

38. Ibid., 188–91, 245, 134–42; CO 5/9, 66, 68–69.

39. See, e.g., *A Letter From an Old Whig in Town, to a Modern Whig in the Country, Upon the late Expedition to Canada* (London, [1711]); [Jeremiah Dummer], *A Letter to a Friend in the Country, on the Late Expedition to Canada: With An Account of former Enterprizes, a Defence of that Design, and the Share the Late M——rs had in it* (London, 1712). Thomas Jefferys, *Directions for Navigating the Gulf and River of St. Lawrence* (London, 1760).

40. CO 5/9, 160; *DRCNY* 5:278–79.

41. Peter Kalm, *Travels into North America . . .*, trans. John Reinhold Forster, 3 vols. (Warrington and London, 1770–71), 2:304–5.

42. *DRCNY* 5:279–81, 349, 358; David Baldwin, *The Chapel Royal, Ancient and Modern* (London: Duckworth, 1990), 56–57.

43. Richter, *Ordeal of the Longhouse*, 228–31.

44. Ibid., 230–32; Sivertsen, *Turtles, Wolves, and Bears*, 88.

45. Richter, *Ordeal of the Longhouse*, 232–34.

46. See especially Philip Otterness, *Becoming German: The 1709 Palatine Migration to New York* (Ithaca: Cornell University Press, 2004).

47. Ibid., 78–88; Robert Hunter to Board of Trade, 14 Mar. 1712/13, CO 5/1085, 21–23.

48. New York Council Minutes, 13 July 1710, 10:528–29, NYSA, IIDH reel 7.

49. New York Council Minutes, 20 July 1710, 10:529–30, NYSA, IIDH reel 7; Otterness, *Becoming German*, 88.

50. Reverend Andrews introduced to Mohawks, 14 Nov. 1712, *DHNY* 3:542–43.

51. New York Council Minutes, 10 Apr 1714, 11:235–36, NYSA, IIDH reel 8; *DRCNY* 4:978–79; AO272 9:23; Paul A. W. Wallace, *Conrad Weiser: Friend of Colonist and Mohawk* (Philadelphia: University of Pennsylvania Press, 1945), 14–18.

52. Robert Hunter to Board of Trade, 14 Mar. 1712/13, CO 5/1085 21–23.

53. Hunter to Board of Trade, 12 Mar. 1712/13, CO5/1050, 452–55; compare with *DRCNY* 3:542–43.

54. New York Council Minutes, 10 and 22 Apr. 1714, 11:235–36, NYSA, IIDH reel 8; Albany County Clerk's Office Deed Book, 15 June 1717, 5:370–71, IIDH reel 8.

55. *DRCNY* 5:569; *LIR* 215.

56. These episodes are detailed in Spotswood to President of the Council of New York, 25 Jan. 1719/20, and Keith to President of the Council of New York, 19 July 1720, *MPCP* 3:82–89, 99–100.

57. Minutes of the Board of Trade respecting New York and Virginia, 7 July 1720, *DRCNY* 5:548–49; Spotswood to President, 25 Jan. 1719/20, and Keith to President, 19 July 1720, *MPCP* 3:89, 99–102.

58. Minutes of the Commissioners of Indian Affairs, 6 July 1719; Colonel Schuyler to the Lords of Trade, 9 June 1720, and encl.: Journal of Myndert Schuyler and Robert Livingston, Jr., from Albany to the Senecas, 3 June 1720; Robert Livingston to Peter Schuyler, 23 Aug. 1720, *DRCNY* 5:528–29, 541–45, 559–61.

59. The principal contemporary account of the war is Samuel Penhallow, *The History of the Wars of New-England, With the Eastern Indians . . .* (Boston, 1726). For the English settlement of the region, see Charles E. Clark, *The Eastern Frontier: The Settlement of Northern New England, 1610–1763* (New York: Knopf, 1970); for the Wabanakis, see Christopher J. Bilodeau, "The Economy of War: Violence, Religion, and the Wabanaki Indians in the Maine Borderlands" (Ph. D. diss., Cornell University, 2006); and for Dummer's War, as the fighting from 1722-27 is known, see Richter, *Ordeal of the Longhouse*, 244–46.

60. For Spotswood, see Leonidas Dodson, *Alexander Spotswood: Governor of Colonial Virginia, 1710–1722* (Philadelphia: University of Pennsylvania Press, 1932), 3–5, and Walter Havighurst, *Alexander Spotswood: Portrait of a Governor* (New York: Holt, Rinehart, and Winston, 1967), 3–5; for Burnet (a protégé of his predecessor, Robert Hunter), see Mary Lou Lustig, *Robert Hunter, 1666–1734: New York's Augus-*

tan Statesman (Syracuse, NY: Syracuse University Press, 1983), 162–63. For Keith, see his entry by Mary Rhinelander McCarl, in John A. Garraty and Mark C. Carnes, eds., *American National Biography* (New York: Oxford University Press, 1999), 12:465–66.

61. *DRCNY* 5:657–58.

62. *DRCNY* 5:664–81.

63. *DRCNY* 5:668.

64. *DRCNY* 5:660.

65. *New-England Courant*, published by James and Benjamin Franklin 1721–26, reproduced in photostat in the Massachusetts Historical Society (Boston, 1924–25), nos. 51–54, July–Aug. 1722. Penhallow, *Wars of New-England*, offers a few additional details about the sachems' time in Boston, including a ceremonial exchange of gifts with the lieutenant governor and the spectacle of the Indians killing an ox with bows and arrows: 97–98.

66. This paragraph and those that follow are based on the "Journall of the proceedings of the Commissioners Approved by his Excellency the Governour and Council to Attend the Delegates of the Six Nations Eastward," 10–27 Oct. 1722, MA 29:75–98.

67. *New-England Courant*, no. 66, 29 Oct.–5 Nov. 1722, and no. 68, 12–19 Nov. 1722.

68. Commissioners to Governor Burnet, 9 Jan. 1723, MACIA 1:4a–5a.

69. Minutes of a meeting between the Massachusetts commissioners and the Six Nations, Albany, 23 May–4 June 1723, MA 29:105–30; quote: 124; "Alexander Hamilton's relation . . . whilst he was a prisoner at Canada," 7 Dec. 1723, *CSP*, 1722–23, 407–15; conference proceedings, 14–20 Sept. 1724, *DRCNY* 5:713–25.

70. Richter, *Ordeal of the Longhouse*, 244–46.

71. New York Council Minutes, 12 Sept. 1733, 16:253–54, NYSA, IIDH reel 10.

72. Edith M. Fox, *Land Speculation in the Mohawk Country*, Cornell Studies in American History, Literature, and Folklore no. 3 (Ithaca: Cornell University Press, 1949), 16–17; A0272 10:122, 10:155.

73. Fox, *Land Speculation*, 18–20; A0272 11:60–61.

74. *DRCNY* 5:962–70.

75. New York Council Minutes, 12 Sept. 1733, 16:253–54, NYSA, IIDH reel 10.

76. A0272 11:66. Though Edith Fox originally mapped out these transactions with penetrating insight, she gives the wrong date for this transaction, and also misses the fact that the deed grants 150,000 acres, rather than 86,000, to the Crown. See Fox, *Land Speculation*, 20.

77. Petition to King George II, 12 Dec. 1734, Calvert Papers, MS 174, no. 1093, Maryland Historical Society, Baltimore, IIDH reel 10.

78. AO272 11:161, 162, 163, 164, 168, 173, 175, 189; 12:86 (additional grants from the Butler tract can be found in 12:85, 12:90, 13:6, and 13:23).

79. Sivertsen, *Turtles, Wolves, and Bears,* 119, 24; *DRCNY* 5:963; meeting of the Albany commissioners, 8 Apr. 1735, MACIA 2:61. A conference in June 1737 was delayed while its participants "Condole[d] the Death of the two sachems who lately Dyed"; one of these may have been Hendrick. *DRCNY* 6:99.

3. Hendrick's War

1. Conference between Commissioners of the Colonies and the Indians, 5–14 Oct. 1745, *DRCNY* 6:289–305; quote: 289.

2. *DRCNY* 6:297–98.

3. *DRCNY* 6:292–93.

4. *DRCNY* 6:293.

5. For the role of wonder in early modern accounts of the Americas see Stephen Greenblatt, *Marvelous Possessions: The Wonder of the New World* (Chicago: University of Chicago Press, 1991), especially 79–82.

6. The rapid growth of a cheap, fantastic travel literature in late seventeenth-century England is a complex topic in its own right. It required the creation of new printing methods and practices and the elaboration of marketing networks that distributed literature widely within London and also carried it efficiently to the provinces. One author and bookseller who specialized in this literature, Nathaniel Crouch, produced a wide array of inexpensive books in the late seventeenth and early eighteenth centuries that purported to open to their readers a wider world. These included a sensational biography of Francis Drake, which ran through at least six editions in London and on the continent; a survey of the English empire in America, presented under the pseudonym Richard Burton, which went through at least five editions in London and Belfast; an account of the trip of fourteen Englishmen to Jerusalem, which passed through at least three editions in London, Boston, and Hartford; and a text entitled *Miracles of Art & Nature,* which surveyed the "Several Varieties of Birds, Beasts, Fishes, Plants, and Fruits of Other Countries." On the emergence of trade publishing, which permitted the rapid dissemination of cheap texts, see Michael Treadwell, "London Trade Publishers, 1675–1750," *Library,* 6th ser., 4 (June 1982): 99–134.

7. [Anon.], *The Four Kings of Canada: Being a Succinct Account of the Four Indian Princes lately Arriv'd from North America* (London, 1710), 8–9.

8. [Anon.], *Four Kings of Canada*, 10.

9. Thomas Harriot, *A Briefe and True Report of the New Found Land of Virginia* (Frankfurt, 1590); John Smith, *The Generall Historie of Virginia, New-England, and the Summer Isles* . . . (London, 1624); William Wood, *New England's Prospect* (London, 1634); John Josselyn, *New England's Rarities Discovered* (London, 1672); Josselyn, *An Account of Two Voyages to New-England* (London, 1674); quotes: 125. Influential French accounts included Gabriel Sagard-Théodat, *Le grand voyage du pays de Hurons* (1632), and *Histoire du Canada* (1636), and Louis-Armand de Lom d'Arce, Baron de Lahontan, *Nouveaux voyages* . . . *dans l'Amérique Septentrionale* (The Hague, 1702–3), an English translation of which was published in 1703. For an extended comparison of French and English texts, see Gordon M. Sayre, *Les Sauvages Américains: Representations of Native Americans in French and English Colonial Literature* (Chapel Hill, NC: University of North Carolina Press, 1997).

10. Cadwallader Colden, *The History of the Five Indian Nations Depending on the Province of New-York in America* (New York, 1727; reprint, Ithaca: 1958), 3–15. For Colden's biography, see Alice Mapelsden Keys, *Cadwallader Colden: A Representative Eighteenth-century Official* (New York: Columbia University Press, 1906), and Alfred R. Hoerman, *Cadwallader Colden: A Figure of the American Enlightenment* (Westport, CT: Greenwood Press, 2002). For his connection to Hunter, see Mary Lou Lustig, *Robert Hunter, 1666–1734: New York's Augustan Statesman* (Syracuse, NY: Syracuse University Press, 1983), 10, 144–47; and Ned C. Landsman, "Introduction: The Context and Functions of Scottish Involvement with the Americas," in Landsman, ed., *Nation and Province in the First British Empire: Scotland and the Americas, 1600–1800* (London: Associated University Presses, 2001), 23–24.

11. Colden, *History of the Five Indian Nations*, xxi, xvii, xx, xvii.

12. John Witherspoon, Francis Alison, and William Smith were especially important to the elaboration of Hutcheson's philosophy in British America; see Ned C. Landsman, "The Legacy of British Union for the North American Colonies: Provincial Elites and the Problem of Imperial Union," in John Robertson, ed., *A Union for Empire: Political Thought and the British Union of 1707* (Cambridge: Cambridge University Press, 1995), 311–17; and Peter J. Diamond, "Witherspoon, Smith and the Scottish Philosophy in Revolutionary America," in Richard Sher and Jeffrey Smitten, eds., *Scotland and America in the Age of Enlightenment* (Princeton: Princeton University Press, 1990), 115–32.

13. Colden, *History of the Five Indian Nations*, x–xi. For the views of Enlightenment writers on Indian speech see Edward Gray, *New World Babel: Languages and Nations in Early America* (Princeton: Princeton University Press, 1999).

14. A revised and expanded edition was published twenty years later in London, in the midst of another war with France, that doubled the length of the narrative by taking the story to the Treaty of Ryswick in 1697 and included a set of documents to illustrate Indian relations: Cadwallader Colden, *The History of the Five Indian Nations of Canada, Which are dependent On the Province of New-York in America, and Are the Barrier between the English and the French in that Part of the World* (London, 1747), reprinted (without the documentary appendix) as pt. 2 of Colden, *History of the Five Indian Nations*. A third edition, published in 1755, included additional material from King George's War; see n. 62 below.

15. Alden T. Vaughan, *Transatlantic Encounters: American Indians in Britain, 1500–1776* (New York: Cambridge University Press, 2006), 137–50.

16. Council of Trade to Duke of Newcastle, 20 Aug. 1730, CO 5/4 198–99. Vaughan correctly notes that the treaty of 1730 delivered much more to the Crown than it did to the Cherokees, who were expected to exclude French and Spanish traders from their communities and return runaway slaves to the colony. The treaty, moreover, implied that the king of Great Britain controlled Cherokee territory and granted them the privilege of living on it. See *Transatlantic Encounters*, 146–47.

17. Vaughan, *Transatlantic Encounters*, 150–64.

18. *DRCNY* 6:172–79; George Clarke to the Lords of Trade, 15 Dec. 1741, *DRCNY* 6:206–9, quote: 208.

19. Jean Lunn, "The Illegal Fur Trade out of New France, 1713–60," in *Report of the Annual Meeting of the Canadian Historical Society* (Toronto: University of Toronto Press, 1939), 61–76.

20. *WAIA* 141; Beauharnois to Maurepas, 21 Sept. 1741, *DRCNY* 9:1071.

21. Thomas Elliot Norton, *The Fur Trade in Colonial New York, 1686–1776* (Madison: University of Wisconsin Press, 1974), 152–73; Edith M. Fox, *Land Speculation in the Mohawk Country*, Cornell Studies in American History, Literature, and Folklore no. 3 (Ithaca: Cornell University Press, 1949), 13–14.

22. Fox, *Land Speculation*, 28.

23. Clarke to Secretary Popple, 28 May 1736; Clarke to Newcastle, 26 July 1736, *DRCNY* 6:59–62, 71–72; quotes: 72, 61.

24. Fox, *Land Speculation*, 28–50.

25. Meeting of the commissioners, 11 Feb. 1732, MACIA 1:352a–353.

26. Meeting of the commissioners, 24 Apr. 1732, MACIA 1:355a–356a.

27. Meeting of the commissioners, 26 June 1732, MACIA 2:5–11.

28. Meeting of the commissioners, 24 Nov. 1731, MACIA 1:350a–351.

29. A0272 11:188, 12:87.

30. Meeting of the commissioners, 3 Oct. 1741, MACIA 2:216a.

31. Milton W. Hamilton, *Sir William Johnson: Colonial American, 1715–1763* (Port Washington, NY: Kennikat Press, 1976), 6; Clarke to Newcastle, 12 June 1736, *DRCNY* 6:65–66.

32. Fox, *Land Speculation*, 47; Hamilton, *William Johnson*, 8–9.

33. William Johnson to Peter Warren, 10 May 1739, *PSWJ* 1:4–7; Hamilton, *William Johnson*, 33–34.

34. Johnson to Warren, 10 May 1739, *PSWJ* 1:4–7; Summons from Commissioners of Indian Affairs, 27 July 1743, *PSWJ* 1:19; Hamilton, *William Johnson*, 15–22.

35. Hamilton, *William Johnson*, 40–41; for an especially evocative, though incomplete and sometimes flawed, portrait of Johnson, see Fintan O'Toole, *White Savage: William Johnson and the Invention of America* (New York: Farrar, Straus and Giroux, 2005).

36. Barbara J. Sivertsen, *Turtles, Wolves, and Bears: A Mohawk Family History* (Bowie, MD: Heritage Books, 1996), 26–27, 144–47. While her effort to reconstruct Hendrick's genealogy is plausible, it is also highly conjectural. It is best to regard this account of Hendrick's parentage as likely but not definitive.

37. John Wolfe Lydekker, *The Faithful Mohawks* (Cambridge: Cambridge University Press, 1938), 54–55; A0272, 13:69.

38. On clothing and comportment, see especially Timothy J. Shannon, "Dressing for Success on the Mohawk Frontier: Hendrick, William Johnson, and the Indian Fashion," *WMQ* 53 (1996): 13–42; for laced hats, fine coats, and ruffled shirts as gifts to sachems, see 37–39, and for the gift of boots and a laced coat to Hendrick, 32. Shannon's otherwise excellent treatment of the subject repeats the assertion of a trip to London in 1740. For a thorough discussion of this claim, see Alden T. Vaughan, "American Indians Abroad: The Mythical Travels of Mrs. Penobscot and King Hendrick," *New England Quarterly* 80 (June 2007): 299–316. Though we have no documentary evidence of a gift of clothes from Johnson to Hendrick until 1746, and Hendrick is first described wearing such attire in 1744, I think it almost certain that Johnson either gave or sold Hendrick a similar suit of clothes prior to his public appearance in 1744.

39. *DRCNY* 6:267.

40. *The Diary of Ebenezer Parkman, 1703–1782*, ed. Francis G. Wallett, pt. 1, *1719–1755* (Worcester, MA: American Antiquarian Society, 1974), 99; "The Journals of Christian Daniel Claus and Conrad Weiser: A Journey to Onondaga, 1750," trans. and ed. Helga Doblin and William A. Starna, *Transactions of the American Philosophi-*

cal Society 84, pt. 2 (Philadelphia: American Philosophical Society, 1994), 17; *Diary of Ebenezer Parkman,* 100.

41. See the biographies of Jacob and Johannes Wendell and Elsie Staats Wendell Schuyler, *CASHP,* accessed 6 June 2008.

42. J. E. A. Smith, *The Poet among the Hills: Oliver Wendell Holmes in Berkshire* (Pittsfield, MA: George Blatchford, 1895), 69–74; J. E. A. Smith, *The History of Pittsfield (Berkshire County) Massachusetts, from the Year 1734 to the Year 1800* (Boston: Lee and Shepard, 1869), 69–73 and following.

43. *Diary of Ebenezer Parkman,* 100; Raymond Phineas Stearns, "Joseph Kellogg's Observations on Senex's Map of North America (1710)," *Mississippi Valley Historical Review* 23 (1936): 345.

44. *Boston Weekly News-Letter,* 12 July 1744; Alexander Hamilton, *Gentleman's Progress: The Itinerarium of Dr. Alexander Hamilton,* ed. Carl Bridenbaugh (Chapel Hill, NC: University of North Carolina Press, 1948), 112–13. The Massachusetts Archives contains a sketchy record of the delegation's meeting with the governor prior to their departure for Maine, but no account of the trip itself.

45. Hamilton, *Gentleman's Progress,* 113.

46. *Boston Weekly News-Letter,* 26 July 1744; Hamilton, *Gentleman's Progress,* 112.

47. The official proceedings of the conference, which ran from June 25 to July 4, are in *MPCP* 4:699–737. An especially useful guide is James H. Merrell, ed., *The Lancaster Treaty of 1744 with Related Documents* (Boston: St. Martin's Press, 2008). Quote: Witham Marshe, "Journal of the Treaty Held with the Six Nations, June–July 1744," in Merrell, *Lancaster Treaty,* 111.

48. Eric Hinderaker and Peter C. Mancall, *At the Edge of Empire: The Backcountry in British North America* (Baltimore: Johns Hopkins University Press, 2003), 81–84.

49. Ibid., 84–87; *MPCP* 4:559–86; quotes: 579.

50. *MPCP* 4:735, 726, 730.

51. *MPCP* 4:726. For the efforts of the Ohio Company of Virginia to make good on the cession, see Lois Mulkearn, ed., *George Mercer Papers Relating to the Ohio Company of Virginia in the Darlington Memorial Library* (Pittsburgh: University of Pittsburgh Press, 1954).

52. Lydekker, *Faithful Mohawks,* 55–57.

53. This and the following two paragraphs are based on extracts from Weiser's journal, in Paul A. W. Wallace, *Conrad Weiser: Friend of Colonist and Mohawk, 1696–1760* (Philadelphia: University of Pennsylvania Press, 1945), 226–28.

54. Beauharnois au ministre, 28 Oct. 1745, C11A vol. 83, ff. 102–107v, accessed 8 May 2008; *WAIA* 239–40.

55. *DRCNY* 6:298, 300.

56. Wallace, *Conrad Weiser*, 230–31.

57. For Clinton's woes, see, e.g., his letter to the Duke of Newcastle, 30 Nov. 1745, *DRCNY* 6:312–14. For anti-Dutch sentiments, including Colden's, see, e.g., Patricia U. Bonomi, *A Factious People: Politics and Society in Colonial New York* (New York: Columbia University Press, 1971), 48–55.

58. Clinton to the Duke of Newcastle, 30 Nov. 1745, *DRCNY* 6:305–7; Robert Sanders to William Johnson, 28 Nov. 1745, *PSWJ* 1:42–43; MACIA 2:320–21 (30 Dec. 1745), 2:321A–323A (4 Jan. 1746), 2:324A–327 (6 Jan. 1746), 2:339–41 (25 Feb. 1746), 2:349–50A (29 Mar. 1746).

59. MACIA 2:352A–54 (5 Apr. 1746), 2:356A–58 (12 Apr. 1746); *WAIA* 246.

60. Johnson to John Catherwood, 14 Apr. 1746, *PSWJ* 1:49; MACIA 2:356A–58 (12 Apr. 1746); *WAIA* 248–49 n. 2.

61. Hamilton, *Sir William Johnson*, 51.

62. Cadwallader Colden, *History of the Five Indian Nations . . .* , 3rd ed., 2 vols. (London, 1755), 2:126.

63. Clinton to the Lords of Trade, 3 June 1749, *DRCNY* 6:485–87, quote: 487.

64. Colden, *History*, 3rd ed., 2:121–22, 126, 125.

65. Ibid., 2:127.

66. Ibid., 2:128.

67. MACIA 2:394–96A (19 July 1746); Colden, *History*, 3rd ed., 2:119–23, 145; quotes: 119, 120–21.

68. *DRCNY* 6:319–20.

69. *DRCNY* 6:319, 320.

70. *WAIA* 248 n. 1; *DRCNY* 6:319, 322.

71. Colden, *History*, 3rd ed., 2:142–43 (italics removed from the second quote).

72. Ibid., 2:119, 131, 149, 153; Clinton to Johnson, 16 Sept. 1746, *PSWJ* 1:64.

73. The conflict over pay for the troops in Albany was part of a larger conflict between Clinton and the Assembly; see, e.g., Clinton to Duke of Newcastle, 23 July 1747, and Captains of the Pennsylvania Companies to Clinton, 8 June 1747, *DRCNY* 6:357–58, 375–76.

74. Clinton to Duke of Newcastle, 9 Dec. 1746, and Petition of Mohawk Warriors to Governor Clinton [n.d.], *DRCNY* 6:312–15. The petition refers to Livingston's claim on Onowedage Flats, but later events suggest this was the tract on Canajoharie Flats. See pp. 154, 218.

75. Clinton to Jacob Glen, 30 July 1746, *PSWJ* 1:55–56; Colden, *History*, 3rd ed., 123–25; Lydekker, *Faithful Mohawks*, 59 (Barclay's claim may or may not have been true; the Mohawks traveled to New York to complain about him, so it was in his

interest to cast aspersions on them); meeting of the Albany commissioners, 25 Feb. 1746, MACIA 2:339–41; quote: 339a–40.

76. MACIA 2:402–5 (24 Nov. 1746).

77. Ibid.; "Journal of Occurrences in Canada; 1746, 1747," *DRCNY* 10:89; "Occurrences in Canada . . . 1747–8," *DRCNY* 10:159.

78. Johnson to Clinton, 18 Mar. 1747, and Clinton to Johnson, 25 Mar. 1747, *PSWJ* 1:81, 84; Clinton to the Duke of Newcastle, 9 Dec. 1746, and Petition of Mohawk Warriors to Governor Clinton [n.d.], *DRCNY* 6:312–15.

79. See Johnson's speech of 25 Apr. 1747 and Johnson to Clinton, 7 May 1747, *DRCNY* 6:358–63: quote: 361. A prisoner from Schenectady informed a French commander that Hendrick's party numbered seventy: *DRCNY* 10:105.

80. "Journal . . . 1746, 1747," *DRCNY* 10:91, 97–98; Johnson to Clinton, 7 May 1747, *DRCNY* 6:362.

81. "Journal . . . 1746, 1747," and "Occurrences in Canada . . . 1747–8," *DRCNY* 10:105, 122, 159.

82. "Relation d'un Coup . . . ," 8 Oct. 1747, C11A, vol. 89, ff. 237–40, translated as "Report of an incursion into the Island of Montreal . . . , 1747," *DRCNY* 10:81–83; "Journal of Occurrences in Canada; 1746, 1747," *DRCNY* 10:108–9. For the difficulty of travel from Montreal to Albany, see, e.g., Lewis Evans, "An Analysis of a General Map of the Middle British Colonies, the Country of the Confederate Indians, &c.," in *Geographical, Historical, Political, Philosophical and Mechanical Essays* (Philadelphia, 1755), 19, reproduced in facsimile in Lawrence Henry Gipson, *Lewis Evans* (Philadelphia: Historical Society of Pennsylvania, 1939), 163.

83. Shirley to Clinton, 15 Aug. 1747, Clinton to Newcastle, 30 Jan. 1748, and Johnson to Clinton, 17 July 1747, *DRCNY* 6:384–85, 414–16, 386–87; quote: 386.

84. Johnson to Clinton, 17 July, 4 Aug., and 14 Aug. 1747, *DRCNY* 6:386–89; quote: 387; Speech of the Indians to Governor Clinton, 17 July 1747, *DRCNY* 6:390–91; quote: 391.

85. Johnson to Clinton, 19 Aug. 1747, *DRCNY* 6:389.

86. Shirley to Clinton, 15 Aug. 1747, and Clinton to Newcastle, 30 Jan. 1748, *DRCNY* 6:384–85, 414–16; "Journal . . . 1746, 1747," *DRCNY* 10:113; Johnson to Clinton, 28 Aug. 1747, and Col. John Roberts to Clinton, 18 Sept. 1747, *DRCNY* 6:390, 397.

87. Johnson to Clinton, 28 Aug. 1747, *DRCNY* 6:390.

88. *DRCNY* 10:128; Johnson to Clinton, 15 Mar. 1747, *PSWJ* 1:146–47, and 16 Mar. 1747, *DRCNY* 6:422–23 (these are variants of the same letter).

89. Johnson to John Catherwood, 16 Mar. 1748, and Clinton to Johnson, 18 Mar. 1748, *PSWJ* 1:149–52; *DRCNY* 10:179.

90. Lords of Trade to Clinton, 29 June 1748, Clinton and Shirley to Lords of Trade, 18 Aug. 1748, Clinton to Galissonière, 29 July 1748, Galissonière to Mascarene, 15 Jan. 1749, and Mascarene to Galissonière, 25 Apr. 1749, *DRCNY* 6:427–28, 437–40, 478–81.

4. Apotheosis

1. *DRCNY* 6:781.

2. *DRCNY* 6:782.

3. Patricia U. Bonomi, *A Factious People: Politics and Society in Colonial New York* (New York: Columbia University Press, 1991), 140–58. Johnson's uncle Peter Warren married DeLancey's sister; as Warren's star rose in England, he became one of DeLancey's most important champions. This is one element of the estrangement between Warren and Johnson, which was confirmed on Warren's death when Johnson learned that he had been written out of his uncle's will. See Johnson to Warren, 24 July 1749, *PSWJ* 1:238–41, and Milton W. Hamilton, *Sir William Johnson: Colonial American, 1715–1763* (Port Washington, NY: Kennikat Press, 1976), 75.

4. Bonomi, *Factious People,* 158–66.

5. For Galissonière, see *DCBO,* accessed 10 Sept. 2008; on Oswego in 1749, see Lieutenant Lindesay to Governor Clinton, 23 Sept. 1749, *DRCNY* 6:537–38; on destruction of the western trade, see also Clinton to the Lords of Trade, 3 June 1749, *DRCNY* 6:487.

6. Clinton to Bedford, 7 July 1749, Hamilton to Clinton, 2 Oct. 1749, and Hendrick's speech to Johnson, 2 Feb. 1750, *DRCNY* 6:515–16, 530–31, 548–49.

7. Michael N. McConnell, *A Country Between: The Upper Ohio Valley and Its Peoples, 1724–1774* (Lincoln: University of Nebraska Press, 1992); Eric Hinderaker, *Elusive Empires: Constructing Colonialism in the Ohio Valley, 1673–1800* (New York: Cambridge University Press, 1997), 18–45, 66–77.

8. Lois Mulkearn, ed., *George Mercer Papers Relating to the Ohio Company of Virginia* (Pittsburgh: University of Pittsburgh Press, 1954).

9. Galissonière to Clinton, 25 Aug. 1748, Clinton to the Lords of Trade, 3 June 1749, Desligneris to Clinton, 19 Oct. 1748, *DRCNY* 6:488–89, 485–87, 490–91; quotes: 491, 486, 490. A list of forty-four prisoners from New York and New England held in Montreal is in Johnson to Clinton, 16 Sept. 1748, *PSWJ* 1:186–88.

10. Governor Shirley (Mass.) to Galissonière, 29 July 1748, Galissonière to

Clinton, 25 Aug. 1748, Clinton to Galissonière, 10 Oct. 1748, Galissonière to Clinton, 29 Dec. 1748, Desligneris to Clinton, 10 Apr. and 14 Apr. 1749, Johnson to Clinton, 28 Apr., 26 May, and 25 June 1749, *DRCNY* 6:452–54, 488–89, 491–94, 496–500, 501–2, 505–6, 512–13, 520; quotes: 520; Clinton to Johnson, 6 Feb. 1749, Pieter D. Schuyler to Johnson, 16 July 1749, *PSWJ* 1:211–13, 237–38.

11. Jonquière to Clinton, 22 Aug. 1749, Clinton to Jonquière, 30 Oct. 1749, Jonquière to Phips, 7 Mar. 1750, Clinton to Jonquière, 7 June 1750, Order of George R., 6 Feb. 1750, *DRCNY* 6:527, 539–40, 562–67, 544–45; The King to M. de la Jonquière, 28 Feb. 1750, Minutes of the Exchange of Prisoners, 28 June 1750, *DRCNY* 10:199, 211–16; "A Journal of the Proceedings of Conrad Weiser . . . ," 1750, *MPCP* 5:470.

12. Johnson to Clinton, 18 Aug. 1750, *DRCNY* 6:589–91.

13. Johnson to Clinton, 18 Aug. 1750, *DRCNY* 6:589–91.

14. Johnson to Clinton, 26 May 1749, 25 June 1749, 19 Aug. 1749, 22 Nov. 1749, 6 Jan. 1750, Clinton to the Duke of Bedford, 7 July 1749 and 22 Nov. 1749, Clinton to Lords of Trade, 28 July 1749, 17 Mar. 1750, *DRCNY* 6:512–13, 520, 525–26, 540–42 (quote: 540–41), 546 (quote), 514–16, 533–34, 520–21, 545–46; Peter Schuyler to Johnson, 16 July 1749, *PSWJ* 1:237–38.

15. Hamilton to Clinton, 20 Sept. 1750, *DRCNY* 6:593–94.

16. "A Journal of the Proceedings of Conrad Weiser . . . ," 1750, *MPCP* 5:471.

17. Hamilton, *William Johnson*, 37–38.

18. Johnson to Peter Warren, 24 July 1749, Johnson to Samuel and William Baker, 31 Dec. 1748, Johnson to Capt. James Ross, 30 May 1749, Peter Felinck to Johnson, [1748], *PSWJ* 1:239–40, 198, 229–30, 201–4.

19. "A Journal of the Proceedings of Conrad Weiser . . . ," 1750, *MPCP* 5:472.

20. *WAIA* 155; Arent Stevens and company petition for license to purchase thirty thousand acres, 30 June 1752, bk. 14:164, deed to Stevens and others, about twenty thousand acres, 19 Oct. 1752, bk. 15:18, Stevens, Barent Vrooman and others for license to be granted patent, 16 Nov. 1752, bk. 15:24, and return of survey, 5 Feb. 1753, bk. 15:37, A0272–78; for the Mohawks' complaint, which was voiced by Hendrick, see pp. 217–18.

21. These grievances are usefully summarized in the "Report of the Privy Council upon the State of New York," which includes a remonstrance by the Assembly and a response from Clinton, both dated in 1747: *DRCNY* 6:614–39.

22. Lords of Trade to Privy Council, 2 April 1751, and Clinton to Lords of Trade, 13 June 1751, *DRCNY* 6:638, 703–4.

23. Clinton to Lords of Trade, 13 June 1751, *DRCNY* 6:638, 703–4.

24. Clinton to Bedford, 18 June 1751, *DRCNY* 6:712–13.

25. Private conference with the governor, 2 July 1751, *PSWJ* 1:339–40.

26. Conference minutes, 6–10 July, 1751, *DRCNY* 6:717–26; quotes: 717, 719.

27. *DRCNY* 6:719, 720, 725.

28. Clinton to Bedford, 18 July 1751, and Clinton to the Lords of Trade, [n.d.], *DRCNY* 6:726–27, 762–63.

29. Sergeant to Johnson, 1 July 1749, *PSWJ* 1:233–34; Jonathan Edwards to Thomas Hubbard, 31 Aug. 1751, *MHSC1* 10:142–53; quote: 143.

30. Patrick Frazier, *The Mohicans of Stockbridge* (Lincoln: University of Nebraska Press, 1992), 1–96.

31. Barbara Sivertsen, *Turtles, Wolves, and Bears: A Mohawk Family History* (Bowie, MD: Heritage Books, 1996), 137, 145.

32. Edwards to Hubbard, 31 Aug. 1751, *MHSC1* 10:142–53; quotes: 144, 145; Frazier, *Mohicans of Stockbridge*, 99.

33. This paragraph and the one following are based on Colden, "The present state of the Indian affairs . . . ," 8 Aug. 1751, *DRCNY* 6:738–47. Additional rumors of French mobilization reached Johnson in the summer of 1751, when he learned of twelve hundred soldiers and two hundred Indians passing Oswego on their way to the Ohio country; Johnson to Clinton, 27 July 1751, *DRCNY* 6:729. In the fall, Clinton reported that the Assembly had refused to honor his claims against the government for Indian affairs; Clinton to the Lords of Trade, 19 Nov. 1751, *DRCNY* 6:749–51.

34. For Duquesne, see *DCBO*, accessed 30 Sept. 2008; Lords of Trade to Privy Council, 2 Apr. 1751, Johnson to Clinton, 20 Apr. 1753, Capt. Stoddart to Johnson, 15 May 1753, and Lieut. Holland to Clinton, 15 May 1753, *DRCNY* 6:638, 778–81; quote: 779.

35. This paragraph and next: Clinton to Johnson, 5 Nov. 1782, *PSWJ* 1:383.

36. This and the following eleven paragraphs are based on conference minutes, 12–16 June 1753, *DRCNY* 6:781–88; quote: 781.

37. Quote: *DRCNY* 6:783.

38. Quotes: *DRCNY* 6:783.

39. Quotes: *DRCNY* 6:783–84.

40. Quotes: *DRCNY* 6:784.

41. Quotes: *DRCNY* 6:784.

42. Quotes: *DRCNY* 6:786.

43. Quotes: *DRCNY* 6:786.

44. Quote: *DRCNY* 6:787.

45. Quotes: *DRCNY* 6:788.

46. *DRCNY* 6:788.

47. See David Preston, "George Klock, the Canajoharie Mohawks, and the *Good Ship Sir William Johnson:* Land and Legitimacy in the Eighteenth-century Mohawk Valley," *New York History* 86 (2004): 473–99.

48. For Colden and New York politics, see Bonomi, *Factious People*, 152–54.

49. Here and in the paragraphs that follow, I touch on themes that are developed perceptively and at greater length in Timothy J. Shannon, *Indians and Colonists at the Crossroads of Empire: The Albany Congress of 1754* (Ithaca: Cornell University Press, 2000), esp. 52–82.

50. Archibald Kennedy, *Observations on the Importance of the Northern Colonies under Proper Regulations* (New York, 1750); [Kennedy], *The Importance of Gaining and Preserving the Friendship of the Indians to the British Interest, Considered* (New York, 1751); quotes: 5, 6; [Kennedy], *An Essay on the Government of the Colonies* (New York, 1752). For Kennedy's background and connection to Hunter, see his entry by Harry M. Ward in *American National Biography*, 12: 564–65; and Ned C. Landsman, "Introduction: The Context and Functions of Scottish Involvement with the Americas," in Landsman, ed., *Nation and Province in The First British Empire: Scotlandand the Americas, 1600–1800* (London: Associated University Presses, 2001), 23–24. For his appointment to the council, see Lords of Trade to Burnet, June 24, 1726, *DRCNY* 5:779–80. For the attribution of the anonymous pamphlets, see Lawrence C. Wroth, *An American Bookshelf 1755* (Philadelphia: University of Pennsylvania Press, 1934), 118–26.

51. [Archibald Kennedy], *Serious Considerations on the Present State of the Affairs of the Northern Colonies* (New York, 1754); quote: 5. Kennedy published two additional pamphlets in 1755 that are not considered here. The theme of Louis XVI's aspiration to universal monarchy is also developed in T. C., *A Scheme to Drive the French out of All the Continent of AMERICA* (Boston, 1755). The contrast between British liberty and French tyranny, which was coupled with the specter of a universal monarchy, was a conventional feature of eighteenth-century British thought; see, e.g., Linda Colley, *Britons: Forging the Nation, 1707–1837* (New Haven: Yale University Press, 1992), esp. chaps. 1–2; and Eliga H. Gould, *The Persistence of Empire: British Political Culture in the Age of the American Revolution* (Chapel Hill: University of North Carolina Press, 2000), 3–4 and following.

52. [John Huske], *The Present State of North America, &c. Part I*, 2nd ed., with Emendations (London, 1755), 42–43, 19, 20, 23, 24, 26–27, 25. For Huske's authorship, see Wroth, *American Bookshelf*, 132–42.

53. [Anon.], *State of the British and French Colonies in North America, With Respect to Number of People, Forces, Forts, Indians, Trade and other Advantages* (London, 1755), 20, 23–24. Huske took strong exception to this pamphlet's discussion of British depredations against Native Americans and disparaged the sources from which they were drawn (see *Present State*, 41–43), but in other ways its arguments are consonant with his.

54. [Anon.], *State of the British and French Colonies*, 29, 53–69, 81–82.

55. This political discourse coincided with the origins of a Romantic understanding of Indians in transatlantic culture; for an introduction to that topic, see Tim Fulford, *Romantic Indians: Native Americans, British Literature, and Transatlantic Culture, 1756–1830* (New York: Oxford University Press, 2006).

56. For Halifax, see Shannon, *Crossroads of Empire*, 76–78; for Osborne, DCBO, accessed 10 Sept. 2008.

57. Lords of Trade to Osborne, 18 Sept. 1753, and to the governors of New Jersey, Virginia, Massachusetts, New Hampshire, Maryland, and Pennsylvania, 18 Sept. 1753, *DRCNY* 6:800–802.

58. Pownall to Lords of Trade, 14 Oct. 1753, and DeLancey to Lords of Trade, 15 Oct. 1753, *DRCNY* 6:802–4.

59. Thomas Pownall to the Lords of Trade, 30 Oct. 1753, *DRCNY* 6:804–5.

60. Conference proceedings, 26–27 July 1753, *DRCNY* 6:808–9.

61. Ibid.

62. Frazier, *Mohicans of Stockbridge*, 96–104.

63. Weiser's Journal, 24 July–30 Aug. 1753, *DRCNY* 6:795–99; quote: 797.

64. Conference proceedings, 8–10 Sept. 1753, *DRCNY* 6:809–15; quotes: 810.

65. *DRCNY* 6:812.

66. *DRCNY* 6:813, 814.

67. Fred Anderson, *Crucible of War: The Seven Years' War and the Fate of Empire in British North America, 1754–1766* (New York: Knopf, 2000), 42–45.

68. Ibid., 45–49; Shannon, *Crossroads of Empire*, 83–84 and following.

69. For weather in Albany, see "[Theodore Atkinson's] Memo Book of my journey as one of the Commissioners on Treaty with the Six nations of Indians, Viz., 1754," in Beverly McAnear, "Personal Accounts of the Albany Congress of 1754," *Mississippi Valley Historical Review* 39 (1953): 732–36; Lords of Trade to Osborne, 18 Sept. 1753, and Lords of Trade to Governors, 19 Sept. 1753, *DRCNY* 6:800–802.

70. Shannon, *Crossroads of Empire*, 105–8; quote: DeLancey to Lords of Trade, 24 Dec. 1753, *DRCNY* 6:817.

71. "[Atkinson's] Memo Book," 730–33; *DRCNY* 6:858–63.

72. Ibid., and Pownall to [Halifax], 23 July 1754, in McAnear, "Personal Accounts," 735, 740–41.

73. *DRCNY* 6:867.

74. Shannon, *Crossroads of Empire*, 127–28.

75. *DRCNY* 6:865–66; Georgiana C. Nammack, *Fraud, Politics, and the Dispossession of the Indians: The Iroquois Land Frontier in the Colonial Period* (Norman: University of Oklahoma Press, 1969), 53–69.

76. Nammack, *Fraud, Politics, and Dispossession*, 53–69; quote: 59.

77. "[Atkinson's] Memo Book," 735.

78. The official proceedings of the conference are in *DRCNY* 6:853–92; DeLancey's opening speech, 861–63.

79. Pownall to [Halifax], 23 July 1754, 741.

80. This and the following six paragraphs: *DRCNY* 6:868–71.

81. Italics in original; in the manuscript version, this passage is underscored. See CO5/6 184.

82. Though it is not italicized in the printed version of the proceedings, this passage, too, is underscored in manuscript: CO5/6 185.

83. *DRCNY* 6:871–74.

84. *DRCNY* 6:878–80; Shannon, *Crossroads of Empire*, 157–58.

85. The Penn and Peters report is in *MPCP* 6:110–29; quotes: 110, 113, 116.

86. Quotes: *MPCP* 6:117, 127.

87. For the Susquehannah Company, see Julian P. Boyd and R. J. Taylor, eds., *The Susquehannah Company Papers*, 11 vols. (Ithaca: Cornell University Press, 1962–71). The deed to Wyoming is in 1:101–21, and see 101 n. 5; see also *PSWJ* 1:405, where Hendrick is mistakenly identified as one of the signers. The subsequent complaint against Lydius, which was delivered by an Onondaga sachem a year later, is in *DRCNY* 6:984. See also Shannon, *Crossroads of Empire*, 168–71.

88. Anderson, *Crucible of War*, 5–7, 50–65, 78; Pownall to [Halifax], 23 July 1754, in McAnear, "Personal Accounts," 742.

89. *DRCNY* 6:884.

90. *DRCNY* 6:883–84.

91. *The Gentleman's Magazine, and Historical Chronicle*, vol. 25 (London, 1755), 252–56; quote: 252. The American newspapers that ran reports were the *New-York Gazette, New-York Mercury, Pennsylvania Gazette, Boston Gazette, Boston Weekly News-Letter, Boston Evening-Post,* and *Boston Post-Boy;* see Shannon, *Crossroads of Empire*, 205–6.

92. Pownall to [Halifax], 23 July 1754, in McAnear, "Personal Accounts," 743–44.

93. Anderson, *Crucible of War*, 66–73, 86–93.

94. Shirley to Johnson, 9 Dec. 1754, *PSWJ* 1:425–26.

95. Morris to Hendrick Peters, 16 Nov. 1754, *MPCP* 6:252–53.

96. Daniel Claus, *Daniel Claus' Narrative of His Relations with Sir William Johnson and Experiences in the Lake George Fight* (n.p.: Society of Colonial Wars in the State of New York, 1904), 3–7; quotes: 7.

97. Ibid., 7–8. They received a similar escort out of town a week and a half later; see the *Pennsylvania Gazette*, 21 Jan. 1755. The official proceedings of Hendrick's visit are in *MPCP* 6:276–93.

98. "Extract of a Letter from Trent Town, New-Jersey, Apr. 18, 1755," in William Nelson, ed., *Documents Relating to the Colonial History of the State of New Jersey*, vol. 19 (Paterson, NJ: The Press Printing and Publishing Co., 1897), 486–88; Nicholas B. Wainwright, *The Schuylkill Fishing Company of the State in Schuylkill, 1732–1982* (Philadelphia: Schuylkill Fishing, 1982), 12–13; David Howard Dickason, *William Williams: Novelist and Painter of Colonial America, 1727–1791* (Bloomington: Indiana University Press, 1970), 5–28 and following. Dickason notes that until the mid–twentieth century, Williams was an obscure figure. No works had been positively attributed to him; he was known only as the man who gave Benjamin West, then a boy of nine, his first painting lesson. By 1970, a dozen or so paintings had been attributed to Williams, while "reliable records . . . indicate that Williams painted more than two hundred forty pictures" (138–39). The Hendrick portrait remains unidentified and is apparently lost.

99. George Croghan to [?], 16 Oct. 1754, Claus to Richard Peters, Oct. 1754, and Claus to Peters, 9 Oct. 1754, *MPCP* 6:180–83.

100. This paragraph and the following: Hendrick's speech, 17 Jan. 1755, *MPCP* 6:281–84.

101. *MPCP* 6:285.

102. Commission from Edward Braddock, 15 Apr. 1755, and Johnson to Colden and Kelly, 9 June 1755, *PSWJ* 1:465–66, 570–71.

103. Mohawks to Johnson, 7 Feb. 1755 and DeLancey to Johnson, 3 May 1755, *PSWJ* 1:452–54, 484–85; Conference between Major-General Johnson and the Indians, 21 June–4 July 1755, *DRCNY* 6:964–89; quotes: 965, 968.

104. Quote: *DRCNY* 6:973.

105. Johnson to DeLancey, 8 Aug. 1755, and to Robert Orme, 1 Aug. 1755, *PSWJ* 1:841–42, 813–16; Anderson, *Crucible of War*, 108–12.

106. Anderson, *Crucible of War*, 115.

107. Johnson to Thomas Pownall, 24 Aug. 1755, *PSWJ* 1:882–83.

108. Johnson to the Lords of Trade, 3 Sept. 1755, *DRCNY* 6:993–97.

109. Anderson, *Crucible of War*, 115–18.

110. Claus, *Narrative*, 12–13.

111. Anderson, *Crucible of War*, 118–19.

112. Claus, *Narrative*, 13–14.

113. Ibid., 14.

114. Anderson, *Crucible of War*, 119–23; Claus, *Narrative*, 15.

115. Claus, *Narrative*, 16–17.

116. Conference between Johnson and the Indians, 11 Sept. 1755, *DRCNY* 6: 1011–13.

117. The report of Paulus's reaction to the news of Hendrick's death appeared first in *New York Mercury*, 22 Sept. 1755; it was reprinted in the *Pennsylvania Gazette*, 25 Sept. 1755, and *Gentleman's Magazine*, Nov. 1755, 519. I have followed the quotation in *Gentleman's Magazine*, which alters the sentence to make better sense. The original reads: "[he] *swore his Father was still alive in that Place, and that there stood his son.*" John Ogilvie, "The Diary of the Reverend John Ogilvie, 1750–1759," ed. Milton W. Hamilton, *Bulletin of the Fort Ticonderoga Museum* 10 (1961): 360–61.

118. Anderson, *Crucible of War*, 121–23; Claus, *Narrative*, 18–19; Pownall to Johnson, 2 Dec. 1755, *DRCNY* 6:1022.

119. *New-York Mercury*, 15, 22, and 29 Sept., 6, 13, and 27 Oct. 1755; *Pennsylvania Gazette*, 15 and 25 Sept., 9, 16, and 23 Oct. 1755; *Gentleman's Magazine*, Oct. 1755, 474; Nov. 1755, 519, 527.

120. *PSWJ* 9:509, 534; the Indian King Hendrick: *Pennsylvania Gazette*, 8 Apr. 1756; the King Hendrick: *Pennsylvania Gazette*, 7 Feb. 1760, 6 Mar., and 4 Sept. 1760, 12 Mar., 6 Aug., 15 Oct., 29 Oct., and 31 Dec. 1761, 19 Aug. 1762, and 6 Aug. 1764; ships: *Pennsylvania Gazette*, 23 June and 15 Sept. 1757, 23 Feb., 11 May, 22 June, and 21 Sept. 1758; Christopher Waterman, "Sloop King Hendrick's Log, 1757," John Carter Brown Library, Brown University, Providence.

121. Note, however, that the weapon in the "brave old Hendrick" print looks more like a medieval European battle-ax than an Indian tomahawk—a fact that only adds to the confusion surrounding the print's origin. I am indebted to Timothy Shannon for this observation. For a penetrating analysis of the pipe tomahawk—an artifact closely related to these weapons—see Shannon, "Queequeg's Tomahawk: A Cultural Biography, 1750–1900," *Ethnohistory* 52 (2005): 589–633.

Conclusion

1. Rufus Alexander Grider Albums, 1886–1900, 9 vols., VC22932, NYSL, 6:8.

2. Fred Anderson, *Crucible of War: The Seven Years' War and the Fate of Empire in British North America, 1754–1766* (New York: Knopf, 2000).

3. Barbara Graymont, *The Iroquois in the American Revolution* (Syracuse, NY: Syracuse University Press, 1972); Peter C. Mancall, *Valley of Opportunity: Economic Culture Along the Upper Susquehanna, 1700-1800* (Ithaca, NY: Cornell University Press, 1991), 130–59; Colin G. Calloway, *The American Revolution in Indian Country: Crisis and Diversity in Native American Communities* (New York: Cambridge University Press, 1995), 108–57; Alan Taylor, *The Divided Ground: Indians, Settlers, and the Northern Borderland of the American Revolution* (New York: Knopf, 2006), 3–141 and following.

4. Jeremy Belknap, *Journal of a Tour from Boston to Oneida, June, 1796*, ed. George Dexter (Cambridge: John Wilson and Son, University Press, 1882), 13–14.

5. Ibid., 14.

6. Ibid., 13.

7. See Carla Gerona, "Imagining Peace in Quaker and Native American Dream Stories," in William A. Pencak and Daniel K. Richter, eds., *Friends and Enemies in Penn's Woods: Indians, Colonists, and the Racial Construction of Pennsylvania* (University Park, PA: Penn State University Press, 2004), 52–53. I am indebted to Daniel Richter for calling my attention to this passage.

8. For a brief biographical sketch of Grant, see *CASHP*, accessed 6 July 2008. Grant's memoirs were originally published in two volumes: Anne Grant, *Memoirs of an American Lady: with Sketches of Manners and Scenery in America, as they existed previous to the Revolution* (London, 1808). They have gone through many editions; later editions combined the volumes. The citations that follow refer to Grant, *Memoirs of an American Lady* (New York: George Dearborn, 1836; reprint, Bedford, MA: Applewood Books, n.d.).

9. Ibid., 29.

10. Ibid., 233–34.

11. See, e.g., Daniel K. Richter, *The Ordeal of the Longhouse: The Peoples of the Iroquois League in the Era of European Colonization* (Chapel Hill: University of North Carolina Press, 1992), 260–62.

12. *Appleton's Cyclopaedia of American Biography*, ed. James Grant Wilson and John Fiske, 7 vols. (New York: D. Appleton, 1888–1901; reprint, Detroit: Gale, 1968), 5:425.

13. This paragraph and next: Henry Schoolcraft, *Notes on the Iroquois: Or, Contributions to the Statistics, Aboriginal History, Antiquities and General Ethnology of Western New York* (New York, 1846), following title page.

14. This paragraph and the next: Henry Rowe Schoolcraft, *Notes on the Iroquois: or Contributions to American History, Antiquities, and General Ethnology* (Albany, 1847), 413–21.

15. For a sustained examination of the idea that Hendrick visited London in 1740, see Alden T. Vaughan, "American Indians Abroad: The Mythical Travels of Mrs. Penobscot and King Hendrick," *New England Quarterly* 80 (2007): 299–316.

16. This paragraph and next: Philip J. Deloria, *Playing Indian* (New Haven: Yale University Press, 1998), 71–94; *Appleton's Cyclopaedia*, 4:403.

17. Lewis H. Morgan, *League of the Ho-de-no-sau-nee or Iroquois*, 2 vols. (1851; reprint, New York: Dodd Mead, 1901.)

18. Entry for Edmund Bailey O'Callaghan in *DCBO*, accessed 9 Oct. 2008; *DHNY; DRCNY;* Peter Force, ed., *American Archives,* 9 vols. (Boston, 1837–53); Jared Sparks, ed., *The Diplomatic Correspondence of the American Revolution,* 12 vols. (Boston, 1829–30); Hezekiah Niles, *Principles and Acts of the Revolution in America; Or, an Attempt to Collect and Preserve Some of the Speeches, Orations, and Proceedings . . .* (Baltimore, 1822).

19. *Appleton's Cyclopaedia*, 5:705–6.

20. William Leete Stone, *The Life and Times of Sir William Johnson, Bart.,* 2 vols. (Albany, 1865), 1:164–65, 257, 393–400, 451–58, 464, 502–12, 549–51.

21. Ibid., 1:551; William W. Campbell, *Annals of Tryon County; Or, The Border Warfare of New York, during the Revolution,* (N.Y.: J. & J. Harper, 1831) app. n. B, 11.

22. Peter Hastings Falk, ed., *Who Was Who in American Art, 1564–1975,* 3 vols. (Madison, CT: Soundview Press, 1999), 2:1375; William H. Gerdts, ed., *Art across America: Two Centuries of Regional Painting,* 3 vols. (New York: Abbeville Press, 1990), 1:267.

23. Rufus Alexander Grider Albums, 1886–1990, 9 vols., VC22932, NYSL, 1:16, 9, 15.

24. Ibid., 2:26.

Acknowledgments

I have received assistance from many individuals and institutions, and accumulated many debts, in writing this book. I am grateful to the National Endowment for the Humanities and the staff of the John Carter Brown Library, then led by Norman Fiering, who supported me as I began my research and drafted an article on the "four Indian kings." Susan Danforth, Dan Slive, and Richard Hurley all assisted me directly in my work there, while fellow scholars Edward Gray, Lieve Jooken, María Isabel Grañén Porrúa, and Calhoun Winton made my time in residence especially memorable. Among the faculty at Brown, I am grateful to Douglas Cope, Tim Harris, and Gordon Wood for the fruitful conversations I enjoyed with them. I also had the great good fortune while in Providence to meet the Reverend Steele W. Martin, an Episcopal priest who was descended from Hendrick Peters Theyanoguin. He took a strong interest in my project and shared information about his grandfather, Peter Martin, who was born on the Grand River in 1859. I regret that Reverend Martin died before he could see this book; in its writing I have been constantly mindful of him and the many other Mohawk descendants in the United States and Canada who continue to identify with the two Hendricks and their lost Mohawk Valley world.

I was fortunate to publish the "four Indian kings" article in the *William and Mary Quarterly*. I want to thank its staff, the article's referees, and the journal's then editor, Michael McGiffert, who taught me a thing or two about writing as he helped me make vast improvements to the manuscript I submitted. In Albany, the staffs of the New York State Library and Archives and the Albany Institute of History and Art have been very helpful. Farther afield, I have benefited enormously from the hard work and dedication of the staffs at the Library and Archives of Canada, the National Archives of the United Kingdom, the British Museum, and the British Library. Melanie Clews offered welcome hospitality while I was in London.

At the University of Utah, I owe a debt of gratitude to colleagues and adminstrators who have been unfailingly supportive of my work. Ray Gunn was a model department chair who helped me find the time I needed to begin this research. Later, when I became chair myself, Dean Robert Newman of the College of Humanities continued to encourage and support my research. The College's Faculty Development Committee and the University Research Committee both provided time off for writing, as did the Office of the President of the University of Utah. As work on the manuscript has drawn to a close, Jim Lehning, who replaced me as department chair, has capably relieved me of administrative burdens in an especially challenging time. I have benefitted, directly and indirectly, from conversations with many of my colleagues, past and present, including Lindsay Adams, Matt Basso, Ben Cohen, Ed Davies, Nadja Durbach, Ray Gunn, Paul Johnson, Anne Keary, Jim Lehning, Dean May, Colleen McDannell, Isabel Moreira, Peggy Pascoe, Paul Reeve, and Anand Yang. Rebecca Horn, my colleague in colonial Latin American history, has been an indispensable influence and support during the years we have worked together. The staff of the Marriott Library, particularly in Interlibrary Loans and Special Collections, has always provided the help I needed.

I am grateful to several audiences that commented upon earlier versions of the argument presented here. Participants in the Sixth Annual Conference of the Omohundro Institute for Early American History and Culture in Toronto, and those at a symposium honoring the research and teaching of Bernard Bailyn, offered useful criticism of my early attempts to place Iroquois relations in a transatlantic context. The contributors to a symposium on British Asia and the British Atlantic at the University of Sussex, organized by Huw Bowen, Elizabeth Mancke, and John Reid and splendidly hosted by Trevor Burnard, helped me hone a more mature statement of that effort; I am especially grateful to Michael Fischer for his comments on that essay. And a roundtable discussion at the USC-Huntington Early Modern Studies Institute offered the opportunity to explore the problem of one-sided source materials in Indian history, especially as they relate to land fraud. I am grateful to Carole Shammas and Peter Mancall for arranging and hosting the visit, and to Matthew Dennis, Joseph Hall, Kirk Swineheart, and the roundtable participants for a stimulating and entertaining conversation.

Two working groups in early American history have been especially important to me. The Front Range Early American Consortium—the FREACs—has been a fixture of the Rocky Mountain region for a generation, and its meetings have brought me into regular contact with a terrific group of colleagues. More recently, the Rocky Mountain Seminar in Early American History has enlivened the intellectual life of the greater Salt Lake area. I am thankful for the friendship and support of both groups' members.

I have received professional assistance from many individuals. Philip Schwartzberg, of Meridian Mapping in Minneapolis, designed the two beautiful maps that appear in the book. Colleen Hallenbeck tracked down land records in the New York State Archives in Albany, and Ann Aronson Photography took pictures of documents held in the New York State Library and Archives. Stefan Bielinski kindly responded to my queries about early Albany and its environs, and Dr. James D. Folts, historian of the First Church in Albany, advised me on surviving artifacts from the seventeenth-century church building. At the British Museum, Agata Rutkowska helped me track down an especially elusive illustration. Daniel Rolph of the Historical Society of Pennsylvania aided me in an ultimately futile search to learn more about the William Williams portrait of the second Hendrick.

Many sharp-eyed readers have offered comments that improved the book. Daniel Richter and Timothy Shannon served as referees for Harvard University Press. Though they may continue to have reservations about some aspects of my argument, they both offered acute criticism that strengthened the book. Tim also helped me work through several conundrums relating to the two Hendricks. Alden Vaughan generously shared his own research with me and has followed the progress of this book with interest. Fred Anderson, Peter Mancall, and Brett Rushforth read the manuscript and offered important suggestions for improvement; each of them contributed in indispensable ways to the book's final form. I have been fortunate to work with Lisa Adams of Garamond Agency, who secured the contract for the book, discussed its scope and argument with me, and carefully read a draft. At Harvard University Press, I am especially grateful to Kathleen McDermott, who expressed confidence in the project from the beginning, commented very usefully on the manuscript, and helped with the title, and Kathleen Drummy, who capably shepherded the book through the editing and production process. Tonnya Norwood and the staff of NK Graphics copyedited the manuscript with care, intelligence, and insight.

Near the beginning of my career, I had the good fortune to teach Jared R. Larson in one of my classes. He has gone on to an extraordinarily successful business career, but he has retained his love of history and has created a research fund in early American history at the University of Utah that has immeasurably aided my work. I owe Jared a very special debt of thanks.

The support of those closest to me has been a constant. I am grateful to my parents, Irving and Eula Hinderaker, for shaping me; to my brothers and their families, for giving flesh to the idea of family; and to Carrie, Michael, and Samuel, for the love and humor that sustain me every day. When I began research on this project, Samuel was an infant and Michael a preschooler. As this book goes to press, Sam is finishing ninth grade and Michael is graduating from high school. I suppose I could wish that I had written the book faster, but I prefer to be thankful that I have had so many moments with them, and with Carrie, in the intervening years.

Index